The Three Mountains

The Three Mountains

Samael Aun Weor

GLORIAN

The Three Mountains

A Glorian Book / 2015

Originally published in Spanish as "Christmas Message 1972-1973" ("Las Tres Montañas").

This Edition © 2015 Glorian Publishing

Print ISBN 978-1-934206-28-7

Glorian Publishing is a non-profit organization delivering to humanity the teachings of Samael Aun Weor. All proceeds go to further the distribution of these books. For more information, visit our website.

gnosticteachings.org

Contents

The Third Mountain: The Mountain of the Ascension

Illustrations

Foreword to the Reader

Without wanting to hurt delicate susceptibilities in any way, we must emphasize the basic idea that a variety of venerable institutions coexist within the cultural-spiritual environment of contemporary humanity that very sincerely believe they know the secret path. Nonetheless, they do not know it.

Allow me the freedom of stating with great solemnity that we do not want to utter any destructive criticism. We are making an emphasis, and it is clear that this is not a crime.

Obviously, and because of a very simple and profound respect towards our fellowmen, we will never proclaim ourselves against any mystical institution.

No human being should be criticized for being ignorant of something that has never been taught to him. The secret path has never been publicly unveiled.

We will state in rigorous Socratic terms that there are many erudites who pretend to know the path of the razor's edge in depth. Not only do they ignore, but moreover they ignore that they ignore.

Without wanting to indicate or point to any type of spiritual organization and without having the intention of taunting anyone, we will simply state that the learned ignoramus not only does not know, but moreover does not know that he does not know.

In all the books of ancient times, the secret path is cited. This path is quoted and mentioned in many verses, yet people do not know it.

Beloved reader, to unveil, to show, and to teach the esoteric path that leads to the final liberation is certainly the purpose of this book that you have in your hands. This is one of the books of the Fifth Gospel.

The great German initiate Goethe wrote, "Every theory is gray, and only the tree of the golden fruits of life is green."

Certainly, what we deliver in this new book are transcendental, lived experiences. It is what we have verified, what we have directly experienced.

It is imperative to trace the maps of the path, to indicate each step with precision, to point out the dangers, etc.

A short time ago, the Guardians of the Holy Sepulcher told me, "We know that you will depart, but before your departure you must deliver the maps of the path and your words to humanity."

I answered by saying, "That is what I will do." Since that time, I solemnly promised myself to write this book.

Chapter I
My Childhood

It is not irrelevant to solemnly testify that I was born with enormous spiritual longings. To deny this would be an absurdity...

Even though some will look at this as unusual and incredible, the concrete fact is that there are those in the world who can completely remember the totality of their existence, even the event of their own birth. I want to affirm that I am one of those who can do so.

Following all the well-known processes of birth, very clean and beautifully dressed, I was gently placed on the maternal bed close to my mother...

Approaching the sacred bed was a certain very gentle giant with a sweet smile who was contemplating me. He was my father.

It is important to clearly and plainly state that at the dawn of any one of our existences we originally walk on four legs, then on two, and finally on three. Obviously, the latter indicates the cane of the elders.

My case cannot be in any way an exception to the general rule. When I was eleven months old I wanted to walk, and it is evident that I did it by firmly sustaining myself upon my two feet. Still, I plainly remember that marvelous instant in which, by interlacing my hands over my head, I solemnly executed the Masonic sign of help: "**Elai Beni Al Manah.**"

Since I still have not lost my capacity for astonishment, I have to state that what happened to me then was marvelous. To walk for the very first time with the body that Mother Nature grants us is without a doubt an extraordinary prodigy.

Very serenely, I directed myself towards the old window from which I could see the varied conjunctions of people who were appearing and disappearing here, there, and everywhere in the picturesque little street of my town. To hold myself by the bars of such an old window was for me the first adventure.

Fortunately, my father, who was a very prudent man, greatly conjured beforehand any danger by placing a screen of wires on the balustrade, for the purpose of stopping me from falling onto the street.

Such a very ancient window from that high floor... how well I remember it! Such a big and old centenarian house where I walked my first steps....

Certainly, at that tender age I loved the enchanted toys with which children enjoy themselves, but this was not in any way interfering with my practices of meditation.

In those first years of life in which one learns how to walk, I trained myself to sit in the oriental style in order to meditate.

Then, retrospectively, I studied my previous reincarnations. It is clear that many people of ancient times were visiting me.

When the ineffable ecstasy concluded, I then returned into the normal, ordinary state, in order to painfully contemplate the old walls of that centenarian, paternal house, where I, in spite of my age, looked like a strange cenobite....

How small I felt before those rough walls! I cried... yes, as children cry... I lamented by saying, "Once again in a new physical body! How painful life is! Woe! Woe! Woe!..."

My good mother always came in those precise instances with the intention of helping me. At the same time she exclaimed, "The child is hungry, thirsty," etc.

Never could I forget those instances in which I happily ran through the ancestral corridors of my house.

Then, unusual cases of transcendental metaphysics began happening to me. My father called me from his bedroom. I saw him in his sleeping clothes, but when I tried to approach him, he vanished, disappearing into an unknown dimension...

Although I sincerely confess that this type of psychic phenomena was very familiar to me, I simply entered into his bedroom to directly verify that his physical body was sleeping within his perfumed, mahogany bed. I told myself the following, "Ah! What happened is that the soul of my father is outside, because his physical body is sleeping in these moments."

In those times, the silent movies had just been introduced. Many people gathered in the public square at night in order to distract themselves by watching movies. These movies were in open fields on rudimentary screens made by a very tempered sheet nailed onto two sticks properly separated...

In my house I had a very different movie. I closed myself in a dark room and I fixed my sight on the wall or fence. After a time of spontaneous and pure concentration, the fence definitively disappeared and the wall became very splendidly illuminated, as if it were a multidimensional screen. Then, from the infinite space surged a living landscape of Mother Nature, with playful gnomes, airy sylphs, salamanders of fire, undines of the water, and neraides of the immense sea. These are fortunate creatures, infinitely happy beings who played with me.

My movie was not silent; Rudolph Valentino was not necessary in it, nor was the famous Vilma Banky of those times. My movie was also with sound. All the creatures who appeared on my special screen sang or uttered very pure lores in the divine and primeval language, which as a river of gold runs through the dense, sunny jungle.

Later on, when my family multiplied, I invited my innocent little siblings to share this incomparable joy with me by serenely watching the astonishing astral figures on the wall of my dark bedroom...

I was always a worshipper of the sun, and as much at dawn as in the evening, I climbed upon the roof of my abode (because in those times balconies did not exist). Seated in the oriental style as an infantile yogi upon the roof tile made of baked clay, I contemplated (in a state of ecstasy) the Sun King. In this way I immersed myself into profound meditation. My noble mother was always very frightened upon seeing me walking about on top of our home...

Whenever my elderly father opened the old door of the wardrobe, I felt as if he would give me that unique coat (a purple diplomat's coat) upon which golden buttons glittered.

It is an old garment from the apparel of the age of chivalry which I wore (in an ancient reincarnation) with elegance when I was named Simeon Bleler. Sometimes in my mind I imagined that within this old wardrobe could be found hidden swords and fencing foils from such ancient times.

I do not know if my father understood me. I thought that maybe he would deliver the objects of that past existence to me. The elder only looked at me, and instead gave me a long narrow cart to play with, a toy of innocent enjoyments for my childhood...

Chapter II
Religion

Being raised with good manners, I needlessly and frankly confess that I was educated according to the official religion of my town.

To be mischievous with somebody in the garret during a liturgical service always seemed abominable to me...

Since my childhood, I had a sense of veneration and respect. Never did I want to shrug my shoulders while in full public worship. Never did I like to exclude myself from my sacred duties, neither laugh, nor mock holy things.

Now, without wanting to entangle myself amongst thorns and brambles, I need to state that in that mystic sect (the name of which does not matter) I found religious principles that are common in all the confessional religions of the world. To cite them now is relevant for the good of the Great Cause.

Heavens

We find them in all the confessional religions, although with different names. Nonetheless, there are always nine, as the Florentine Dante stated with so much assertion in his classic poem *The Divine Comedy*.

1. Heaven of the Moon, the astral world
2. Heaven of Mercury, the mental world
3. Heaven of Venus, the causal world
4. Heaven of the Sun, the Buddhic or Intuitive World
5. Heaven of Mars, the Atmic World, region of Atma
6. Heaven of Jupiter, or Nirvana
7. Heaven of Saturn, the Paranirvanic World
8. Heaven of Uranus, the Mahaparanirvanic World
9. Heaven of Neptune, the Empyrean World

It is evident that these nine heavens are also within us, here and now. They interpenetrate each other without being confused. Obviously, these nine heavens are found located in nine superior dimensions. Clearly, they are nine parallel universes.

Infernos

It is good to emphatically remember the diverse religious infernos that we are stating in this 1972-1973 esoteric Christmas message... Let us solemnly evoke, let us bring to mind, all of the multiple pre-historic and historic infernos.

Remembrances, reminiscences about Chinese, Mohammedan, Buddhist, Christian (etc.) infernos exist everywhere. It is unquestionable that all of the various infernos serve as a symbol for the submerged mineral kingdom...

Dante, the marvelous disciple of Virgil, the poet of Mantua, clearly discovered with mystical astonishment the intimate relationship existing between the nine Dantesque circles and the nine heavens...

The Bardo Thodol, the Tibetan book that talks about the spirits of the world of the afterlife, stands out magnificently before our eyes, letting us see the crude reality of the infernal worlds located within the interior of this planetary organism on which we live.

It is indubitable that the nine Dantesque circles within the interior of the Earth are scientifically correlated with the nine submerged infradimensions below the tridimensional region of Euclid.

The cosmic existence of the infernal worlds in any world of the infinite space is evident and clear. Obviously, the submerged mineral kingdoms are certainly not something exclusive to the planet Earth.

Angelology

The whole cosmos is directed, watched, and animated by a series of almost interminable hierarchies of conscious beings. Each one of them (whether they are called by one name or another, such as Dhyan Chohans, Angels, or Devas, etc.) have a mission to accomplish, and are messengers only in the sense that they are agents of the karmic and cosmic laws. They vary in their respective degrees of consciousness and intelligence infinitely. All of them are perfect humans in the most complete sense of the word.

Multiple angelical services characterize divine love. Each Elohim works within his specialty. We can and must appeal for angelical protection.

God

All religions are precious pearls strung upon the golden thread of divinity.

The love that all mystic institutions of the world feel for the divine is noticeable: for Allah, Brahma, Tao, Zen, I.A.O., INRI, God, etc.

Religious esotericism does not teach atheism of any kind, except in the sense that the Sanskrit word *nastika* encloses: no admission of idols, including that anthropomorphic God of the ignorant populace. It would be an absurdity to believe in a celestial dictator who is seated upon a throne of tyranny and throws lightning and thunderbolts against this sad human ant hill.

Esotericism admits the existence of a Logos, or a collective Creator of the universe, a Demiurge architect.

It is unquestionable that such a Demiurge is not a personal deity as many mistakenly suppose, but rather a host of Dhyan Chohans, Angels, Archangels, and other forces. God is gods.

It is written with characters of fire in the resplendent book of life that God is the Army of the Voice, the great Word, the Verb.

> *In the beginning was the Word, and the Word was with God, and the Word was God.*
>
> *All things were made by him, and without him was not any thing made that was made.* - John 1:1-3

For this reason, it is evident that any authentic human being who really achieves perfection enters into the Current of Sound, into the celestial army constituted by the Buddhas of Compassion, Angels, Planetary Spirits, Elohim, Rishi-Prajapatis, etc.

It has been said to us that the Logos sounds, and this is obvious. The Demiurge, the Verb, is the multiple, perfect unity.

Whosoever adores the gods, whosoever surrenders worship unto them, is more capable of capturing the deep significance of the diverse divine facets of the Demiurge architect.

When humanity began to mock the holy gods, then it fell mortally wounded into the gross materialism of this Iron Age.

Lucifer

We can and must radically eliminate all of the subjective, tenebrous, and perverse psychological aggregates that we carry within. Nonetheless, it is unquestionable that we will never dissolve the shadow of the Inner Logos within ourselves.

It is clear and evident by all means that Lucifer is the antithesis of the Creator Demiurge. Lucifer is the projected, living shadow within the profound depth of the microcosm, the human being.

Lucifer is the guardian of the door who alone is entrusted with the keys of the lumisial, wherein no one may enter save the anointed ones who have the secret of Hermes.

So then, we have just written this name that is detestable to the pitiful ears of the common people. It is necessary to also convey that the esoteric Lucifer of the archaic doctrine is not what the theologians (such as the famous Desmouss-Eaux and the Marquis of Mirville) mistakenly supposed, but the contrary. He is the allegory of good, the symbol of the highest sacrifice (Christus-Lucifer) of the Gnostics, and the god of wisdom under many names.

Lucifer is light and shadow, mysterious symbiosis of the Solar Logos, multiple, perfect unity, INRI.

Demons

Through diverse religious theologies, we are given a picture of those divine Logoi as being punished for committing the unforgivable error of falling into animal generation when reincarnated in human bodies.

Those tenebrous genii are fallen angels, authentic demons in the most complete sense of the word.

It is absurd to affirm that such rebels gave the mind to the human being.

It is obvious that those fallen angels are truly cosmic failures.

At this moment, it is very opportune to remember the inhuman names of Andrameleck, Belial, Moloch, Bael, etc., whose horrendous abominations can be studied in the Akashic records of Nature by any adept of the White Lodge.

Let us distinguish between an esoteric **downfall** and a **descent**. Evidently, these rebel angels did not descend, they fell, and this is the difference.

Limbo

Being versed in the history of the universe, we know with certainty what the Orco is of the classic Greeks and Latin Romans, and the Limbo of the Christian Esotericists.

Certainly, it is not irrelevant to emphasize the transcendental idea within this treatise that Limbo is the antechamber of the infernal worlds.

All of the known and unknown caves form a broad and uninterrupted net that embraces the planet Earth in its entirety. As we have mentioned in a previous paragraph, this constitutes the Orco of the classics, the authentic Limbo of Gnostic esotericism... In short, it is the other world, where we live after death.

Limbo corresponds to that mystical and tremendous allegory that states, "Those innocent children who died without having received the waters of baptism live there."

Within Gnostic esotericism, such waters are of a Genesiatic type, and constitute the **Ens Seminis** (the entity of semen, as stated by Paracelsus).

Sexual Yoga, Maithuna, Sexual Magic, is symbolized within diverse religious cults with the sacrament of baptism. The clue to salvation is found in the spinal medulla and in the semen; indeed, salvation can only be achieved in this manner, in this way; anything else is a worthless waste of time.

Those "innocent children" are the saints who did not work with the spermatic waters of the first instant. They are virtuous people who believed in achieving the realization of their Innermost Being without accomplishing the commitment of the sacrament

THE SECRET PATH HIDDEN IN A MEDIEVAL ILLUMINATION AS BAPTISM.

of baptism. They did not know about Sexual Magic, or they emphatically rejected it.

Only Mercury, the chief and evoker of souls, while holding the caduceus of wisdom with his dexterous hand, can summon to a new life the unhappy, innocent creatures who are precipitated into the Orco.

Only Mercury, the arch-magi and arch-hierophant, can help these souls be reborn in propitious environments in order for them to perform the fertile and creative work in the "forge of the Cyclops."

Thus, this is how Mercury, the nuncio and wolf of the Sun, escorts the souls out of Limbo in order to initiate them into the celestial militia.

Purgatory

Let us define purgatory as follows: an inferior molecular region, a sub-lunar type zone, submerged astral (secondary Kama Loka).

We need to fry the seeds of evil, to annihilate infrahuman larvae of any type, to purge ourselves from any corruption, to radically purify ourselves in the purgatorial world.

When speaking about purgatory, Dante Alighieri states:

"Close to the top, we reached a point from where
I saw a gate (it first appeared to be
merely a gap, a break within the wall)
And, leading up to it, there where three steps,
each one a different color; and I saw
the silent figure of someone on guard.
I slowly raised my eyes: I saw that he was sitting on the highest
step, his face
too splendid for my eyes – looked away!
And in his hand he held a naked sword;
so dazzling were the rays reflected thence,
each time I tried to look I could not see.
He said to us: "Speak up from where you are.
What is it that you want? Where is your guide?
Beware, you may regret your coming here."
"A while ago, a lady sent from Heaven
acquainted with such matters," replied my guide,
"told us: 'Behold the gate. You must go there.'
"May she continue guiding you to good,"
the courteous keeper of the gate replied,
"and so, come forward now up to our stairs."
We reached the step. White marble was the first,
and polished to the glaze of a looking glass;
I saw myself reflected as I was.
The second one was deeper dark than perse,
of rough and crumbling, fire-corroded stone,
with cracks across its surface-length and breadth.
The third one, lying heavy at the top,
appeared to be of flaming porphyry,
red as the blood that spurts out from a vein;
upon this step the angel of the Lord
rested his feet; he sat upon the sill
which seemed to be of adamantine rock.
Up the three steps my master guided me
benevolently, saying: "Ask him now,
in all humility, to turn the key."
Falling devoutly at his holy feet,
in mercy's name I begged to be let in;

but, first of all, three times I smote my breast.
Then with his sword he traced upon my brow
the scars of seven P's. "Once entered here,
be sure you cleanse away these wounds," he said.
Ashes, or earth when it is dug up dry —
this was the colour of the robes he wore;
he reached beneath them and drew out two keys.
One key was silver and the other gold;
first he applied the white one, then the yellow —
with that the gate responded to my wish.
"Whenever either one of these two keys
fails to turn properly inside the lock,"
the angel said, "the road ahead stays closed.
One is more precious, but the other needs
wisdom and skill before it will unlock,
for it is that one which unties the knot.
I hold these keys from Peter, who advised:
'Admit too many, rather than too few,
if they but cast themselves before your feet.'"
Then, pushing back the portal's holy door,
"Enter," he said to us, "but first be warned:
to look back means to go back out again."
And then the pivots of that sacred gate,
fashioned of heavy metal, resonant,
turned slow inside their sockets. The rolling roar
was louder and more stubborn than Tarpeia's,
when it was robbed of vigilant Metellus —
its treasury made lean from that time on.
And as the grating pivots rolled, I turned,
for I heard chanting: Te Deum Laudamus —
accompanied by the sweet notes of that door.
This Harmony of sounds made me recall
just how it seems in church when we attend
to people singing as the organ plays:
sometimes the words are heard, and sometimes lost."

— Purgatory IX, The Divine Comedy of Dante Alighieri

MARY MAGDALENE, WIFE OF JESUS

The Divine Mother

Mary, or better said, **RAM-IO**, is the same Isis, Juno, Demeter, Ceres, Maia, the Divine Cosmic Mother; She is the serpentine power which lies beneath the living depth of all organic or inorganic matter.

Mary Magdalene

Beautiful Magdalene is without a doubt the same Salambo, Matra, Ishtar, Astarte, Aphrodite, and Venus.

All the priestess wives of the world constitute the solar aura of the repented Magdalene.

Blessed be those men who will find shelter in that aura, because theirs will be the kingdom of heaven.

Christ

Christ is Ormus, Ahura-Mazda among the Persians, who is the antithesis of Ahriman (Satan).

Christ is Vishnu in the sacred land of the Vedas. He is the Second Logos, sublime emanation of Brahma, the First Logos.

The Avatar Krishna is the Hindustani Jesus. The gospel of this master is similar to the gospel of the divine rabbi of Galilee.

Fu Xi is the Cosmic Christ among the ancient Chinese, the one who wrote the famous *I Ching*, the book of laws, and who designated Dragon Ministers for the good of humanity.

Osiris was in fact the Christ in the sunny country of Khem, in the land of the Pharaohs, and whosoever incarnated him was an Osirified One.

Quetzalcoatl is the Mexican Christ, who is now dwelling in distant Tule. He is the "white god."

Immaculate Conceptions

It is urgent to really comprehend what immaculate conceptions are. These conceptions are abundant in all the ancient cults. Fu Xi, Quetzalcoatl, Buddha, and many others are the result of immaculate conceptions.

The sacred fire makes the waters of life fertile in order for the master to be born within us.

Certainly, every angel is a child of the Divine Mother Kundalini. Really, she is virginal before, during, and after childbirth.

In the name of truth, we solemnly affirm the following: the Third Logos, the Holy Spirit, Shiva, the first begotten of creation, our inner individual Monad, or more correctly, our super-individual Monad, is the husband of Devi Kundalini, our particular Cosmic Mother.

Chapter III
Spiritualism

I was still a boy of twelve springs when I, as someone who was eagerly investigating the mysteries of beyond, diligently proposed to inquire, inspect, investigate, the disquieting field of Spiritualism.

Then, with the constancy of a clergyman in a cell, I studied innumerable metaphysical books. It is not irrelevant to cite that some of those authors included Luis Zea Uribe, Camille Flammarion, Kardec, Leon Denis, Caesar Lombroso, etc.

Certainly, the first book from a series by Kardek looked very interesting to me, but I had to read it three times with the indisputable longing of integrally understanding it.

Afterwards, when I really converted myself into a true bookworm, frankly and plainly speaking, I confess that I became impassioned with *The Book of Spirits*. I then continued with many other volumes of substantial content.

I enclosed myself within my house or in the public library for long hours with a mind impenetrable to anything that was not of these types of studies, and with the evident longing of searching for the secret path.

Now, without boasting of wisdom and without any vainglory, I wish to write in this chapter the knowledge of the results of my investigations in the field of Spiritualism.

Mediums

Mediums are passive and receptive subjects who grant their matter, their body, to metaphysical phantoms from beyond the grave.

It is unquestionable that **epilepsy** is the karma of mediumism. Obviously, epileptic people were mediums in their past lives.

Experiments

1 A certain lady (whose name I do not wish to mention) was constantly seeing the phantom of a dead woman. This phantom was revealing many things to her in her ear.

The lady fell into a trance during a solemn spiritist meeting. The obsessive phantom showed the alluded medium a specific place in the house in order to excavate, because there, said the phantom, she would find a great treasure.

The indications of the phantom were followed, but unfortunately the treasure was not found.

It is unquestionable that the so-called treasure was only a simple mental projection from the subjective psyche of the attendants. Obviously, these types of people are always greedy within their depths.

2 Distantly, long ago, very far from this beloved Mexican land of mine, I had to go inland into Zulia, a state of Venezuela in South America.

As a guest in the campestral abode of my host, I must state that I was then an eyewitness to an unusual metaphysical event.

It is important to note for the good of my readers that my host was without a doubt and plainly speaking a very humble person and of the colored race. It is unquestionable that this good man, certainly very generous with the needy, acquired big costly meals with ease, grace, and satisfaction, at his own expense.

To abide in any hotel among cultivated people or to be resentful against someone for any reason was impossible for this man. Certainly, he preferred to resign himself to the fate of labor, in the hard misfortune of work.

It is not irrelevant to state in a great manner that such a mentioned gentleman seemed to have the power of ubiquity, since he was seen in all places, here, there, and everywhere.

One given night among others, this distinguished gentleman invited me with much secrecy to a meeting of Spiritism. I did not wish in any way to decline such a courteous invitation.

Three persons were reunited under the rural roof of his ranch. We sat down around a table with three legs.

Full of immense veneration, my host opened a small box that he never abandoned in his trips and took an indigenous skull from it.

Subsequently, he recited some beautiful prayers and cried out with a great voice, calling the phantom from that mysterious skull.

It was midnight; the sky was cloudy with large black clouds that were sinisterly shadowing that tropical space. Rain, thunder, and lightning shook the whole district.

Strange knocks were felt underneath the piece of furniture (the table). Then, definitively violating the law of gravity, like mocking the ancient texts of physics, the table arose from the floor.

Afterwards, the most sensational thing occurred: the invoked phantom appeared within the room and came close to me.

Finally, the table was inclined towards my side and the skull that was upon this piece of furniture came towards me to lay on my arms.

"That's enough," cried out my host. "The tempest is very strong and under these conditions these types of invocations become very dangerous." At that very moment a frightful thunder made the face of the invoker turn pale.

3 One day, walking on one of those old streets of Mexico City, moved by a strange curiosity, I felt I had to enter with other people into an ancient, large house, where for good or for bad, a Spiritist or Spiritualist center was functioning.

There was an extra-superior, exquisite hall that had many small bells and many emotive and delicate people, great in their kind.

Very respectively, without pretending in any way to expose myself to any risk, I took a seat in front of the platform.

Certainly, my purpose for entering into such a place was not for saturating myself with the doctrine of the Spiritist mediums or to start arguing with evilness in friendly terms, with fake meekness and pious postures. I was only going to take note of all details with a flexible understanding and singular prudence.

To train oneself for a speech that one is going to recite in public, to prepare oneself with anticipation, is certainly something excluded at any time from the Spiritist mentality.

Patiently, the sacred confraternity of mystery was waiting with mystic longing for the voices and words that would come from beyond the grave.

A gentleman of a certain age, independent from the diagnostics of the others, suitable for something very ominous, fell into a trance. Convulsively, he shook himself as any epileptic; he rose up to the platform, occupied the tribune of eloquence and took the floor.

That unfortunate possessed man cried out with a great voice, "Here, among ye, Jesus of Nazareth, the Christ."

In those frightful instants, the altar of the Baalim, the platform adorned with candles and flowers, horrifyingly vibrated and all the prostrated devotees fell to the ground.

Without wanting to disturb anyone in their performance, I serenely dedicated myself to study the medium with my sixth sense.

Pierced with anguish, I could certainly verify the crude reality of that unusual metaphysical case. Obviously, the medium was possessed by a sinister, leftist impostor, who was exploiting the credulity of others by posing as Jesus Christ.

With my clairvoyant sense, I observed a black magician dressed in a blood red tunic.

The gloomy phantom (inserted within the physical body of the medium, while imparting advice to the consulters) was trying to speak with a Jesus Christ tone, with the goal of not being uncovered by those fanatical people.

When that horrifying meeting concluded, I withdrew from that precinct with the ardent desire of not returning to that place ever again.

4 To live with one's heart content, with one's family in good will, at peace, in order to work by dint of magic upon the Earth is certainly something very romantic.

Nonetheless, to rush impetuously towards all risks seems to be indispensable sometimes, when one tries to obtain all the good possible for others.

Flanked by intellectual walls, I wanted to flourish with wisdom. So, without weakening my forces, I traveled throughout many places of the world while still very young.

Long ago, within the remote distance of a South American district popularly known with the name of Quindio, I, being very flexible with understanding, became acquainted with a Spiritist medium who was working as a blacksmith.

Without ever jumbling himself in any argument, that laborer was quietly working in his reddish forge.

He was a strange, Spiritist blacksmith, a mystic man with a bronzed figure and an athletic coenobite personality.

Bless my soul, oh God and hail Mary! I saw this man in a sinister, leftist, mediumistic trance being possessed by Beelzebub, prince of demons.

I still remember those tenebrous words with which the power of darkness closed the assembly:

> "Bel tengo mental la petra y que a el le andube sedra, vao genizar le des." (Then, the signature, Beelzebub).

What a paradoxical anchorite blacksmith! I found him repented the next day, after that leftist, Spiritist, Witches' Sabbath session. Then he solemnly swore in the name of the eternal living God not to lend his physical body to the horror of darkness anymore.

Sometimes, I found him in his forge, very sincerely consulting the Spiritist prayer book of Kardec.

Afterwards, the alluded gentleman, full of mystical enthusiasm, invited me to other exhaustive mediumistic sessions, where with infinite eagerness he evoked "Juan Hurtado el Mayor."

Without any exaggeration, and for the good of my beloved readers, I must now opportunely affirm that the mentioned phantom who was talking through the tongue of the medium

KRISHNA (THE CHRIST) GUIDES ARJUNA (THE HUMAN SOUL) TO ELIMINATE HIS DEFECTS

in trance boasted of having the power of manifesting himself through one hundred and fifty mediums simultaneously.

To conclude a speech to people with cunning, with rhyming words, is certainly very normal. Nonetheless, to pluralize himself into one hundred and fifty simultaneous and different discourses seemed to be something astonishing to me at that time.

It is unquestionable that in that epoch of my life, I still had not analyzed this theme about the plurality of the "I," of the "myself."

The Ego

Obviously, the alluded ego lacks of any self-ennobling and dignifying divine aspect.

Allow us the liberty of disagreeing with those people who presuppose the existence of two "I's," one of a superior type and another of an inferior type.

Certainly, and in the name of the truth, we certify without any discord the tremendous well-informed reality of the fact that in each person there exists only the terribly perverse pluralized "I."

This deep conviction is made firm with the vivid experience of the author of this present esoteric treatise. In no way do we need to exteriorize immature ideas. We will never commit the nonsense of affirming preposterous utopias. Our assertion has very abundant documentation in all of the sacred books of ancient times.

As a living example of our assertion, it is good to remember the bloody battles of Arjuna against his beloved relatives (the "I's") found in *The Bhagavad Gita* ("The Song of the Lord"). Clearly, these subjective psychic aggregates evidently personify the complete conjunction of psychological defects that each one of us carries within.

In rigorous experimental psychology, the bottling up of the consciousness within such subjective "I's" is evident. Then what continues beyond the sepulcher is the ego, a bunch of devil-"I's," the psychic aggregates.

The affiliation of such psychic aggregates with the Spiritist or Spiritualist centers is obvious and manifest. It is well-known and evident that such devil-"I's," because of their multiplicity, can enter into many mediumistic bodies in order to manifest themselves, as was the case of Juan Hurtado el Mayor.

Any master of samadhi can clearly verify when in the state of ecstasy the following: that which is manifested through the mediums of Spiritism are not the souls or the spirits of the dead, but the devil-"I's" of the dead, which are the psychic aggregates that continue beyond the burial chamber.

It has been said to us with much emphasis that during the postmortem (after death) states the mediums continue to convert themselves into beings who are possessed by a demon or demons. It is unquestionable that after a certain time the mediums conclude by divorcing themselves from their own divine Being. Then they enter into the submerged devolution of the infernal worlds.

Chapter IV
Theosophy

I do not want to boast at all about very delicate and multiple philosophical and metaphysical themes, but I frankly confess with full sincerity that even though I had not yet arrived to the sixteenth spring of my present existence, nonetheless, I was already engulfed within many subject matters of substantial content.

With infinite longings, I proposed myself to analyze in detail and in the light of modern science the problems of the spirit.

The experiments of the English physicist William Crookes, illustrious member of the British Royal Society, prominent discoverer of matter in the radiant state and of thallium, became extremely fascinating to me.

The famous materializations of the specter of Katie King in the middle of the laboratory seem to be astounding to me. Such a theme is exposed by Crookes in his *Measurement of Psychic Force*.

What struck me as excellent, exceptional, and marvelous were many sacred themes of antiquity like the serpent of paradise, the donkey of Balaam, the words of the Sphinx, the mysterious voices of the statues of Memnon at dawn, the terrible MENE-TEKEL-PERES at Belshazzar's banquet, the Seraphim of Teheran, Father of Abraham, the Oracle of Delphi, the betyles or the speaking stones of destiny, the oscillating and magical Menhirs of the Druids, the enigmatic voices of all bloody necromantic sacrifices (authentic origin of all classic tragedies, which cost the initiate Aeschylus his life because of his indiscreet revelations in *Prometheus*, *The Choephori,* and *Eumenides*), the words of Tiresias the diviner evoked by Ulysses in *The Odyssey* at the edge of the gap, full with the blood gushed from the propitiatory Black Lamb, the secret voices commanding the destruction of the sinful Rome which were heard by Alarico, and that the maiden of Orleans also heard and commanded of her the destruction of the English, etc.

Trained with good manners, when I was seventeen years old I dictated lectures in the Theosophical Society, without being rehearsed in oratory with the aim of speaking in public.

I received the Theosophical diploma from the hands of Jinarajadasa, the illustrious president of that august Society, whom I had the good fortune of knowing personally.

Being confident in myself, in my character, I was very well informed about the strange and mysterious knocks of Rochester, the classic psychic phenomena of the Eddy farm, where the very Theosophical Society was born. I had accumulated many data related with those evoked tripods of the Pythonesses of ancient times. I knew about enchanted houses and about post-mortem apparitions. As well, I knew in depth about all telepathic phenomena.

Unquestionably, with all of those metaphysical data accumulated within my poor mind, I converted myself into a very challenging erudite.

Nonetheless, I wanted very sincerely to mold my heart with the good Theosophical criteria. Therefore, I felt an allure for the books that I found in its rich library.

I discovered, with mystical astonishment, an inexhaustible spring of divine wisdom in the wonderful pages of *The Secret Doctrine*, an extraordinary work of the venerable, great Master Helena Petrovna Blavatsky, a sublime martyr of the nineteenth century.

Let us read now the following notes which are certainly very interesting:

> 1885. The Col. H. S. Olcott writes on the 9th day of January in his diary. H.P.B. has received from the Master M. the plan for The Secret Doctrine. It is excellent; Oakley and I did intend to do it on the previous night, but this one is much better.
>
> H.P.B. was forced to leave Adyar and to travel in March into Europe because of the conspiracy of the married couple Coulomb. She took with herself the precious manuscript. When I was prepared to board the ship, Subba Row recommended that I write The SECRET DOCTRINE and to weekly send him what was written. I promised him I

HELENA PETROVNA BLAVATSKY

will... since he is going to add notes and commentaries, and afterwards the Theosophical Society will publish it.

It was in that year when the Master K.H. wrote: The Secret Doctrine, when ready, will be the triple production of M., Upasika, and mine.

It is evident that such notes invite us to meditate. It is clear that the venerable Master H.P. Blavatsky interpreted and adapted these teachings to the epoch.

When the theoretical studies of the Theosophical type was over and done with for me, I then practiced with intensity Raja Yoga, Bhakti Yoga, Jnana Yoga, Karma Yoga, etc.

I acquired multiple psychic benefits with these practical Yogas that were made known by this venerated institution.

However, since her excellence Master H.P.B. always considered Hatha Yoga as greatly inferior, I will clarify: I was never interested in such a branch of the Hindustani Yoga.

Much later in time, I was invited to a great assembly of the venerable White Lodge where in a plain agora Hatha Yoga was qualified as authentic black magic.

Chapter V
The Rosicrucian Fraternity

I was already an adolescent of eighteen springs in this present reincarnation when I was granted the high honor of entering into the ancient Rosicrucian School. This meritorious institution was happily founded by the excellent Sir Doctor Arnold Krumm-Heller, medic/colonel of the glorious Mexican army, illustrious veteran of the Mexican revolution, eminent professor of the Medical University of Berlin, Germany. He was also a notable scientist and extraordinary polyglot.

As an impetuous boy, I presented myself with certain arrogance in that "Aula Lucis," which was directed then by an illustrious gentleman of noble intelligence. Without indulging myself into giving many compliments, neither beating around the bush, I frankly confess and speak plainly that I started out arguing and I ended up studying.

In the end, what seemed best to me was to go near the wall and place myself at the corner of the classroom enraptured in ecstasy.

It is not irrelevant to state in a great manner, yet without much pomposity, that saturated with many intricate theories of substantial content, I only yearned with infinite longings to find my ancient way: the path of the "razor's edge."

By excluding very carefully all pseudo-pietism and vain, insubstantial, empty words of ambiguous chatter, I decisively resolved to combine theory and practice.

Without prostituting intelligence for gold, I certainly preferred to humbly prostrate myself before the Creator, Demiurge of the universe.

I joyfully found an inexhaustible, wealthy spring of exquisite splendors in the books of Krumm-Heller, Hartmann, Eliphas Levi, Steiner, Max Heindel, etc.

Without excessive verbosity, I emphatically, seriously, and sincerely declare that in such an epoch of my current existence I methodically studied the whole Rosicrucian library.

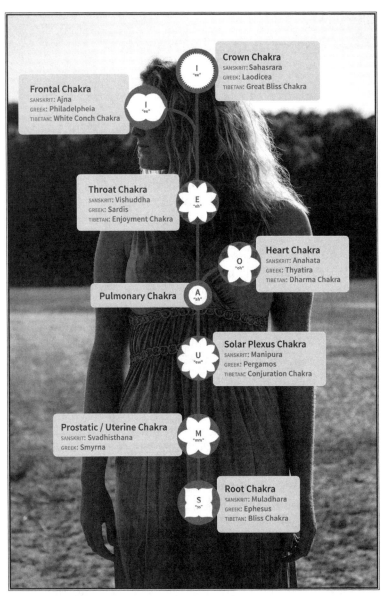

Crown Chakra
SANSKRIT: Sahasrara
GREEK: Laodicea
TIBETAN: Great Bliss Chakra

I
"ee"

Frontal Chakra
SANSKRIT: Ajna
GREEK: Philadelpheia
TIBETAN: White Conch Chakra

I
"ee"

Throat Chakra
SANSKRIT: Vishuddha
GREEK: Sardis
TIBETAN: Enjoyment Chakra

E
"eh"

Heart Chakra
SANSKRIT: Anahata
GREEK: Thyatira
TIBETAN: Dharma Chakra

O
"oh"

Pulmonary Chakra

A
"ah"

Solar Plexus Chakra
SANSKRIT: Manipura
GREEK: Pergamos
TIBETAN: Conjuration Chakra

U
"eu"

Prostatic / Uterine Chakra
SANSKRIT: Svadhisthana
GREEK: Smyrna

M
"mm"

Root Chakra
SANSKRIT: Muladhara
GREEK: Ephesus
TIBETAN: Bliss Chakra

S
"ss"

CHAKRAS AND VOWELS

Along my way, I was searching with infinite longings for a sojourner who could possess some precious balm in order to heal my painful heart.

I was suffering frightfully and crying out in solitude while invoking the holy masters of the great White Lodge.

The great Kabir Jesus said, *"Knock, and it shall be opened unto you, Ask, and it shall be given you, Seek, and ye shall find."*

In the name of That, which is the Reality, I declare the following: by accomplishing the teachings of the Christian gospel, I asked, and I received; I sought, and I found; I knocked, and it was opened to me.

It is unquestionable that in no way can we deal with such extensive and complex studies like the ones of the Rosicrucians within the limited frame of this present chapter; obviously, we will not fit the agenda. Therefore, I will limit myself to synthesize and conclude.

> The **frontal chakra** is developed with the intonation of the vowel **I** like this: *Eeeeeeeeeeeeeeeee* (as in "bee"). FACULTY: Clairvoyance.

> The **laryngeal chakra** is developed when chanting the vowel **E** like this: *Ehehehehehehehehehehehehe* (like "egg"). FACULTY: Magical Ear.

> The **cardiac chakra** is developed while vocalizing the vowel **O** like this: *Ooooooooooooooooooooooooo* (as in "toe"). FACULTY: Intuition, astral projections.

> The **umbilical chakra** is developed by intoning the vowel **U** like this: *Uuuuuuuuuuuuuuu* (as in "you"). FACULTY: Telepathy.

> The **pulmonary chakra** is developed by singing the vowel **A** like this: *Aaaaaaahhhhhh* (as in "tall"). FACULTY: Memory of past lives.

I.E.O.U.A. is the order of the vowels. All of the mantras are formed with these letters.

Dr. Krumm-Heller stated that one hour of daily vocalization is better than reading a million books of pseudo-esotericism and pseudo-occultism.

I would then inhale with supreme eagerness the Christonic Prana, the vital breath of the mountains, and then I would slowly exhale while making the resounding of the correspondent vowel.

For better clarity, I state that each vowel was preceded by an inhalation and was only resounding in the exhalation (it is obvious that I was inhaling through the nostrils and exhaling through the mouth).

Concrete Results

All of my astral chakras or magnetic centers were intensifying their vibratory activity by positively spinning from left to right like the needles of a clock, seen not at one's side, but frontward, afar from us.

Observed from within one's own body, the positive rotation of the chakras is clockwise. The same rotation, observed from afar by someone else, appears counter-clockwise.

POSTIVE ROTATION LOOKING FROM INSIDE OUT AT ONE'S OWN CHAKRAS.

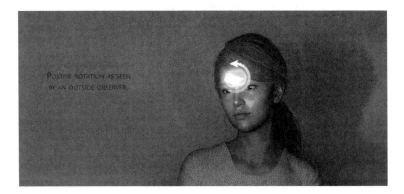

POSTIVE ROTATION AS SEEN BY AN OUTSIDE OBSERVER.

Retrospective Exercise

The teacher taught us with much didacticism a certain marvelous retrospective exercise.

He advised us that upon the instant of awakening not to ever move while on our bed. He explained to us that with such a movement the astral body is agitated and the memories of our dreams are lost.

It is unquestionable that during the hours of sleep the human soul travels out of the physical body. What is important is not to forget the inner experiences when returning into the physical body.

He indicated to us to practice a retrospective exercise in that precise moment, with the intelligent purpose of remembering experiences, occurrences, and places visited during those dreams.

Results

I solemnly declare that such a psychic exercise became astonishing to me because my memories became more vivid, intense, and profound.

Daily (preferably at sunrise), I sat comfortably on a delectable chair with my face toward the east, in accordance with the instructions of the teacher.

I then imagined in an extraordinary way a gigantic golden cross, having the Sun King as its basic center, coming from the east of the world, projecting divine rays that after traveling through infinite space penetrated within my solar plexus.

Delighted, I then intelligently combined such an exercise with the intonation of the vowel **U**, prolonging the sound in the right way: *Uuuuuuuuuuuu*.

The effect of such an exercise was the unexpected awakening of my telepathic eye (which is located, as we have already said, in the region of the navel). I became exquisitely hyper-sensible.

This was due to the fact that such a magnetic chakra possesses astonishing functions, such as the attraction and accumulation of the radiant energy of the solar globe. It is obvious that for such reason my lotus flowers, or my astral wheels, could receive major electromagnetic charges which more intensified their vibratory radio-activity.

It is for a very good purpose to remind our beloved readers in this moment that the solar plexus with its solar radiations supplies energy to all of the chakras of the human organism.

Undoubtedly and without any exaggeration, I am allowed to make a certain emphasis in order to solemnly asseverate that because each one of my astral chakras were extraordinarily developed, the perceptions of clairvoyant and clairaudient types, etc., were intensified.

Departure

A little while before leaving such a meritorious institution, the alluded teacher uttered the following, "Let not one of those who are present here dare to qualify himself as a Rosicrucian, because we are nothing but simple aspirants of Rosicrucianism." Then he added with great solemnity, "Rosicrucians are Buddha, Jesus, Moria, K.H., etc."

Chapter VI
The Corsair

For a great number of superficial people, the theory of reincarnation is a cause for laughter. To others who are very religious, it can signify a taboo or a sin. For the pseudo-occultists, this is a very firm belief. For the scoundrels of the intellect, this is a disheveled utopia. Yet for us, the ones who can remember our prior existences, reincarnation is a fact.

In the name of truth, I have to solemnly affirm that I was born remembering all of my past reincarnations, and to swear to this is not a crime. I am a man with an awakened consciousness.

Obviously, we must make a frank differentiation between **reincarnation** and **return** (two very distinct laws), although this is not the objective of this present chapter. After this preamble let us get to the facts, to the point.

In olden times, when the seas of the world were infested with pirate vessels, I had to pass through a tremendous bitterness. At that time, the Bodhisattva of the Angel Diobulo Cartobu was reincarnated. It is not worthless to affirm with a certain emphasis that such a being was in possession of a feminine body of splendid beauty. It is clear that I was her father.

Unfortunately, in an ill starred hour, the cruel piracy that did not respect lives or honor kidnapped all the beautiful girls after having isolated that European town where many citizens abided in peace. It is clear that my daughter, an innocent maiden of those forgone times, was among those beauties.

In spite of the terror of many villagers, I courageously achieved (placing my own life in danger) the confrontation of the treacherous captain of that corsair ship. "You take my daughter out of that hell in which you have placed her, and I promise you that I will take your soul out from that hell in which it already is!" Such were my painful exclamations.

The dreaded corsair, while looking at me with fierceness, had pity on my insignificant person, and with an imperative voice commanded me to wait for a while.

I watched with infinite longing as the filibuster returned to his black ship. I understood that he knew how to deceive his sea wolves with astuteness because moments after, he gave my daughter back to me.

Bless my soul, oh God, and hail Mary! Who would think that after various centuries I was going to re-encounter the ego of that dreaded corsair re-incorporated within a new human organism?

Thus, this is the law of the eternal return of all beings and things. Everything is repeated in accordance with another law called **recurrence**.

One night, with great spiritual longings, I found him joyous among the select group of those aspiring to be Rosicrucians.

That old corsair also spoke the English language, and he even told me of having traveled a lot, because he was a sailor for a North American naval company.

However, our friendship became an "ignis fatuous," a "sudden blaze of straw," because I very soon plainly verified that this man, in spite of his mystical longings, continued in his more intimate depths as an ancient corsair dressed for modern times.

With much enthusiasm, that gentleman narrated to me his astral experiences, because it is unquestionable that he knew how to astral project himself at will.

One given day among others, we arranged a transcendental metaphysical meeting to be realized in the Summum Supremum Sanctuarium of Berlin, Germany.

For me, this was a relatively new experience, because it did not occur to me until then to perform an experiment of the voluntary projection of the Eidolon. However, I knew that I could do it. Therefore, I daringly accepted such a meeting.

With complete clarity, I remember those solemn moments in which I was converted into a spy of my own dream...

In mystical lurking, I waited for the instant of that transition that exists between vigil and dream. I wanted to take advantage of those marvelous moments in order to escape from my physical body.

The state of lassitude and the first dream images were enough in order to completely understand that the awaited for moment was arriving...

I arose from my bed delicately, and walking very slowly, I left my house feeling possessed by a certain spiritual, exquisite, and delicious voluptuousness...

It is unquestionable that when I arose from my bed in the instant of drowsiness, the astral projection, the natural separation of the Eidolon, was performed.

With that very extraordinary shining of the astral body, I departed from all of those surroundings, yearning to arrive at the temple of Berlin...

Clearly, I had to marvelously travel over the boisterous waters of the Atlantic Ocean...

By serenely floating in the radiant astral atmosphere of this world, I arrived at the lands of old Europe and immediately directed myself to the capital of France...

I silently wandered as a phantom through all of those old streets which in other times served as the scenario for the French Revolution...

Suddenly, something unusual happened. A telepathic wave reached my solar plexus, and I felt the absolute imperative necessity of entering into a precious abode...

I never in any way would regret having trespassed the wealthy threshold of such a noble mansion, because there I had the immense joy of finding a friend of my past incarnation...

That fellow was wonderfully floating, submerged in the fluidic astral environment, out of his dense body that was sleeping within the perfumed bed of mahogany...

In the nuptial bridal bed, the delicate physical body of his well-beloved was sleeping as well. The sidereal soul of this one was sharing the wonderful joy of her husband and was floating out of her mortal receptacle...

I saw two tender infants of splendid beauty happily playing within the magical enchantment of that abode...

I saluted my ancient friend and also his ineffable Eve, but the children were frightened by my unexpected presence...

It seemed better for me to withdraw from there and go along those streets of Paris. My friend did not reject my idea and conversing together we departed from that mansion of delights...

We walked slowly, slowly, along all of those streets and avenues that go from the center towards the periphery...

All of a sudden (as is usually said), I proposed to him to visit the temple of Berlin in Germany together. The initiate very gently declined this invitation with the objection that he had a spouse and children and therefore wanted only to concentrate his attention on the economical problems of life...

With great sorrow, I moved away from that awakened man, lamenting that he was postponing his esoteric work...

Suspending myself in the astral light of marvels and prodigies, I passed above an old and very ancient wall...

Joyfully, I traveled along the winding way that in a serpentine form unfolded here, there, and everywhere...

Intoxicated with ecstasy I arrived at the temple of transparent walls. The entrance of that holy place was certainly very remarkable...

I saw a type of park that people usually enjoy on Sundays, filled with very beautiful plants and exquisite flowers that exhaled a breath of death...

The temple of splendors was shining solemnly in the extraordinary depth of such an enchanted garden...

The iron railed grille doors that gave access to the precious park of the sanctuary opened sometimes in order for someone to enter; sometimes they were closing...

The whole delicate and marvelous conjunction appeared illuminated with the immaculate light of the universal spirit of life...

Before the sancta sanctorum, I joyfully found many noble aspirants of diverse nationalities, towns, and languages...

These mystic souls, moved by the force of their longing, had escaped from the dense and mortal form in order to come to the sancta during the hours in which the physical body sleeps...

All of these sublime devotees conversed about ineffable things. They were talking about the law of karma. They were discoursing about extraordinary cosmic matters... They were exuding from themselves the perfume of friendship and the fragrance of sincerity.

In this state of happiness, I wandered here, there, and everywhere, searching for the daring filibuster who boldly proposed to me such a tremendous meeting...

I interrupted many groups asking for the alluded to gentleman of long ago, but none could give me an answer...

I then understood that such an ancient pirate did not accomplish his pledged word. I was ignorant of his motives, I felt deceived...

Silently, I resolved to approach the glorious door of the temple of wisdom. I tried to penetrate within the holy place, but the guardian closed the door while telling me, "It is not yet the hour, withdraw..."

Serenely, and comprehending everything, I joyfully sat on a symbolic stone, very close to the gate of mystery...

In those instants of plenitude, I observed myself in an integral way. Certainly, I am not a being with a subjective psyche. I was born with an awakened consciousness and I have access to objective knowledge...

How beautiful the astral body looked to me! (This body was a splendid result of very ancient transmutations of the libido).

I remembered my physical body that was now lying asleep in the remote distance of the occidental world, in a town of America.

While observing myself, I committed the error of comparing the true astral and the physical vehicles. By such a comparison, I lost the ecstasy and instantaneously returned into the interior of my dense material shroud...

I arose from my bed moments after. I had achieved a marvelous astral projection...

When I severely questioned the old filibuster as to his reason for not being capable of accomplishing his word, he did not know how to give me a satisfactory answer.

Thirty-five years passed since that epoch in which that old sea wolf and I arranged such a mysterious meeting...

Beyond time and distance, that strange person was already only a written memory within the dusty pages of my old chronicles...

Nonetheless, I confess and plainly speak that after so many years, I became astonished by something unusual...

One spring night, while absent from the dense, perishable form, I saw the Lord Shiva (the Holy Spirit), my sacred super-individual Monad, with the ineffable resemblance of the Ancient of Days...

With great severity, the Lord was reprimanding the old corsair of the seas. It is unquestionable that the physical body of this man was lying down in bed during those hours of the night...

With longing, I wanted to intervene as a third in the discussion. The Elder of the Centuries in a categorical way commanded my quietude and silence...

Long ago, that pirate returned my daughter to me. He had taken her from that hell within which he himself put her...

Now my real Being, Samael, was struggling in order to liberate him, to emancipate him, in order to take him out of the infernal worlds...

Chapter VII
Meditation

Flanked by intellectual walls, weary of so many complicated and difficult theories, I decided to travel towards the tropical coasts of the Caribbean Sea.

There, far away, seated as a hermit of forgone times under the taciturn shadow of a solitary tree, I resolved to put into oblivion all of that difficult compilation of vain rationalism...

I, with the mind blank, starting from a radical zero, engulfed within profound meditation, was searching inside of myself for the Secret Master...

Plainly speaking, I confess with complete sincerity that I took very seriously that phrase from the testament of ancient wisdom that literally states:

> *Before the false dawn came over this earth, those*
> *who survived the hurricane and the storm gave*
> *praise to the Innermost, and to them appeared the*
> *heralds of the dawn.* - The Testament of Learning

Obviously, I was searching for the Innermost. I worshipped him within the secrecy of meditation. I surrendered devotion unto him...

I knew that within myself, within the deep unknown hidden places of my soul, I would find him. The results did not take much time in coming...

Later on in time, I had to depart from that sandy beach in order to find shelter in other lands and other places...

However, wherever I went, I continued with my practices of meditation. While laying down on my bed or on the hard floor, I placed myself in the form of the flaming star, open legs and arms towards the left and right, with the body completely relaxed...

I closed my eyes in order not to be disturbed by anything from the world.

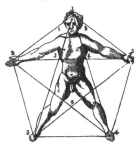

PENTAGRAM

Afterwards, I intoxicated myself with the wine of meditation in the cup of perfect concentration.

Unquestionably, as I was intensifying my practices, I really felt that I was approaching the Innermost...

The vanities of the world were not of interest to me. I knew well that everything from this valley of tears is perishable...

The Innermost, with his instantaneous and secret answers, was my single interest...

There are extraordinary cosmic festivities that can never be forgotten. This is well known by those divine and human...

In the moment I write these lines, the pleasant dawning of a venturous day comes into my memory...

Out of the planetary body, from the interior garden of my abode, humbly kneeled, I cried out with a great voice while calling the Innermost...

The blessed one crossed the threshold of my mansion. I saw him coming towards me with a triumphant step...

With precious zephyr dress and an ineffable white tunic, the beloved one came to me. I joyfully contemplated him...

The crown of the hierophants glowed splendidly upon his heavenly head. The whole nature of his body was that of happiness...

All of those valuable gems, the ones that the Apocalypse of Saint John speaks of, shone preciously on his dexterous hand...

With great firmness, the Lord was grasping the rod of Mercury, the scepter of kings, the staff of patriarchs...

Taking me in his arms, the venerable one sang with a voice of paradise, saying things that terrestrial beings are incapable of understanding...

The Lord of Perfection then took me to the planet Venus, very far away from the bitterness of this world...

Thus, through the secret path of profound interior meditation I approached the Innermost. Now I utter this because...

Chapter VIII
The Jinn States

Despite the fact that I had occupied my life with so many studies, I also had to deeply investigate the "**Jinn**" states.

Behold, dear readers, how the words of this chapter are a cause for wonder and happiness for us, since we were able to experience in a direct way the real existence of the lands and people in the Jinn state.

> "It will cause astonishment that in the first third of the eighteenth century, when the superstitious Phillips were not reigning any more, the very same Don Juan of Mur and Aguirre, former Governor of San Marcos of Arichoa in Peru, blindly believed in the existence of multiple mysterious islands throughout all the seas of the world.

> "This was due to the more or less fantastic information that was sent to the general and to the royal audience about the repeated apparitions of those dreamt of islands. Such information did produce," says Viera, "new feverish outbursts in all the spirit towards what is marvelous, and moved us to attempt the discovery of the **Nontrabada** Island for the fourth time.

> "The truth is that the **Nontrabada** or **Uncovered** has not been seen by the mortals since the eighteenth century. The aggressive skepticism that has reigned in the world since the encyclopedia does not deserve anything but to make the veil of Maya more dull and dense to those kind of uncovered ethereal mysteries, or mysteries of the fourth dimension."

> "The **Nontrabada** or **Uncovered** Island, more generally known as island of San Borondon," says Benitez in his history of the Canary Islands, "is one of those enchanted countries that has preoccupied the modern people as much as the golden fleece of the ancients. Certainly, they had powerful reasons for this, because effectively from the islands of Palma, Gomera, and Hierro, they were used to seeing O.S.O. from the first one and the O.N.O. from the last on. Running in the direction N. to S. was a kind of mountainous land that in accordance to the most generally

admitted computation, would be forty leagues of distance from the Palma, and that could have (we do not know how it was measured) about 87 leagues long by 28 leagues wide and that could be at 28 and some minutes of a latitude north, because sometimes it was shown from the southwest of Tenerife.

"The third day of April of 1570, the Doctor Hernan Perez de Grado, First Regent of the Audience of the Canaries, delivered a recommended order to the islands of Palma, Gomera, and Hierro, with the purpose of performing an exact investigation with all the people who observed the apparition of such a land, or, that had proof of its existence from any other sources.

"Because of such information, from the island of Palma he removed the Portuguese pilot Pedro Vello, native of Setubal, who said that because of a tempest, he disembarked on the island **Nontrabada** with two persons from his crew, and that there, he contemplated such and such marvels (extraordinary phenomena, giant prints, etc.).

"Then, the sky became cloudy at dawn, the hurricane blew horizontally, and being afraid of losing the ship, he returned to board it very quickly.

"In the moment of setting sail they lost sight of that land, and when the tempest ended they tried to go back to it, but it was impossible for them to discover it from any point of view. Therefore, they were disappointed, especially for two men of the crew who were abandoned within the thickness of the jungle."

This true Jinn story that is represented here for you, dear reader, is taken at face value from old chronicles.

Ancient traditions, truly, very respectable traditions, tell us that in the golden age of Lacio and of Liguria, the divine king Jano or Saturn (I.A.O., Bacchus, Jehovah) reigned over those holy people, all Aryan tribes, though from diverse epochs and origins. Then, it may be said that in the same epoch with the Hebrew people, those Jinns and mankind lived happily together.

The Jana, Yana, Jnana, or Gnosis is nothing but the science of Jano, meaning the science of initiatic knowledge, the science of Enoichion, or the seer. The variants of his name are so many that there is one in each language, such as Jan, Chhan or Kan, Dan, Dzan, D'Jan, Jain, Jian, Ioan, Kwan, Swan, Thanos, Thoan, Chohan. All of them are equivalent to the most sublime conception of a planetary spirit, the regent of Saturn, a nazada, a kabir in the most complete sense of the word.

The Jinn sciences are not an opinion for me, but an established truth, and if you want me to show this with my lived experience, listen with patience to the following narrative.

Thirty times had I seen the autumn leaves fall in my present reincarnation when I had to work consciously and positively with the doctrine of the Jinns or of Jano.

On one night of marvels, Litelantes, my priestess-spouse, proposed to me a sublime invitation...

I was resting with my relaxed body, face up (lying down position) on the nuptial bridal bed...

I must affirm with a certain solemnity and for the good of the Great Cause that in those moments I was in the state of alert novelty, alert perception.

I was dozing with attention and vigilance as a watchman in an epoch of war.

Obviously, I was longing with infinite thirst for something extraordinary.

After the well known rigorous invocations, I felt as if another human being was lodged upon my relaxed body, exactly upon the sheets, blankets, or bedclothes that delicately protected me from the cold of the night.

Unquestionably, that being was Litelantes. I recognized her because of her voice when, in a forceful way, she called me by my Christian name...

Clearly, that adept-lady, by means of the extra help of some Jinn people, had managed to place her physical body within the fourth dimension.

"Come on," she told me, "come on, come on!"

I, who with infinite longing always waited for this instant, promptly arose from my bed.

It is obvious and evident that when I arose from the bed, being helped like this, I passed through the crossing gate of the speed of light. Then I stood beside my anchoritic bed of penitence with my physical body fully submerged within the fourth dimension.

Any sincere Gnostic could certainly perform the same if in the initial moments of falling asleep he concentrates himself intensely in his particular, individual Divine Mother Nature...

The following is a very special magical formula:

I believe in God.
I believe in my Mother Nature.
I believe in White Magic.
My Mother, take me with my body.
Amen.

This prayer must be prayed thousands of times in the instants when we want to sleep.

Nonetheless, it is important not to forget a common saying that states, "*Strike with thy rod while thou beg to thy God.*"

When slightly asleep, get up from your bed while begging, and then jump with the intention of floating in the surrounding environment. Have faith even the size of a grain of mustard seed, and you might move mountains.

If you do not achieve floating, go back into your bed again and repeat the experiment.

Many are those who triumph immediately, and others persevere months and even entire years in order to attain their entrance into the Jinn paradises...

After this small but important, indicative type of divergence, let us continue with our story.

I left my bedroom with a steady and decisive step. I passed through a small patio, and directed my steps towards the street.

Granting me the way with a lot of reverence, a certain group of elderly women respectfully bent before my insignificant person who has no value. I thanked them for this special deference.

I left the city, very closely followed by this group of Jinn people. I directed myself towards the neighboring mountains.

THE JINN STATE
"With the help of the Divine Mother Kundalini, we can place the physical
body into a Jinn state in order to travel throughout the cosmos."

I felt as if I was submerged into a very ancient, sub-lunar, distant past. I understood that I had penetrated within an inferior cosmos...

I was submitted to ordeals of courage, being forced to fly over profound precipices...

By floating in the surrounding environment of the fourth dimension in the company of Litelantes and the whole procession of Jinn people, I traversed the boisterous ocean and arrived at a certain secret place in old Europe...

I courageously entered into a certain castle where I admired with astonishment a strange symbol that had a crucifix underneath it...

The return to my mansion was relatively easy, because it is a law in the fourth dimension that everything returns to its original point of departure.

Litelantes and I very happily talked about all of this. Obviously, we had achieved a marvelous triumph.

Some days after, we continued with these experiments, learning to place the physical body into a superior cosmos...

Today we know by direct experience that with the help of the Divine Mother Kundalini, we can place the physical body into a Jinn state in order to travel throughout the cosmos.

ΗΦΑΙΣΙΟΣ   ΔΙΟΝΥΣΟΣ

Dionysus

Chapter IX

The Dionysian Wave

Unquestionably, Mammon and Dionysus can never be conciliated, because they are incompatible in their summaries as well as in their contents.

In an irrefutable, axiomatic way, we can and even must define **Mammon** with two terms:

1. Intellectualism

2. Money (gold, material wealth)

It is urgent to correctly define **Dionysus** in the following precise and blunt way:

1. Voluntary transmutation of the sexual libido

2. Transcendental mystical ecstasy

Now it is opportune to cite (amongst the lucky dates of this wretched, pygmoid humanity) the date February 4, 1962, and the hour between 2:00 and 3:00 in the afternoon, in which all the planets of our solar system were reunited in a supreme cosmic council precisely under the brilliant constellation of Aquarius, in order to initiate the new Age within the august thunders of thought.

Since that memorable date and under the regency of Uranus (the very venerable and very meritorious Lord of Aquarius), the Dionysian wave intensely vibrates within all of Nature.

It is important to emphasize within this present chapter the transcendental news that such a cited planet has been, is, and always shall be the brilliant star that intelligently rules and governs the endocrine sexual glands.

Now you will be able to comprehend for yourselves the intrinsic motive that the intensive Dionysian vibration originates in these moments.

Nonetheless, the concrete fact that the terrestrials in their overwhelming majority were not at the same level of the circumstances is evident, clear, and manifest. Earthlings were not capable of positively polarizing themselves with such a cosmic wave...

Therefore, to define the two aspects, positive and negative, of this cosmic vibration is relevant, urgent, and indispensable.

DIONYSUS AND HIS WIFE ARIADNE

1. **Positive Dionysian Pole:** sexual enjoyment by means of sublimation; voluntary transmutation of the entity of semen; awakened consciousness; objective knowledge; superlative intuition; transcendental music of the great classical Masters, etc.

2. **Negative Dionysian Pole:** sexual degeneration; infrasexuality of many types; homosexuality, lesbianism; demonic pleasures within the infernal worlds by means of drugs, mushrooms, alcohol, etc., infernal music such as the "music" of these modern days, etc.

To comprehend in depth the intimate processes of these two poles of the Dionysian wave is something very urgent...

As a living example of these pair of diametrically opposite poles that correspond to the mentioned undulation, it is now opportune to cite here as a mode of illustration two contemporary revolutionary movements.

Plainly speaking, I want to clearly and delicately refer to the **universal, international, Christian, Gnostic movements**, and also to the obverse of the Dionysian coin known with the ill-famed or infamous name of the **hippie movement** and subsequent cultures.

Unquestionably, the two mentioned psychological antipodes constitute, "per se," a living, manifested demonstration of these pair of opposite poles of the tremendous Dionysian vibration.

When judiciously arriving at this part of the present chapter, the necessity of a didactic confrontation is unavoidable.

THE FOLLOWERS OF DIONYSUS: THE MAENEDS AND THE SATYRS. SOME USE
THE ENERGY OF DIONYSUS POSITIVELY, AND SOME USE IT NEGATIVELY.

Dionysian inebriation, ecstasy, Samadhi, is obviously indispensable when one is trying to experience that which is the Truth, the Reality. Such exaltation is one hundred percent possible by means of the technique of **meditation**.

Psychedelia is different. This term must be translated as this: *psyche* = "soul"; *delia* = "drug."

Specifically, we will state: **psychedelia is the antithesis of meditation.** The inferno of drugs is within the interior of the planetary organism on which we live, under the very epidermis of the terrestrial crust.

Hallucinatory mushrooms, L.S.D., pills, marijuana, etc., evidently intensify the vibratory capacity of the **subjective** powers, but it is clear that they could never originate the awakening of the consciousness.

Psychedelic drugs fundamentally alter the sexual genes and this is already scientifically demonstrated. The birth of monstrous children is evidence of the sequence of such negative, genetic mutations.

Meditation and psychedelia are incompatible, opposite, and antagonistic. They can never be mixed.

Unquestionably, these two factors of the Dionysian inebriation refer to and indicate psychological rebellion.

Gnostics and hippies were annoyed with the vain intellectualism of Mammon. They were bored with so many theories. They arrived at the conclusion that the mind, as an instrument of investigation, is abundantly miserable...

Zen? Jnana Yoga? These are superlative. Faculties of cognition that are infinitely superior to the mind exist in a latent state within us. We can experience that which is the Reality, that which is not of time, in a direct way, by means of these faculties.

Unfortunately, the hippie movement preferred the inferno of drugs. Indubitably, they defined themselves perversely.

We, the Gnostics, plainly disappointed with the stubborn intellectualism of Mammon, drink the wine of meditation from the cup of perfect concentration.

Radical and in depth **psychological changes** are urgent when we are disappointed with the scoundrels of the mind.

To return to the original point of departure is what is wise. Only thus is a radical transformation possible.

Sexology? Bless my soul, oh God, and hail Mary! This theme horrifies the puritans...

It is written in the sacred scriptures with words of fire that sex is a stumbling stone and a rock of offense...

The evidence stands out; we are not the offspring of any theory, school, or sect.

In the crude root of our existence, we only find the coitus of a man and a woman...

We were born nude; somebody cut our umbilical cord; we cried, and then we searched for the maternal breast...

Clothing? Schools? Theories? Erudition? Money, etc.? All of these came later on, as an addition.

Beliefs of all types exist everywhere. However, the unique force that can transform us in an integral and unitotal way is the force that placed us on the carpet of existence. I am referring to the creative energy of the first instant, to the **sexual potency**.

The delightful love, the erotic enjoyment, is by logical sequence the greatest joy...

To know how to wisely copulate is indispensable when a definitive psychological change is sincerely longed for.

The hippies forebode all of this when they revolted against Mammon, but they erred in their way. They did not know how to synchronize themselves with the positive pole of Dionysus.

We, the Gnostics, are different; we know how to enjoy. To transmute and sublimate the libido is enjoyable for us. This is not a crime.

The hippie movement and subsequent cultures resolutely march on the devolving, descending path of infrasexuality.

The universal, international, Christian, Gnostic movements victoriously progress on the ascendant, revolutionary path of suprasexuality.

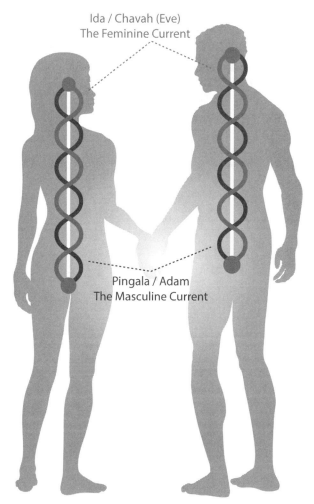

Ida / Chavah (Eve)
The Feminine Current

Pingala / Adam
The Masculine Current

THE CADUCEUS AND THE BODY

Chapter X
The Sexual Fire

The sexual transmutation of the **Ens Seminis** into creative energy is made possible when we carefully avoid the abominable spasm, the filthy orgasm of the fornicators.

The bi-polarization of this type of cosmic energy in the human organism was analyzed since ancient times in the initiatic colleges of Egypt, Mexico, Peru, Greece, Chaldea, Rome, Phoenicia, etc.

The ascension of the seminal energy to the brain is performed thanks to a certain pair of nervous cords that, in the form of an eight, splendidly unfold to the right and to the left of the dorsal spine.

We now have arrived at the Caduceus of Mercury with its wings of the Spirit that are always opened.

CADUCEUS

This mentioned pair of nervous cords can never be found with the bistoury [scalpel], because they are of a semi-ethereal, semi-physical nature.

These two nervous cords are the two witnesses of the Apocalypse, *"the two olive trees and the two candlesticks standing before the god of the earth, and if any man will hurt them, fire proceeded out of their mouth, and devoured their enemies."*

In the sacred land of the *Vedas*, these two nervous cords are known with the Sanskrit names **Ida** and **Pingala**. The first one is related with the left nasal cavity, and the second one with the right.

It is obvious that the first one of these two nadis or canals is of a lunar type. It is clear that the second one is of a solar type.

Many Gnostic students may be a little surprised to find that although **Ida** is of a cold and Lunar nature, **Ida** has its roots in the right testicle.

Many disciples of our Gnostic movement might receive the news as unexpected and unusual that although **Pingala** is of a strictly solar nature, Pingala really emerges from the left testicle. Nevertheless, we should not be surprised, because everything in nature is based on the law of polarities. The right testicle finds its exact antipode in the left nasal cavity, as has already been demonstrated. The left testicle finds its perfect antipode in the right nasal cavity and obviously this is the way it must be.

Esoteric physiology teaches us that in the feminine sex the two witnesses emerge from the ovaries. It is unquestionable that within women the order of these two olive trees of the temple is harmoniously reversed.

Old traditions which surge forth from within the profound night of all ages state that when the solar and lunar atoms of the seminal system make contact in the Triveni close to the coccyx, then as a simple electric induction a **third force** awakens; I mean the marvelous fire of love awakens.

It is written in old texts of ancient wisdom that the inferior orifice of the medullar canal is found hermetically closed in common and current people. The seminal vapors open this canal in order for the sacred fire of sexuality to enter within it.

A marvelous combination made of various canals is processed along the medullar canal. These canals interpenetrate each other without being confused. This is due to the fact that these canals are located in different dimensions. Let us remember Sushumna, and others, like the Vajra, the Chitra, the Centralis, and the famous Brahmanadi. The fire of sexual enjoyment rises through this last one when we never commit the crime of spilling the semen.

It is an absurdity to emphasize the mistaken idea that the erotic fire of all enjoyments undertakes a return trip towards the coccyx after the incarnation of the Being (the Jiva-atman) within the heart of the human being.

Horrifyingly false is the concept that torpidly affirms that the divine flame of love separates itself, venturing on a return trip through the initial path, after having its enjoyable union with Paramashiva. Such a fatal return, that descent towards the coccyx, is only possible when the initiate spills the semen. Then the initiate falls, fulminated by the ray of cosmic justice.

The ascension of the sexual fire along the medullar canal is performed very slowly, in accordance with the merits of the heart. The fires of the cardias (heart) wisely control the miraculous ascension of the flame of love.

Obviously, that erotic flame is in no way automatic or mechanical, as many sincere but mistaken people suppose. This serpentine fire awakens exclusively with the sexual enjoyment of a man and a woman united by a true love.

The erotic flame will never ascend through the medullar canal of a man and a woman united by mere personal convenience.

The ascension of the holy flame within the dorsal spine of adulterous men and women is impossible.

The fire of sexual enjoyment will never rise in the dorsal spine of those who betray the Guru.

The sexual fire can never ascend through the medulla of drunkards, homosexuals, lesbians, drug-addicts, assassins, thieves, liars, slanderers, exploiters, coveters, blasphemers, the sacrilegious, etc.

The fire of sexual enjoyment is similar to a serpent of marvels which, when awakened, emits a peculiar sound very similar to any viper which is incited with a stick.

The sexual fire, whose Sanskrit name is **Kundalini**, is developed, revolves, and ascends within the aura of the Maha-Chohan.

Indeed, the ascension of the flame of ardent enjoyments along the spinal canal from vertebra to vertebra, from degree to degree, advances very slowly. This flame will never instantaneously ascend, as some people who do not possess correct information mistakenly suppose.

It is not irrelevant to significantly state, yet without much pomposity, that the thirty-three degrees of occult masonry esoterically correspond with the thirty-three spinal vertebrae.

When the alchemist commits the crime of spilling the "cup of Hermes" (I refer to the seminal spilling), he obviously loses masonic degrees, because the fire of amorous enchant-

THE COILED KUNDALINI. HINDU.

ments descends one or more vertebrae in accordance with the magnitude of the fault.

To recuperate the lost degrees is frightfully difficult. However, it is written that there is more happiness in the cathedral of the soul for a repented sinner than for a thousand righteous ones who have no need for repentance.

We are always assisted by the Elohim in the magisterium of love. They advise and help us.

The adhyatmic university of the wise periodically examine the aspirants who, after having renounced mammon (intellectualism and material wealth), wisely enjoy the delights of love in the bridal nuptial chamber.

The clue of redemption is found in the medulla and in the semen, and anything that is not through this way, through this path, as a fact signifies a useless waste of time.

The serpentine fire (Kundalini) appears as a snake coiled three and a half times within a certain magnetic center situated in the coccygeal bone, at the base of the dorsal spine.

When the sexual serpent awakens in order to initiate its journey inwardly and upwardly, we pass through six transcendental mystical experiences that we can and must clearly define with the following six Sanskrit terms:

1. **Ananda:** A specific type of spiritual bliss.

2. **Kampana**: Electric and psychic type of hyper-sensibility.

3. **Utthana:** Progressive development of **self-cognizance**, astral projections, transcendental mystical experiences in the superior worlds, etc.

4. **Ghurni:** Intense divine longings.

5. **Murccha:** States of lassitude, relaxation of muscles and nerves in a very natural and spontaneous way during meditation.

THE COILED KUNDALINI. AZTEC.

6. **Nidra:** A specific mode of dream which, when combined with profound interior meditation, is transformed into a resplendent Samadhi (ecstasy).

Unquestionably, the fire of love confers unto us infinite transcendental powers.

The sexual flame is without any doubt simultaneously a **Jehovistic** and **Vedantic** truth.

The sexual flame is the goddess of the Word always worshipped by the wise. When it awakens, it confers illumination unto us.

The erotic flame confers unto us that divine wisdom which is not of the mind and which is beyond time.

She is the one who gives the **mukti** of final beatitude, and the **jnana** of liberation.

DI-ON-IS-IO, DIONISIO, the voluntary transmutation of the libido during the paradisiacal coitus, becomes extraordinary when syllabling this magical word, this mantra of marvels.

Magical Results of this Mantra

1. **DI:** Intensifies the vibration of the creative organs.

2. **ON:** Intelligent movement of the creative energy in the entire sexual nervous system until being submerged within the consciousness.

3. **IS:** This mantric syllable reminds us of the Isiac mysteries, and to its correspondent name **ISIS.** Obviously, the vowel **I** and the letter **S** when prolonged as a sweet and gentle whistle invoke the sexual serpent in order to victoriously rise through the medullar spinal canal.

4. **IO: Isolda,** the luni-solar androgyne. **Osiris-Isis** has sparkled with terrible divinity since the profound creation of all ages. **I,** with its deep significance, is certainly the phallus (**the lingam**), the Hebrew י **iod. O** is the eternal feminine, the uterus (**the yoni**), the famous Hebrew ה **hei.**

IO: The integral transmutation of the libido is performed when we intone this last syllable of the magical word during the sexual trance.

Thus, this is how the igneous serpent of our magical powers awakens in order to initiate its exodus along the medullar canal.

Obviously, the maternal aspect of the sacred flame, which in a serpentine form ascends through the dorsal spine, is evident.

The flame with the form of a snake, the divine sexual flame, is the very sacred Mother **Kundalini**.

Out of the physical body our particular Cosmic Mother (because everyone has their own) always assumes the presence of a marvelous Virgin Mother.

Once upon a time when I was out of the physical body — the date and hour do not matter — I met with my sacred Mother within the interior of a precious hall.

After all the well-known hugs between son and mother, she sat on a comfortable chair in front of me, an opportunity that I took advantage of in order to ask questions which are necessary.

QUESTION: "Am I doing well, my Mother?"

ANSWER: "Yes, my son, you are doing well."

QUESTION: "Do I still need to practice Sexual Magic?"
ANSWER: "Yes, you still need it."
QUESTION: "Is it possible that in the physical world there could be someone who could Self-realize without the necessity of Sexual Magic?"

The answer to this last question was tremendous:
ANSWER: "Impossible, my son; that is not possible."

I frankly confess and with plain words that this pronouncement from the Beloved One left me astonished. I then remembered with supreme pain so many pseudo-esotericist and pseudo-occultist people who in truth are longing for the final liberation but who do not know the **Sahaja Maithuna** — Sexual Magic — the marvelous clue of the Great Arcanum.

Unquestionably, the path that leads towards the abyss is paved with the stones of good intentions.

THE GODDESS OF HEAVEN IN EGYPTIAN SYMBOLISM

Chapter XI
The Sacred Cow

Before the second Transapalnian catastrophe, which fundamentally altered the aspect of the terrestrial crust, an old continent existed that now remains submerged within the boisterous waters of the Atlantic Ocean.

I am emphatically referring to "Atlantis." Innumerable traditions exist everywhere about it.

Behold, or not, the Atlantean foreign names, or names of barbarian languages which the cretinous Greeks alluded to when wanting to kill **Anaxagoras**, who dared to say that the Sun was a little bigger than half of Peloponnesus.

Names, I say, which were translated into the Egyptian language by the Saiphic priests, and restored into their primary significance by Plato the Divine, in order to later marvelously pour them into the language of Attica.

Behold the diamantine thread of the millenary tradition from the Saiphic priests to Solon and then continuing with the two Cristias and the Master Plato...

Behold, I tell you, the extraordinary descriptions of botany, geography, zoology, mineralogy, politics, religion, customs, etc., which come from the Atlanteans.

Behold as well, with the eyes of a rebel eagle, the veiled allusions of the first divine kings of such an ante-delugean old continent, divine kings who simultaneously have many references in Mediterranean Paganism and in very ancient sacred texts from the oriental world.

Behold those astonishing notes of Diodorus Siculus — that for us are still material for study — which give a detailed account of those sublime kings.

Behold at last — and this is what is most interesting — the similar characteristics of the sacrifice of the sacred cow of Brahmans, Hebrews, Mohammedans, the European Gentiles, and thousands of other populaces...

It is unquestionable that our most celebrated and indestructible taurine circus is in its depth nothing but a very ancient ancestral survival from that Atlantean sacrificial festivity whose description is still found in many archaic secret books.

There are in reality many legends in the world about the bulls that were released in the Temple of Neptune. These animals were not brutally subdued with banderillas and swords as in these times, but with ropes and other ingenious arts of classic tauromachy.

The symbolic beast already defeated in the sacred bull ring was immolated in honor to the holy gods of Atlantis, gods who, as the very Neptune, had devolved from the primitive solar state, becoming a people of the lunar type.

The classic art of tauromachy is certainly something initiatic and related with the mysterious worship of the sacred cow...

Behold the Atlantean bull ring from the Temple of Neptune, and the present one.

Certainly they are nothing but a living zodiac in which the honorable public are seated as the constellations.

A TORERO IN HIS SYMBOLIC SOLAR GARMENTS

The Initiator or Hierophant is the **Master**, the walking baderilleros are the **Companions**, and the mounted bull fighters are the **Apprentices**.

Therefore, the Apprentices ride on the horse, in other words, on all the ballast of their untamed body, which falls dead in hard battle.

The Companions already feel superior since they are putting the banderillas or the lances into the wild bull, into the animal ego; in other words, they are already (like Arjuna from *The Bhagavad Gita*) the persecutors of the Secret Enemy.

The Master with the cape of his hierarchy, which signifies the domination over **Maya**, is the one (as a resemblance to the God Krishna from that old poem) who grasps with his dexterous hand the flaming sword of willpower. He becomes not the persecutor but the killer of the "I," or the beast, a horrifying, roaring monster which was also seen in **Camelot**, **Kamelok** or **Kamaloka** by the very King Artus, supreme chief of the illustrious Knights of the Round Table.

The resplendent Atlantean tauromachy is a profoundly significant royal art, since it teaches us through its brilliant symbolism the hard battle that must lead us to the dissolution of the "I."

Any retrospective glance related with taurine esotericism can indubitably conduce us to mystical discoveries of a transcendental order.

As a fact of the present actuality, it is worthy to cite the profound love which the Torero feels for the Virgin. It is clear that he totally delivers himself to her before appearing with his sparkling suit in the bull ring.

This reminds us of the Isiac mysteries, the terrible sacrifice of the sacred cow and the archaic worship of IO, whose origins have become solemn on our planet Earth since the dawn of life.

It becomes thrilling, clear, and defined that truly only IO, Devi Kundalini, the sacred cow of five legs, the Divine Mother, possesses that serpentine magical power that permits us to reduce the animal ego, the roaring beast within the ring of existence, to cosmic dust.

The vowels IO constitute in themselves the number **ten** of generation, and the reason for the circumference of the diameter.

Obviously, 10 is then the number of Pi (Pithar), the tremendous masculine-feminine mystery.

IO is also the swastika, fohat, or transcendental sexual electricity which is represented by

A Greek vessel in honor of IO, the Goddess who was turned into a cow.

the cross within the circle, symbol of the Earth, a theme upon which a book can be written.

It is written with letters of fire in the book of life, that such a swastika symbol has existed in all the countries of the Earth since the night of the centuries, in the form of coordinating mathematics.

We need with entirely undeferable urgency to convert ourselves into "ox herders," in other words, into wise conductors of the "sacred cow."

The venerable, great Master H.P.B. really did see an authentic cow with five legs in India. This was a real caprice of nature, an immaculate, very white, ineffable miracle... Don Mario Roso de Luna said that such a unique creature carried the fifth leg on its back, and that with this leg it scared flies or scratched itself...

The curious animal was herded by a young boy from the Sadhu sect. This virgin boy nourished himself exclusively with the milk of this mysterious cow. The esoteric, marvelous, and resplendent symbolism of the "cow with five legs" stands out as obvious and unmistakable. This is a very vivid manifested expression of the five unfoldments of our very particular Divine Mother **Kundalini**...

Let us remember the sign of the infinite, the horizontal eight which is equal to the number five, which when read literally is "infinite equal to five"; in other words, the infinite is equal to the Pentalpha, equal to the ineffable cow with five legs, equal to the star of five points or the starry, regular pentagon, which stopped **Mephistopheles** when he came to the bewitching invocation of Dr. Faust...

THE SIGN OF THE INFINITE. THE PENTALPHA: PENTA (5) + ALPHA (A).

To define these five aspects is indispensable for the good of all and each one of our students:

1. The unmanifested **Kundalini**

2. Ineffable **ISIS**, chaste Diana (wisdom, love, power).

3. The Greek **Hekate**, the Egyptian **Proserpine**, the Aztec **Coatlicue** (the queen of the infernos and death, terror of love and law).

4. The **individual, particular Mother Nature** (the one who created our physical body).

5. The **instinctive, elemental, female magi** (the one who originated our instincts).

The "ox herder," the conductor of the "sacred cow," can and must work in the magisterium with these five powers of the Pentalpha...

Solemnly, emphatically, I declare the following: I directly work with the five powers of the sacred cow.

To illustrate, clarify, and teach about the Pentalpha is an obligation, but I prefer to do it with lived stories:

First Story

It is said that between the sublime and the ridiculous, there is but one step, and this is axiomatic.

You may remember for a moment the Bacchantes when they were in their orgiastic period of rage. These were feminine beauties positively polarized with the Dionysian wave, Nymphs of the forests and mountains who were persecuted by the lascivious Sileni.

Behold now the ridiculous Maenads, who were negatively polarized with the wave of Dionysus... They were licentious dancers in the rage of their sacred madness, "hippie" women of ancient Greece... They were feminine prostitutes who were excited by drugs in complete Dionysian inebriation... the human and animal sacrifices were making them even more dangerous.... The lustful Maenads were the ones who killed Orpheus, and the marvelous lyre fell upon the floor of the temple and was broken into pieces.

The Maenads drink the ambrosia-wine of the god Dionysus (center). Note the laurel around his sexual organs. Greek vase, 4-3rd centiry, B.C.

Once upon a time, I was narrating to my friends some comic episodes from a Bohemian past...

Obviously, the fermented fruit of the vineyard and the Bacchantes at the breaking point of their orgiastic rage could not be absent in such comicality...

These were ridiculous scenes of those ancient times in which I walked as a fallen Bodhisattva on this world of **Kali Yuga**.

Nonetheless, starry moments of humanity exist, and a cosmic recollection is truly very necessary...

Out of the physical vehicle, in the **astral body**, under the tridimensional zone of Euclid, I had to enter within the subterranean world...

What happened afterwards was exceedingly frightful. What I saw in that horrifying submerged zone was the same that was seen by the Hoffmans, the Edgar Poes, the Blavatskys, the Bulwer-Littons of all times. It was the same as the poet Espronceda portrayed through his demoniacal chorus, as the anguishes of the poet, and as the discordant voices of those who pilot the vessel of life without course, when trusting themselves as madmen to the wind of passions and to the tenebrous sea of doubt in the good work. It was as those who are fatally betrothed with destiny, as those who proudly want to build Towers of Babel with their stubborn ambitions, as those who lie, those who combat for mundane glories, those who wallow in the muddy pleasures of orgies, those who covet gold, as the lazy ones who hate the fertile and creative work, as those evil ones, those hypocrites and other victims of the Proteus of egoism. To that end... claws, teeth, horns, snouts, darts, wrasses, sawing wings, tearing rings appeared which were threatening to annihilate me as a vile worm...

Many horrifying sounds were heard in those moments through my magical ear: wailing, howling, whistling, neighing, squeaking, bellowing, gagging, meowing, barking, snorting, snoring, and croaking.

Submerged, I was within the mud of so much misery. Anguish possessed me; I was anxiously waiting for a balm to heal my painful heart...

The lucubrations of those great seers of the astral who were called alchemists, kabbalists, occultists, esotericists, yogis, gnostics, or simply poets, were not in vain.

Suddenly, something unusual happened beyond the muddy waters of Acheron. The horrible door that gives access to the abode of Pluto turned upon its hinges of steel...

Intensely moved, I shook myself. I forebode that something amazing had happened. I was not mistaken... I saw her, it was she, the **unmanifested Kundalini**. She had crossed the threshold where the lost souls abide...

Magnificent Madonna, excellent, extraordinary, and terrifically divine, she approached me with a magistral step. I did not know what to do. I was confused. I simultaneously felt fear and love...

A cosmic reminder? Recrimination? The Beloved One spoke with a voice from paradise. She blessed me, and then continued on her way as if she was going towards the frightful walls of the city of Dis.

In those moments, from within the depth of my consciousness, I felt that she wanted also to help the others who dwelled around that city of pain where no one can enter without just indignation...

While looking from the high tower of an ardent summit, it is said that Dante saw the three infernal furies who unexpectedly appeared. Those furies had, as is said, movements and limbs of a feminine nature.

I instantaneously remembered all of this. I did not want in any way (I, a miserable slug from the mud of the earth) to become another inhabitant of the city of pain. Fortunately, I had the immense joy of being able to depart from within the bottom of the Averno in order to appear in the sunlight...

The next day: very early, someone knocked at my door; it was an old professor of secondary schooling... That good person invited me to a graduation party. His daughter had concluded her studies with complete success...

It was impossible to decline such an invitation! He was my friend, and I even owed him certain services. In no way was I able to reject him...

After all the well-known personal arrangements, Litelantes and my insignificant person who does not have any value departed from home with the longing of arriving at the professor's abode.

Many very warm and elegantly dressed people welcomed us into the illustrious mansion...

Delicious music resounded in the estate. Happy people were coming, going, here, there, and everywhere. Joyfully, the couples danced upon the soft carpet.

Many times my splendid host came towards us with the purpose of offering fermented wine...

Very closely, I saw time and time again the resplendent cups of fine baccarat. However, I energetically rejected **Bacchus** and his orgies. I was remorseful in my heart. My host became caustic, incisive, and even a little offensive.

Unquestionably, he was converted into my worst enemy. He mistakenly supposed that I was being ungracious at his party... Later on, he propagated against me diverse defaming lies. He threw against my insignificant person the whole poison of his criticism...

Not being happy with all of this, he appealed to public calumny, by accusing me before tribunals of justice for certain crimes that until now I am ignorant of...

This gentleman of foregone times died a short time later, involved in a disgraceful automobile accident.

Today I think that I certainly acted like any ignorant person would at that party. I lacked diplomacy.

There are guests in all the halls of the world who know how to play with the devil. They pass the whole night with one cup in their hand and marvelously defend themselves. Each time when there is a new toast they show that they are drinking, but in reality they do not drink. They mock the demon of alcohol...

DIANA OF VERSAILLES, A ROMAN COPY OF A GREEK STATUE OF ARTEMIS,
THE TWIN SISTER OF PHOEBUS APOLLO. FOURTH CENTURY B.C.

Second Story

Let us now go into a very singular new story in which we will not talk of marvelous feasts neither of Heliogabalian banquets...

> "What a rested life
> for the one who escapes from mundane strife
> and follows the concealed path
> on where have walked
> the few wise who in the world have lived!
>
> "Do not be turbid of the chest
> as the great arrogants' condition,
> neither of the golden ceiling nest
> be wondrous, whose construction
> by the wise moor, is on jasper's foundation!..."

The hunter Venus, who descends from the high summits with the purpose of helping her son Aeneas, the Trojan hero who has disembarked on the land of Libya, brings me an unusual remembrance...

Isis, Adonia, Tonatzin (the second aspect of my Divine Mother **Kundalini**), came to me more rapidly than the blow of Eurus...

She did not have the common face of mortals. Instead, she possessed a beauty impossible to describe with words. She resembled the sister of Phoebus Apollo...

I found myself within her very loving immaculate arms. The Beloved One resembled a *Mater Dolorosa*, like the one of the Christian gospel...

I was hungry and she gave me to eat, thirsty and she gave me to drink, sick and she healed me. To forget her words is impossible:

"My son, without me, at the hour of death you will be completely orphaned." Then she continued, saying, "You, without me, would be completely alone in the world. What would your life be without me?"

Posteriorly, I repeated, "Certainly, without you, oh Mother of mine, I would be orphaned. I recognize that in the hour of death, without your presence, I would be very lonely."

Life becomes a desert when one has died within oneself. Without the help of our Divine Mother Kundalini in the whole presence of our Being, we would then find ourselves interiorly orphaned...

Oh beloved Mother! You have manifested the Prana, electricity, strength, magnetism, cohesion, and gravitation in this universe.

You are the divine occult energy within the unknown profundities of each creature.

Oh Maha Sarasvati! Oh Maha Lakshmi! You are the ineffable spouse of **Shiva** (the Holy Spirit).

Third Story

The legend of the celestial cow whose milk is ambrosia, life, and immortality is in no way without solid foundations. We the adepts, like the divine Gautama or Buddha, conductor of the cow, work very seriously with the magisterium of the five aspects of **Devi Kundalini**.

It greatly pleases us, the Gnostics, to nourish ourselves with the apples of gold, or of Freya, that give immortality to the gods...

We joyfully drink the liquor of Soma or Biblical Manna with which we feel ourselves so invigorated and comforted as in the best moments of our flourishing youth...

A certain cosmic, transcendental, divine event comes into my memory in the instant in which I write these lines.

Many years ago, it happened on a night of the full moon that I was transported to an extraordinary monastery of the universal White Fraternity...

How happy I felt in that mansion of love! Certainly, there is no better pleasure than feeling oneself released in the soul... In those instants, time does not exist, and the past and future are joined within an eternal now.

Following my friends through royal chambers and galleries, we arrived at a very refreshing patio which made the one from the lions of Alhambra look like a miniature.

In this enchanting patio, various springing water fountains, as those from the divine water spring of Castalia, mur-

mured amongst flowers that have never been seen or mentioned.

However, the best was displayed in the center of the patio, and I contemplated it with the mystical astonishment of a penitent anchorite...

I want to emphatically refer to the "stone of the truth." This stone had a divine, human form...

It was the sexual prodigy of the blessed Goddess Mother Death, a funereal, spectral marvel...

It was the third aspect of my Divine Mother Kundalini, a living, petrous sculpture, a tremendous representation of that which greatly frightens the mortals...

Plainly speaking, I confess before the divine and before humans that I embraced the terrible Mother Death while in complete Dionysian inebriation...

To reconcile myself with the law was indispensable. This was what the brothers of the Order of Saint John, those venerable ones who had already performed in themselves the Hyperborean mystery, had said unto me...

When concluding that cosmic festival, I then had to reunite myself with some ladies and gentlemen of the Holy Grail in the refectory of the monastery...

With much secrecy and great enthusiasm, we the brothers and sisters commented about that extraordinary event while dining...

Unquestionably, the "Animated Stones," which in ancient Arcadia radically modified the way of thinking of the wise man Pausanias, can be classified into two types: Ophite and Siderite, the "Serpent Stone," and the "Star Stone."

Eusebius especially never separated himself from his Ophites, which he carried in his bosom. He received oracles from them, which were uttered by a small voice that sounded like a fine whistle...

Arnobio narrates that whenever he found a stone of this type, he would never stop asking questions, which were answered by a little, clear, and sharp voice...

It seemed to me that Hekate, Proserpine, Coatlicue, within the living animated stone, was emerging from the "Field of Death," or from some tomb of Carnac.

Fourth Story

What the common people know of the reality of shamanism is very little, and even this very little has been adulterated, the same adulteration that has occurred in the rest of the non-Christian religions.

Shamanism used to be called, without any right, the "Paganism of Mongolia," since it is one of the most ancient religions of India. It refers to the cult of the Spirit, the belief in the immortality of souls, and that these, beyond death, keep presenting the same characteristics of the human beings whom they were animating here on the earth. This occurred even when their bodies had lost their objective form, when the human being substituted its physical form for the spiritual one because of death.

In its present form, such a belief is a sprout from the primitive theurgy, and a practical fusion of the visible world with the invisible one.

When a foreign person who is naturalized in this country wishes to enter into communication with his invisible brothers, he has to assimilate their nature, that is, he must find these beings by walking half of the way that separates him from them. Then, enriched with an abundant provision of spiritual essence given by them, he then endows them in return with a part of his physical nature, in order to place them, through this action, in the condition of being able to sometimes show themselves in their semi-objective form, a form that they ordinarily lack.

Such a process is a temporal change of nature, which is commonly called theurgy.

Shamans are called sorcerers by vulgar people, because it is said that they invoke the spirits of the dead with the goal of exercising necromancy. But true shamanism cannot be judged based on its degenerated ramifications in Siberia, in the same way that the religion of Gautama Buddha cannot be confused with the fetishism of some people in Siam and Burma who call themselves its followers.

Unquestionably, theurgical invocations become simpler and more effective when they are magically operated with the physical body totally submerged within the fourth dimension.

By walking inwardly and upwardly half of the way (that half which separated us from the beloved brothers), we are able to find ourselves face to face with our beloved dead. Obviously, this whole process becomes easier by walking the totality of the way.

Like Iamblicus, we can invoke the holy gods in order to personally talk with them, by submerging the physical body within the fourth parallel.

Nonetheless, it is clear that we need with extreme urgency a fulcrum point, a lever, which really permits us to jump with the entire physical body into the fourth dimension.

Opportunely, it is good to place here that famous phrase of Archimedes, "Give me a lever of support and I will move the universe."

In the eighth chapter of this book, we already spoke with much emphasis about the magical agent of the **Jinn** states. I want to clearly refer to the fourth aspect of **Devi Kundalini**. (This is the lever of support for the fourth dimension).

In the moments in which I write these lines, some remembrances, magnificent, divine evocations, come into my mind...

It happened that in an autumn night I resolved to drink of the wine of meditation in the cup of perfect concentration.

The motive of my meditation was **my particular Divine Mother**, the fourth aspect of the igneous serpent of our magical powers.

To pray is to talk with God, and I talked with the Beloved One, begging her with a silent verb to take me with my physical body to the terrestrial paradise (the fourth dimension).

What took place afterwards in that night of mystery was astonishing: being assisted by the Beloved One, I rose from my bed...

When I left my abode and went out to the streets, I could evidence that my physical body had penetrated into the fourth dimension...

She took me into the most profound forest of Eden, where the rivers of pure water of life flow with milk and honey...

Virgin, lady of wooded summits! Everything becomes silent before thee, the non-cultured Iberia, the moody Gallic who challenges even when dying, and the fiery Sicambro who when finally surrendering his weapons, humbly respects you.

Beloved Madonna of mine, by the gods who from the high heaven govern the mortals on the Earth, I always beseech thine help...

The countenance of my Mother Nature was like a paradisiacal beauty, impossible to describe with human words...

Her hair looked like a cascade of gold that deliciously fell upon her alabaster shoulders...

Her body was like unto the mythological Venus. Her hands, with very beautiful conical fingers filled with precious gems, had the Christian form...

I conversed with the Beloved One in the forest. She told me things that terrestrial beings are not able to comprehend...

My Mother was resplendently sublime in the ethereal world, in the fourth vertical, in the fourth dimension...

If therefore nothing produces alleviation for a painful chest, neither marbles of Phrygia, neither resplendent purpura, it is better for one to seek shelter within the delicious bosom of his particular, individual Divine Mother Nature...

She is the author of our days, the true artificer of our physical body...

She was the one that in the human laboratory joined the ovum with the sperm in order for life to have sprouted...

She is the creator of the germinal cell with its forty-eight chromosomes...

Without her, the cells of the embryo would not have multiplied, neither would the cells have formed...

Even when suffering surrenders your soul, keep yourself firm, oh disciple! Humbly deliver yourself to your Mother Nature...

Fifth Story

> "I want to see in the confines of the terrestrial mansion, the ocean and Thetis, to whom we owe our existence."

The loves of Jupiter with the virgin **Io**, she who was transformed into a celestial female calf (or sacred cow for the oriental world) in order to escape from the anger of **Juno**, is something that has very deep significance...

Behold here, the first Jupiter of Greek theology, father of all gods, lord of the universe and brother of Uranus or Ur-Anas, or in other words, the primordial **fire** and **water**, because it is known in accordance with the classics that there are more than three hundred Jupiters within the Greek pantheon.

JOVE or **IOD-EVE** in his other aspect is the male-female יהוה **JEHOVAH**, or the collective androgyny of **Elohim** from the books of Moses, the **Adam Kadmon** of the Kabbalists, the **IA-CHO** or **INACHO** of Anatolia who is also **Dionysus**, whose vibratory wave has become very intense with the entrance of the Sun into the brilliant constellation of Aquarius...

Jesus the great Kabir never surrendered cult to the anthropomorphic **Jehovah** of the Jewish multitudes...

The law of retaliation, "An eye for an eye and a tooth for a tooth," from the avenger **Jehovah,** was overcome by the law of love: *"Ye love one another, as I have loved you."*

If we scrutinize with mystical enthusiasm the sacred scriptures, we can clearly verify the unmistakable and evident fact that the anthropomorphic Hebraic **Jehovah** does not appear in any of the four gospels.

RAM-IO (MARY), the Divine Mother Kundalini, always accompanied the Beloved One, and we see Her at the foot of the cross on the Mount of the Skulls...

"Father, forgive them; for they know not what they do," uttered the divine rabbi of Galilee from the majestic summits of Calvary.

Unquestionably, the blessed lord of perfections only wor-shipped his Father who is in secret and his Divine Mother Kundalini.

In other words, we will state: the great Kabir Jesus pro-foundly loved יהוה **IOD-HEVE**, the divine, interior male-fe-male...

י **IOD** is certainly the particular individual Monad of each one of us, the Hindustani **Shiva**, the arch-hierophant and arch-magi, the first begotten of creation, the golden fleece, the treasury which we must take hold of after defeating the drag-on of darkness...

הוה **HEVE** is the unfolding of י **IOD**; Heve is the divine wife of **Shiva**. She is our individual Mother Kundalini, the sacred cow with five legs, the esoteric mystery of the Pentalpha.

Jupiter and his cow of **Io** (*iiiii ooooo*), keep in exact con-comitance with יהוה **IOD-HEVE**, the interior divine couple of each creature.

We have studied four aspects of the sacred cow of IO. Let us now continue with the fifth mystery...

There are transcendent and transcendental cosmic inter-vals on the esoteric path.

I had to pass through one of those intervals, after having entered into the temple of the Twice-born...

I want to refer in an emphatic manner to a period of sexu-al suspension, to a period of sexual abstention which endured for several years.

During this interim, I dedicated myself with absolute exclusivity to profound, interior meditation...

The objective of this meditation was to dissolve the psy-chological "I," the "myself," the "itself," the one which is cer-tainly a knot within the cosmic energy, a thickness that we must reduce to cosmic dust.

It seemed fundamental to me to comprehend each one of my psychological defects in an integral manner. But I wanted to proceed a little further in the path of meditation.

Comprehension is not everything. We need to capture the **deep significance** of that which we had comprehended, with maximum, expedited urgency.

Any devotee of the royal path may have given himself the luxury of comprehending a psychological defect in all of the territories of the mind. Nonetheless, he still may not have achieved the capture of its deep significance.

By trying to comprehend my own defects in all of the bends of the mind, I resolved to become an enemy to myself.

Each defect was studied in separate and in a very ordinate way. I never committed the error of trying to hunt ten hares at the same time. I did not want in any way to expose myself to failure.

The meditation became exhaustive. It became more and more profound, and when I was feeling dismayed, I left the mind in quietude and in silence as if waiting for some revelation; the truth came in those instants. I captured that which is not of time, the deep significance of the comprehended defect, in an integral manner.

Afterwards, I prayed with vehemence, beseeching, begging my Divine Mother Kundalini for the elimination from my mind of the psychological aggregate, the psychological defect in question.

Thus, little by little, with this didactic, with this "modus operandi," I achieved the elimination of fifty percent of those subjective infrahuman elements that we carry inside and that constitute the **EGO**, the "I," during that sexual pause.

However, it is evident that everything in life has a limit. There are scales and scales, degrees and degrees.

This work became frightfully difficult when I had to confront more ancient infrahuman elements.

Unquestionably, my Divine Mother required far more superior weapons. I remembered the lance of Eros, the marvelous emblem of transcendental sexuality, but I was in a pause. What could I do?

Nonetheless, a cosmic desideratum had already been delivered unto me and a certain categorical command was demanding me to descend again to the "flaming forge of Vulcan" (sex) but I had not comprehended.

I had been transported to the mountains of mystery; I had seen those terrible forces of the Great Arcanum in action. I fought in vain against the categorical commands of the Dionysian wave. Certainly they were frightfully divine, omnipotent...

These supernatural powers looked like an apocalyptic hecatomb. It felt as if those forces could make the Earth jump into pieces.

When I wanted to explore, investigate, inquire, about the origin of such sexual powers and forces, I found myself face to face with the **elemental female magi**, with my Divine Mother Kundalini in her fifth aspect.

Certainly, I had seen her. She was the size of a gnome or pygmy, very small, and very beautiful...

She was dressed with a white tunic and a long black cape that she was dragging on the floor. Her head was covered with a very special magical cornet.

Beside one of the two symbolic columns of occult masonry, the Beloved One had commanded me to a new descent into the "Ninth Sphere" (sex).

Disgracefully, I had believed that it was related with some ordeal, therefore I continued in disobedience. Certainly, I was slow in comprehension and this was stagnating me.

While struggling for some time in mortal fights against a certain very infrahuman psychic aggregate that violently resisted its elimination, I appealed to the lance of Longinus.

I did not have another solution. I appealed to the sexual transcendental electricity. I beseeched my Divine Mother Kundalini during the metaphysical copulation. I eagerly begged her to grasp the lance of Eros.

The result was extraordinary. My sacred Mother, armed with the holy pike, with the divine spear, with the sexual, electric power, could then reduce the horrifying monster, the psychic aggregate which I was in vain trying to dissolve without the chemical coitus, to cosmic dust.

Thus, this was how I abandoned my sexual pause and returned to the "forge of the Cyclops." By working with the holy spear I achieved the reduction of all of the infrahuman elements that constitute the "I" to cosmic dust.

The fifth aspect of Devi Kundalini grants us sexual potency, the natural instinctive force, etc.

The Divine Mother and the Christ-child

The First Mountain

The Mountain of Initiation

JESUS AND HIS DISCIPLES

Chapter XII
The Gnostic Church

Those who have already passed to the other shore are the ones who truthfully know what the rigorous ordeals of initiations are...

It is not a crime to alienate ourselves from the monster of a thousand faces (humanity) in order to efficiently help it.

I was thirty years old when I was submitted to frightful ordeals. What I saw then, what happened to me, is relevant to narrate.

It was during one night of mystery when I felt the howling of the hurricane beside me. I then comprehended...

How lonely I found myself on that night; nevertheless, no matter where I situated myself, here, there, or anywhere, all of a sudden I saw myself always surrounded by crowds. I did not know how all of a sudden all of these people were surrounding me, and then suddenly...

The hurricane was howling again, this is how I comprehended "what was gone with the wind." Today I utter this because...

> What murmur
> so far away reverberates
> which the silence
> in the serene
> black night did interrupt?
>
> Is it perhaps the horse of the speedy race
> that runs at full gallop in the flying escape,
> or the rough roar of the hungry wild beast,
> or perhaps the whistle of the north wind,
> or the hoarse echo of the distant thunder
> which in the deep caverns resounded,
> or the boisterous sea which threatens with its engorged bosom,
> a new Luzbel, for the throne of his God?

All of those specters from that night of mystery were also seen by this great poet who sang as follows:

Dense mist
covers the sky
and by spirits
is inhabited,
wandering,
here is the wind
and there, they go across
vaporous
and numberless
and here they gather
and there they spin
they now adjoin
they detach
they now disappear
they appear
they wander, they fly.

Vague crowd of vain phantoms
of diverse shapes, of assorted colors
riding on goats, on serpents and on crows,
and on canes of brooms, with a silent murmur...

They pass, they flee,
they come, they grow,
diminish,
they evaporate,
become colored,
and within shadows
and reflections
close and distant
now they vanish,
now they evade me
with horror,
now they flurry
with furor
in a fantastic aerial masquerade
on all sides of me.

With all these wails, howls, whistles, neighs, squeaks, bellows, gaggles, meows, barks, snorts, snores, and croaks, the poet seer keeps listening and talking to us with words which are like the vivid and phosphoric strokes of El Greco, and like such extraordinary apparitions as those found in "The Caprices" of Goya.

In many places, there were shields with rampant lions, shells of Compostela, beheaded moors, fleurs de lis and trouts, palaces everywhere and big houses in ruins, poverty and more poverty.

Often, I had to courageously confront the black powers of the air, to which the Apostle Paul of Tarsus refers in chapter II, verse I of the Epistle to the Ephesians.

Unquestionably, the most dangerous adversary in that night had the fatal title of "**anagarika.**" I want to emphatically refer to the demon Cherenzi. That repugnant, tenebrous creature had taught **black tantra** (Sexual Magic with seminal ejaculation) to the world. As a result of that black tantra, just by glancing at him one could see that he has a very developed diabolical tail and horrifying horns.

This leftist tantric demon came before my presence accompanied by two other demons. He appeared to be very satisfied with his abominable **Kundabuffer** organ (a terribly satanic, witch-like tail), an outcome or corollary of black tantra, which is the projected sexual fire from the coccyx, downwards towards the atomic infernos of the human being.

Out of the blue (as it is said), I asked him the following question, "Do you know me?"

His answer, "Yes, I saw you one night in the city of Bacata when I was dictating a lecture."

Certainly, what happened afterwards was not very pleasant: that "Anagarika" had recognized me; infuriated, he threw fire through his eyes and tail... He wanted to hurt me in a violent way. I defended myself with the best conjurations of High Magic, and he finally flew off with his attendants.

While the hurricane was howling, I solitarily continued on my way during that night of mystery...

Within the profound depths of my consciousness I had the strange sensation of departing from everything and everybody...

Panting and tired after having fought repeatedly against the tyranny of the prince of the powers of the air (the spirit that now worked in disobedient children) I entered inside the **Gnostic Church**.

This temple of luminous marble with its unusual reflectivity looked as if it was made out of crystal.

The unconquered terrace of this transcendental church, like a glorious acropolis, dominated the solemn area of a sacred pinery...

From that terrace, the resplendent starry firmament was pictured as in the Atlantean temples of ancient times. Those now buried Atlantean temples were longing for the extraordinary poetry of Maeterlinck. Those temples were where **Asuramaya**, the astrologer, a disciple of **Narada**, made observations in order to discover the chronological cycles of thousands of years, which he then taught to his beloved disciples in the light of the pale Moon, and which is still practiced today by his devout successors.

Slowly I advanced inside of this holy place, walking very quietly and with a reverent attitude.

However, something surprised me: I saw a certain personage who crossed my way and blocked my passage. Another battle? I prepared to defend myself, but this personage very amiably smiled and exclaimed with a voice of paradise, "You do not scare me; I know you very well!"

Ah! Finally, I recognized him... He was my Guru Adolfo, whom I have always called by the diminutive "Adolfito" (little Adolf). Bless my soul, oh God, and Hail Mary! But... what was I doing?

"Forgive me, master! I did not recognize you..."

Then, my guru conducted me by hand towards the interior of the Gnostic Church...

The mahatma took a seat, and afterward invited me to sit by his side. It was impossible to decline such an invitation.

Certainly, the dialogue that occurred afterwards between master and disciple was extraordinary.

"Here, within the Gnostic Church," said the hierophant solemnly, "you can be married only with one woman; you cannot be with two.

"Long ago, in the past, you gave vain hopes to a certain lady 'X' who, for that reason, in spite of time and distance, is still waiting for you.

"Obviously, you are unconsciously performing a very harmful action towards her, because she lives in a city in complete misery waiting for you.

"This lady could well return into the bosom of her family in the country, and it is clear that her economical problems would then be resolved."

Astonished and perplexed when listening to these words, I hugged my guru, with infinite gratitude for his advice.

"Master," I said, "what could you say about my spouse **Litelantes**?"

Answer, "She is worthier for you for Sexual Magic, the **Sahaja Maithuna**... With this adept-lady you can work in the **Ninth Sphere** (sex)."

"Oh, guru, what I hope for with infinite longings, at any cost to me, is the awakening of the **Kundalini** and the union with the Innermost..."

"But, what have you said, oh disciple — at any cost?"

"Yes, master, I have said this..."

"A payment was given to someone on this night, and to him the duty of helping you in the awakening of your **Kundalini** has been entrusted.

"You have passed the **Direne ordeal**," exclaimed the hierophant. Then, while placing on my head a turban of immaculate whiteness that holds a button of gold on the forehead, he said, "Let us go towards the altar..."

Promptly standing, I walked with my holy guru to the holy altar...

Still I remember that solemn instant in which I had to swear a solemn oath as I kneeled before the sacred altar...

"At any cost!" exclaimed my master with a great voice and with intense vibration; this phrase was repeated from sphere to sphere...

I then covered my **solar plexus** with my left hand and extended my dexterous hand upon the **Holy Grail** while saying, "I swear it!"

A tremendous oath!

> "It has been stated that this cup, which was carved out of an enormous emerald, was used by the great Kabir Jesus in his last supper; genuine legends from Castilla, such as the one from Alphonse VII, states how he took away this famous bowl or Grail (better if we call it a cup) from the hands of the Moors of Almeria. Indeed, a terribly divine cup..."

To swear before the Holy Grail?...

Ancient legends state that Joseph of Arimathaea collected the blessed blood that was shed from the wounds of the Beloved One within that cup at the foot of the cross, on the Mount of the Skulls...

Such a vessel was previously granted to Soliman or Solomon, the solar king, by the Queen of Sheba, and was a patrimony (according to others) from the Tuatha Dé Danann, a "Jinn" race from Gaedhil (Gallic Britain).

How this venerated relic came to be found in the hermitage of Saint John of la Peña in the Pyrenees is unknown. From there, its peregrination continues, then to the Galician Salvatierra, then to Valencia during the time of James the Conquistador, and then to Genoa because the Genovese received it in ancient times as a reward for the help they lent to Alphonso VII in the fields of Almeria.

Epilogue

Very early in the morning, I wrote to the noble, suffering lady who was waiting for me in that remote city...

I advised her with infinite sweetness to return to her land with her relatives and that she should forget about my insignificant person who has no value...

Chapter XIII

The First Initiation of Fire

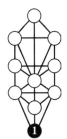 When dealing with transcendental and practical esotericism, we can and even must emphasize the following.

Everything which has been stated in occultism about geomantic boards, astrology, magical herbs, marvelous parchments with cryptographic languages (in spite of being absolutely noble and true) is certainly nothing but **kindergarten**, the minor part of the great wisdom inherited from the East. This wisdom consists of the radical transformation of oneself by means of the revolutionary asceticism of the new Aquarian Age (an extraordinary mixture of the sexual arousal with spiritual longing).

Indeed, we Gnostics are the elect ones, possessors of three great treasures that are:

A) The Philosophical Stone

B) The Clavicle of Solomon

C) The Genesis of Enoch

These three factors constitute the living foundation of the Apocalypse, besides the collections of Pistorius, the Theosophy of Porphyry and many other very ancient secrets.

The absolute radical change within ourselves, here and now, would be impossible without the **Philosophical Stone**.

Clearly and plainly speaking, I declare: the **Ens Seminis** (the entity of semen) is certainly that venerable matter (cited by Sendivogius) with which we must elaborate the Philosophical Stone.

Sexual Magic is the way... Thus, this is what I understood in my present reincarnation when I wanted to elaborate upon the Philosophical Stone.

We can accomplish that alchemical maxim that states *Solve et Coagule* by means of the blessed stone.

We need to dissolve the psychological "I" and coagulate the Hydrogen SI-12 within us in the form of the solar bodies, inner powers, virtues, etc.

It is the Philosophical Stone that valorizes the sexual seed and gives the power of germination to it, like a mystical leaven that creates fermentation and raises the complete metallic mass in order for the king of creation to appear in his integral form, which is not the intellectual animal mistakenly called "human being," but the authentic **human**.

Willpower — **Thelema** — acquires the power of transmutation that converts vile metals into gold, in other words, evil into good, in all circumstances of life. For this reason, **Thelema** demands a minimum quantity of Philosophical Stone or "powder of projection" for the transmutation.

Each vile metal dissolved in the sexual alchemical crucible is always replaced with the pure gold of some new virtue (*Solve et Coagule*). The **modus operandi** is mentioned in the eleventh chapter, fifth story, of this same treatise (for more information you must study my book entitled *The Mystery of the Golden Blossom*).

To light the individual **Fohat**, the flame of Eros, in our sexual alchemical laboratory is certainly the foundation of the Dionysian wave. Thus, this is how I profoundly comprehended it when studying at the feet of my Guru "Adolfito."

Unquestionably, I was always assisted during the meta-physical copulation. The other divine guruji, to whom payment was given in the temple (see chapter twelve), accomplished his pledged word.

This great soul assisted me astrally during the chemical coitus. I saw him making strong magnetic passes upon my coccygeal bone, dorsal spine, and superior part of my head.

When the erotic igneous serpent of our magical powers awoke in order to initiate its inner, upward march, I felt very thirsty and a very sharp pain in my coccyx that lasted for many days.

I was then congratulated in the temple. I can never forget that great cosmic event.

During that epoch, I was dwelling in peace within a small house at the seashore, in a tropical zone on the coast of the Caribbean Sea...

The ascent of the **Kundalini** from vertebra to vertebra was performed very slowly, according to the merits of the heart.

THE SPINAL COLUMN

Cervical
vertebrae
(7)

Thoracic
vertebrae
(12)

Lumbar
vertebrae
(5)

Sacrum
(5 fused
vertebrae)

Coccyx
(4 fused
vertebrae)

Each vertebra is very demanding. We can infer with this that there are difficult ordeals.

As a corollary we affirm: the ascent of the Kundalini to any vertebra is not possible if we do not fulfill the precise moral conditions for it.

These thirty-three spinal vertebrae are denominated in the superior worlds with symbolic terms like "canyons," "pyramids," "holy chambers," etc.

Certainly, the mystical ascension of the flame of love from vertebra to vertebra and from chakra to chakra along the medullar canal was performed upon the foundation of Sexual Magic, as well as sanctification and sacrifice (goodwill).

The assisting mahatma granted me help by conducing the sacred fire from the coccygeal bone (base of the dorsal spine), to the pineal gland, situated, as it is already known by physicians, in the superior part of the brain.

Posteriorly, with great mastery, that "great Ssoul" made my erotic fire flow up to the region of the mid-brow.

The First Initiation of Fire became the corollary when the igneous serpent of our magical powers made contact with the atom of the Father in the magnetic field at the root of the nose.

Certainly, it was during the mystical ceremony of the Last Supper when the cosmic date for the initiation was settled. The Holy Grail, as a sacred ember, flamingly shone upon the table of the Pascal banquet.

The true history of this Holy Grail is written in the stars and does not have its foundation in Toledo, as it is stated by Wolfram von Eschenbach...

The principal known origins of all these chivalrous legends related with the legend of the Holy Grail are:

A) The *History Rerum in Partibus Transmarinis Gestarum* by Guillermo from Tyre (1184), a Latin work translated into French with the title of *Roman D'Eracle*. It is a book which serves as a foundation for the book *Gran Conquista de Ultramar,* translated from French into Castellan in the late thirteenth century or the beginning of the fourteenth century. In this book *Gran Conquista de Ultramar,* the five main branches which refer to the cycle of the First Crusade are summarized: The *Chanso D'Antiocha,* the *Chanson de Jerusalem, Les Chetiis* (or captives), and *Elias* (the Knight of the Swan).

B) The *Dolopathos* by John of Haute-Selve, written in 1190.

C) The poem which Paris called *Elioxa* or *Helioxa* — The Solar Calf — the primitive name of Insoberta or Isis-Bertha from the *Knight of the Swan*. This last work has great analogies, in accordance with Gayangos, and with the famous *Amadis of Gaul.*

D) *Parsifal* and *Titurel* by Eschenbach.

E) *Count of the Grail* by Chrétien de Troyes (1175), *Lohengrin* or *Swan-Ritter* (the Knight of the Swan), an anonymous Bavarian work from the thirteenth century published by Goerres in 1813.

F) *Tristan and Isolde* by Godofrede of Strasbourg (1200-1220), and also there are many analogous "Tristans" found in literature.

G) The "Demand of the Holy Grail" with the marvellous acts of Lancelot and his son Galahad (fourteenth century), with all of its concordant works.

I waited with infinite anxiety for the date and hour of the initiation. The date was related with a very sacred 27th.

I wanted an initiation as the one obtained by Commander Montero in the Temple Chapultepec, or like the initiation obtained by Gines de Lara (the reincarnated deva) in that sancta sanctorum or adytum of the Templar Knights on an extraordinary night of an eclipsed moon.

However, my case was certainly different, and even if this seems to be incredible, I felt disappointed during the night of my initiation.

While resting with infinite anguish on my hard bed within a humble cabin by the shore of the sea, I passed the night uselessly waiting in vigil...

My priestess wife was sleeping, snoring, sometimes moving in her bed, or pronouncing incoherent words...

The frightfully roaring sea was beating the shore with its furious waves, as if protesting...

Daybreak came and nothing! Nothing! Nothing! Oh God, what a "dog's night"... Bless my soul, oh God, and hail Mary!...

What intellectual and moral tempests I had to experience in those mortal, nocturnal hours!

Indeed, there is no resurrection without death, nor a dawn within nature (or within the human being) without darkness, sorrows, and nocturnal agony preceding them, which makes their light more adorable.

All of my senses were tested and tortured in mortal agony that made me exclaim, *"My Father, if it is possible take this cup away from me, but not my will but thine be done."*

When the sun arose like a ball of fire, seemingly emerging from within the tempestuous ocean, Litelantes awoke saying, "Do you remember the festivity that they offered to you up there? You received the initiation..."

"What? But what are you saying? Festivity? Initiation? Which? The only thing that I know is that I passed a night more bitter than bile..."

"What?" exclaimed Litelantes, astonished. "So then you did not bring back any memory to your physical brain? You do not remember the great chain? Did you forget the words of the great initiator?"

Overwhelmed by such questions, I interrogated Litelantes, saying, "What did the great being tell me?"

"He warned you," exclaimed the Adept-lady, "that from now on you will have double the responsibilities for the teachings that you will give to the world... Moreover," said Litelantes, "you were dressed with the white linen tunic of the adepts, of the occult fraternity, and the flaming sword was delivered unto you..."

Ah! Now I understood. While I was passing through so much bitterness in my anchorite, penitent bed, my real inner Being was receiving the cosmic initiation...

Bless my soul, oh God, and hail Mary! But what is happening to me? Why am I so slow-witted?

"I am a little hungry. I think that it is time for us to get up for breakfast..."

Moments later, in the kitchen, Litelantes gathered some dry wood that would serve as combustion for lighting the fire...

Breakfast was delicious; I ate with a great appetite after such a painful night...

Another day of routine: I worked as I always did in order to gain the daily bread, and then close to midday I rested in my bed...

I was certainly tired, and a small nap seemed to me just, and moreover, I was sorrowful within my heart...

I did not have any inconvenience in lying down with my body well-relaxed in the "dorsal decubitus position," in other words, lying on my back, facing up...

Suddenly, while being in the state of vigil, I saw that someone entered my room. I recognized him as a "chela" of the venerable White Lodge...

This disciple held a book in his hands; he wanted to consult me and to solicit a certain authorization...

When I wanted to give an answer, I spoke with the type of voice that even surprised me. It was **Atman** answering through my creative larynx. He is terrifically divine.

"Go," said my real Being, "accomplish the mission that is commanded unto you." The thankful chela left.

Ah! How different I was... Yes, now I understand. Those were my exclamations after the departure of that chela...

Happily, I arose from my hard bed in order to talk with Litelantes. I needed to tell her what had just occurred...

I felt as if something superlative, a transcendental, ethnic change of an esoteric, divine type had operated within the interior of my consciousness.

I was longing for the night. For me, that tropical day was as a vestibule of wisdom. As soon as possible, I wanted to see the sun like a ball of fire sinking once again into the boisterous waves of the ocean.

When the moon started to turn the boisterous water of the Caribbean Sea metallic, precisely when the birds of the sky were withdrawing into their nests, I had to urge Litelantes to conclude her domestic chores.

That night we went to bed earlier than usual; I was longing for something. I was in an ecstatic state...

While laying down again on my anchorite, penitent hard bed in that Hindustani asana of a dead man, "dorsal decubitus" (facing up with a relaxed body, arms along the sides, heels together, with the feet opened like a fan), I was waiting in the state of alert perception, alert novelty.

Suddenly, in a matter of a thousandth of a second, I remembered a distant mountain.

What happened then was something unusual, unexpected...

Instantaneously, I saw myself there, upon the distant summit, very far away from my physical body, affections, and the mind...

I was **Atman** without boundaries, far away from the dense body and in the absence of the supra-sensible vehicles...

The cosmic initiation that I received the previous night was a palpable fact, a living crude reality that I did not even need to remember in those moments of Samadhi...

When I placed my dexterous hand over the golden belt, joyfully I could verify that there I had the flaming sword, exactly at my right side...

All the details that Litelantes had given me had become precise for me. How happy I felt now as a **Spirit-Man**! I was dressed with the tunic of white linen...

I cast myself into the infinite sidereal space while in complete Dionysian inebriation. I joyfully moved away from the planet Earth...

While submerged within the ocean of the universal spirit of life, I did not want to return into this valley of bitterness. So I then visited many other planetary abodes...

While smoothly placing myself upon a giant planet from the unalterable infinite, I exclaimed, "I dominate the whole of this," as I unsheathed the flaming sword...

"The human being is called to be the governor of the whole of creation," answered a hierophant who was at my side.

I then put the flaming sword within its golden sheath and while submerging myself even more within the "sleeping waters of life," I performed a series of extraordinary invocations and experiments.

"Buddhic body, come unto me!"

Then, attending my call, the beautiful Helen, Guinevere, the queen of the Jinn knights, my beloved Spiritual Soul, came to me.

She entered within me and I within her, and between us we formed the famous Atman-Buddhi of which Oriental Theosophy speaks greatly.

It has been said, and with just rightness, that **Buddhi** (the Spiritual Soul) is like a glass of alabaster, fine and transparent, within which the flame of **Prajna** (Atman) blazes.

From within the very depths of the chaos, I continued to perform those singular invocations in a successive order, and I then called my Human Soul, saying, "Causal body, come unto me!"

I saw my Human Soul gloriously dressed with the causal vehicle (the Theosophical Superior Manas).

How interesting that moment was when my Human Soul joyfully entered into me...

At that moment, that Theosophical Triad, known in Sanskrit as **Atman-Buddhi-Manas**, was lucidly integrated in an extraordinary way.

Unquestionably, **Atman** (in other words, the **Innermost**) has two souls. The first is the Spiritual Soul (**Buddhi**), which is feminine. The second is the Human Soul (Superior Manas), which is masculine.

While inebriated with ecstasy, I subsequently called my mind as follows, "Mental body, come unto me!"

I had to repeat this invocation numerous times because the mind is tardy in obeying, but finally it presented itself with great reverence saying, "Lord, here I am. I have concurred to your call. Excuse me for being delayed. Did I accomplish your orders well?"

In those instants in which I was going to give an answer, the solemn voice of my Pythagorean Monad emerged from my profound interior, saying, "Yes! You obeyed well. Enter..."

That voice was like the **Ruach Elohim,** which according to Moses sowed the waters in the dawn of life...

It is not irrelevant to emphatically state that I concluded these invocations by calling the astral body. This body was

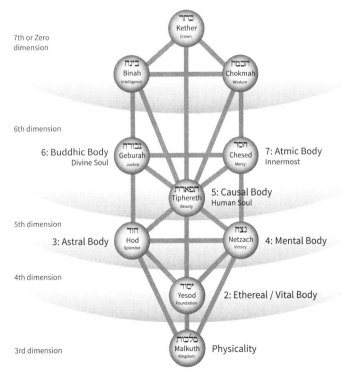

THE KABBALAH AND THE BODIES OF THE HUMAN BEING

also a little delayed in coming to my esoteric call, but finally it entered within me.

I, from within the Chaos (the primitive abyss), already dressed with my supra-sensible vehicles, could have also called my physical body which in those moments was within its anchorite and penitent hard bed. Obviously, this body would have concurred to my call.

This is never impossible: my physical body, which was resting in those very interesting moments within the hard bed, could be helped with the fourth aspect of **Devi Kundalini**. It could have abandoned the three-dimensional region of Euclid in order for it to concur to my call.

However, I then preferred to emerge from within this "vacuum" (vacuum, in the sense of a completely unlimited and profound space), in order to return to the planet Earth...

In those moments, I resembled a solitary ray emerging from the abyss of the Great Mother...

The return to this planet of bitterness, governed by forty-eight laws, was relatively very quick.

Frankly and plainly speaking, I declare: I returned into my physical body with complete **self-cognizance** by penetrating within this body through that marvelous door of the soul cited by Descartes. I am referring to the pineal gland...

It is a pity that Cartesian philosophy ignores what **objective knowledge** is.

Since such a type of pure knowledge is accessible to my cognitive faculties, I have written these lines for the good of our beloved readers...

Chapter XIV
The Second Initiation of Fire

Unquestionably, we can and must asseverate with great emphasis the transcendent and transcendental existence of two types of classic occultism.

Two occultist modalities, from all the conjunctive varieties of historical and pre-historical processes related with the Earth and its human races, are given unto us to infer as follows:

A) Innate occultism

B) Scholastic occultism

Clearly, the first of these two branches is pre-delugean. The second is completely post-delugean.

The exact parallels of these two clearly enunciated forms of occultism must be clairvoyantly discovered within the two modalities of the law:

A) Natural, paradisiacal law (wisdom of gods)

B) Written law, Deuteronomy (the second and more inferior law)

It is written with characters of fire in the book of life that when "the Sons of God," in other words, the **Elohim** or the **Jinns**, knew the daughters of men, then, frightfully, the terrible Atlantean catastrophe or the universal deluge occurred (Genesis 6). Then, the formidable empire of the first law concluded, and the time for the Deuteronomy or the second law arrived.

The terrible imperfection of the written law is excessively visible and evident. It is a law that is a torment for the great men because of its frightful limitations, but a severe protection for the smaller men.

While congregating his people on the plains of Moab, Moses, the illustrious sacred leader of the people of Israel, exposed to the sight of everyone the extraordinary prodigies that the Lord had performed in his favor. When on the Mount of Sinai, the first alliance had been established, and he repeated the law with new illustrations, pronouncing frightful warnings against its transgressors and promising just rewards and happiness of many types to those who faithfully obey it.

After having blessed the twelve tribes of Israel, Moses, when transfigured on Mount Nebo, contemplated the "Promised Land," the Elysian Fields or the Jinn's world, the land which flows with milk and honey, the ethereal world, the fourth dimension...

Moses did not die like the rest of mankind; he disappeared on Mount Nebo. His cadaver was never found. What happened to him? Moses returned into the happy land of the Nordic and Druid chants. He became a "Jinn." He was converted into an inhabitant of paradise...

We have verified in an integral form the unmistakable, clear, and definitive fact that precisely there, in the supra-liminal world, in the fourth dimension, is where the people of the ancient Arcadia joyfully abided. I want to refer specifically to the paradisiacal humanities of ancient times.

When John the Baptist was beheaded, the great Kabir Jesus *"departed into a desert place by ship privately"* (St. Mark 6:32); in other words, into the Jinn lands, into the fourth coordinate of our planet Earth. Here is where he performed with the multitude the miracle of the five loaves of bread and two fish, from which about five thousand men (not to mention women and children) ate, and moreover they took up twelve baskets full of fragments (St. Matthew 14:15-21).

It is clear that the great Gnostic priest Jesus had to penetrate within the fourth dimension; he placed the multitudes within the fourth dimension with the evident purpose of performing the miracle...

Ancient Irish traditions (wisely consigned in the delectable chants of their bards or Nordic rhapsodies) spoke justly about an extraordinary **Cainit** or **Inca** people (in other words, "Priest Kings") called the **Tuatha Dé Danann** who were very skillful in all types of magical arts learned in Thebes.

Obviously, the **Tuatha Dé Danann** are a great Jinn people, prototype of the indefatigable traveler, "the errant Jew."

The Tuatha Dé Danann traversed the Mediterranean countries until arriving at the same Scandinavia where they founded four great magical cities, in addition to having previously founded a lunar and a solar city.

When the Tuatha arrived in Ireland, they disembarked on that island, as Aeneas in Cartagus, protected by a thick magical mist (or the **veil of Isis** of the fourth dimension that hid them).

In other words, we state that the Tuatha returned to Ireland; they arrived there within the fourth dimension.

The very famous battle of **Madura** (Magh Tuiredh), in which the Tuatha, full of glory, defeated the tenebrous **Fir Bolg**, can be found written in old chronicles.

> "The excellency of the **Tuatha Dé Danann** was indeed great, and their hosts so powerful and innumerable that the fields appeared suited with masses of combatants who extended unto the regions where the sun sets as the day declines. Their heroes became immortal before **Tara**, the magical capital of Ireland.

> "The Tuatha did not arrive at Erin on any known ship, neither could anybody grasp and clearly determine whether they were people born on the Earth or descended from Heaven, nor if they were diabolic entities or from a new nation which could not in any way be human, since their veins did not run with the royal blood of the indefatigable Berthach, the founder of the primitive Ceinne."

Definitively, when the great Atlantean catastrophe occurred, the Tuatha Dé Danann entered the fourth dimension.

Some human races joyfully inhabit the ethereal region of our planet Earth. These people still live in a paradisiacal state, even in our days of so much bitterness...

Many magical cities of splendid beauty exist in the fourth coordinate of our planet Earth.

We can discover the elemental paradises of nature with all of its temples, valleys, enchanted lakes, and Jinn lands within the terrestrial fourth vertical...

TARA, THE ANCIENT CAPITAL OF THE TUATHA DE DANAAN IN COUNTY MEATH, IRELAND. ATOP THE MOUND TO THE LEFT IS THE STONE OF FAH WHICH, ACCORDING TO LEGEND, WILL CRY OUT WHEN TOUCHED BY A TRUE KING.

Unquestionably, it is here in the "Promised Land" where we can still joyfully find the **innate occultism** and the **natural, paradisiacal law**...

Those blessed Jinns who happily dwell in the Elysian Fields, in the land that flows with milk and honey, are certainly never under the regency of Deuteronomy or the second law, which is a great torment to the mortals...

Obviously, the Jinn multitudes, those known as the Tuatha Dé Danann, joyfully dwell in Eden under the regency of the first law...

The Tuatha Dé Danann always carried through all the lands of their legendary exodus four magical, esoteric symbols:

A) A gigantic **cup** or **grail** (living symbol of the feminine uterus).

B) An enormous **lance** of pure iron (masculine phallic symbol).

C) A great flaming **sword** (symbol of the sexual fire).

D) The **stone** of truth (symbol of the sexual Philosophical Stone).

If Moses, the great Hebrew leader, would have ignored the deep significance of these four magical symbols, he would never have converted himself into a Jinn on Mount Nebo...

Thus, this is how I comprehended it when prostrated before the **Logos** of the solar system. With complete humility, I asked to enter into the Second Initiation of Fire...

It is impossible to forget those instants in which the Blessed One entrusted to a certain specialist the sacred mission of wisely conducing through my dorsal spine the second degree of the power of the fire...

I wanted to know in depth the mysteries of the fourth coordinate, and to victoriously penetrate into the "Promised Land..."

I needed with maximum and undeferable urgency to restore the igneous powers within my ethereal, vital depth...

I was congratulated in the temple with a great cosmic festivity when the **second serpent** awoke in order to initiate its inward and upward ascension along the ethereal spinal medulla.

The Jinn specialist assisted me during the metaphysical copulation.

Litelantes and I perceived him with our sixth sense.

Clearly, I was not abandoned. That Jinn person helped me with strong magnetic passes that came from my coccyx up to the pineal gland...

A great moral responsibility was cast upon this master's shoulders, which was to intelligently conduce for me the living and philosophical fire along the spinal medullar canal in the famous theosophical **lingam sarira** (the vital depth of the human organism).

Obviously, such a vehicle is just the superior section of the physical body, the tetra-dimensional aspect of our physical body.

"This initiation is more arduous."

This is how the Logos of our solar system spoke unto me. However, I hoped with infinite longings to know the mysteries of the **ethereal world**, to enter into the Promised Land.

The brilliant ascent of the second igneous serpent along the medullar canal, from vertebra to vertebra and from chakra to chakra, was performed very slowly according to the merits of the heart.

Each spinal vertebra of an ethereal type implies determined virtues. It is clear that we must be tested before reaching any vertebra. Let us remember that gold is tested with fire, and virtue with temptation.

The legs of the thrones of the gods have animalistic forms. The tenebrous incessantly attack those that intend to reach any degree of the occult masonry in their dorsal spine. *"The kingdom of heaven suffereth violence and the violent take it by force."* - Matthew 11:12

Mystical agapes exist in the country of *The One Thousand and One Nights*. I was at one of those feasts. The guests were royally attended to by swans of immaculate whiteness on the shore of a crystalline lake...

The following cosmic law was taught to me upon another occasion: **"You must never mix within the same house two contrary forces, because a third force, which is destructive for everybody, is the result of this mixture of two opposite currents."**

The **Vital Body** is constituted of four ethers:

A) Luminous ether

B) Reflective ether

C) Chemical ether

D) Ether of life

The first of these ethers is found intimately related with the diverse functions of **willpower** and **imagination**.

The second ether is found secretly associated with all the sensorial and extra-sensorial **perceptions**.

The third is the foundation of all **biochemical** and **organic processes**.

The fourth serves as a medium for the forces that work with the processes of **reproduction** of the races.

I learned to liberate the two superior ethers in order to travel with them far away from the physical body during the Second Initiation of the Fire.

Unquestionably, clairvoyant and clairaudient perceptions are extraordinarily intensified when one absorbs the two superior ethers in one's astral body.

These ethers permit us to bring into the physical brain the totality of the supra-sensible **memories**.

The vivid esoteric explanation of the mystical **decapitation**, which in a scenic way was showed to me, was certainly extraordinary...

I was invited to a macabre feast and what I saw on the tragic table was certainly frightful...

A profane, bloody head was placed on the silver tray and was decorated with something that is better to omit...

It is clear that its deep significance is that the animal ego, the itself, the myself, must be beheaded...

As a blunt and definitive fact, we can conclude here with great assertion that the head of John the Baptist upon a tray of silver possesses identical significance...

Unquestionably, John the harbinger taught this terrible truth by ascending to the altar of supreme sacrifice...

By exploring old chronicles with the constancy of a clergyman in a cell, we discover the following:

> "The Nazarenes were known as Baptists, Sabians, and Christians of Saint John. Their belief was that the Messiah was not the Son of God, but simply a prophet who wanted to follow John. Origen [Vol. II, page 150] observed that there are some who say that John was the anointed one (**Christus**).

> "When the metaphysical conception of the Gnostics, who saw the Logos and the Anointed One in Jesus, was starting to gain ground, then the primitive Christians were separated from the Nazarenes and were accusing Jesus of perverting the doctrine of John and of changing the baptism in the Jordan for another one." - Codex Nazaraeus, II, page 109

St. John the Baptist, symbolizing the Terrestrial Man,
bows over the Philosophical Stone in order to receive the
decapitation, the symbol of the death of the psychological
"I," the ego. The cosmic executioner gives the head to
Salomé, a symbol of the wife of the initiate, for it is she
who helps her beloved to his initiation, and vice versa.

It is relevant to emphatically asseverate the transcendental fact that John the Baptist was also a **Christus**...

On the other hand, when considering from the point of view of the **Logos** (multiple, perfect unity), it can be said that he has saved those that have died in themselves, those that have decapitated the animal ego, and have defeated the kingdom of darkness or inferno.

As a consequence or corollary, I understood all of this in a unitotal, integral way when seeing the macabre table in the hall of the feast...

The adepts of the occult fraternity gave me a beautiful present when I abandoned that unusual and abysmal den. It is a minuscule instrument of magic with which I can operate as a theurgist by modifying plasticity... Those who have seen my photographs have evidenced for themselves the concrete fact that I control my plasticity voluntarily. The various forms of my face disconcert my best photographers. However, frankly and plainly speaking I confess that it is not I who possesses this power but my Innermost, my real, inner Being, **Atman,** the ineffable one. He operates upon my plasticity when it is indispensable...

My insignificant person has no value; the Great Work is what matters. I certainly am nothing but a simple slug in the mud of the earth...

If I could write in detail the whole of that which we the mystics have experienced in the thirty-three holy chambers of the ethereal world, we would fill many volumes. Therefore, I prefer to speak in synthesis...

When the second degree of the power of the fire reached the height of the creative larynx, I was put in jail.

The accusatory affidavit was textually saying the following: "This man, in addition to committing the crime of healing the ill, is also the author of a book entitled *The Perfect Matrimony,* which is an outrage against public morality and the good customs of the citizens."

It was within the horrifying dungeon of an old South American prison where I then had to pass through the classic ceremony of the decapitation...

Then, I saw at the foot of a large, old, fortified tower my **Divine Mother Kundalini** with the flaming sword in her dexterous hand, decapitating a creature.

"Ah! Now I understand," I exclaimed within the dreadful darkness of that horrible dungeon. Posteriorly, I entered into that delectable state that in high yoga is known as **Nirvikalpa Samadhi**.

Out of this other dungeon which is called the physical body, I experienced in ecstasy within myself the great inner profound Reality...

He, my Monad, penetrated within me, in my soul, and then I became totally transfigured.

I integrally saw myself with lucid plenitude.

He is the fifth of the seven spirits before the throne of the Lamb, and I am his **Bodhisattva**. This comes as a reminder of that phrase of Mohammed, *"Allah is Allah, and Mohammed his prophet..."*

When departing from that prison, I directed my steps towards my house. There, my best friends were waiting for me...

Some days later, the second degree of the power of the fire made direct contact with the atom of the Father, situated in the magnetic field of the root of the nose. Then I saw, envisioned in the night, the flaming star with the eye of God at its center. The resplendent pentalpha was detached from the Sun Christ in order to shine upon my head...

The cosmic festival on that night of the initiation was extraordinary. I saw, from the threshold of the temple, my real Being, the Innermost, crucified on his cross in the very sacred depth of the sanctuary before the brothers and sisters of the occult fraternity.

While he was receiving the initiation, I arranged my affairs with the lords of karma in the vestibule of the temple...

Chapter XV
The Third Initiation of Fire

Unquestionably, death is something profoundly significant. Certainly, it is urgent and undeferable to go deeply into this theme, to go profoundly into it and into all of the levels of the mind with infinite patience, integrity, and sincerity.

As a luminous consequence or corollary, we can and must affirm with solemnity the following postulate: **"We can discover the origin of life only by totally discovering the mysteries of death."**

If the seed does not die, the plant is not born. Death and conception are intimately associated.

We inevitably project through time and space the electronic design of our own existence in the moment when we exhale the last breath of our existence.

Clearly, later on this electro-psychic design comes to impregnate the fecundated egg.

This is how we **return**.

The path of life is formed by the prints of the hooves of the horse of death.

The amorous enjoyments of our future earthly parents are found to be secretly joined with our last moments of agony.

The repetition of our present life, as well as its consequences, will be the destiny that awaits us beyond death.

What continues beyond the burial chamber are "my attachments, my affections, my hatred: I want, I do not want, I envy, I wish, I seek revenge, I kill, I steal, I am lustful, I am anger, I am greedy, etc...."

The whole of this legion of "I's" (a true legion of **demons**), which personify psychological defects, returns, comes back, and is reincorporated.

To talk about one individual "I" would be absurd. It is better to talk with complete clarity about the **pluralized "I."**

Esoteric, orthodox Buddhism teaches that the ego is a summation of psychic aggregates.

The Egyptian book *The Occult Abode* mentions with great emphasis the **red demons of Seth** (the devilish "I's" which constitute the **ego**).

Such quarrelsome, shouting "I's" constitute the tenebrous legions against which Arjuna had to combat under the commands that directly emanated from the Blessed Lord **Krishna** (see *The Bhagavad Gita*).

The personality does not return. The personality is a daughter of its time. It has a beginning and an end. Certainly, what continues after death are a bunch of **devils**.

We can attain immortality in the astral world. However, this is only possible by building the **Eidolon (the astral body)**.

Many diverse authors of a pseudo-esoteric and pseudo-occultist type fall into the error of confounding the **ego** with the astral body.

Modern metaphysical literature talks abundantly about projections of the astral body.

However, we must have the courage to recognize that the aficionados of occultism project themselves with the **ego** in order to travel through time and space within the sub-lunar regions of Nature.

The astral body is not a necessity for physical existence.

It is good to remember that the physical body fortunately has a vital depth or **lingam sarira**, which integrally guarantees its existence.

Unquestionably, the astral body is a luxury that very few people have. The persons who are born with this splendid vehicle are rare.

The Sexual Hydrogen SI-12 is the **alchemical element**, the raw watter of the Great Work, with which we can build the astral body.

Obviously, the cited hydrogen represents the final product of the transformations of food within the marvelous laboratory of our organism.

It becomes evident that this hydrogen is the most important matter with which sex works. The elaboration of this substance is developed in a concordant rhythm with the seven notes of the musical scale.

It is good to comprehend that the "**ens seminis**" and its peculiar Hydrogen SI-12 is a seed and a fruit at the same time.

To create a new life within our existing organism, to give evident form to the "astral or sidereal body" of the **alchemists** and **kabbalists**, factually signifies the transmutation of this portentous **hydrogen** in order to give it an intelligent crystallization into a superior octave.

You must understand that the astral body is born from the same material, from the same substance, from the same matter, from which our physical body is born. The procedures are the only difference.

When the whole physical body, all the cells, remain (as a way of saying) impregnated by the emanations of this matter which is the SI-12, and when these are fully saturated, then the SI-12 matter starts to crystallize.

The formation of the astral body constitutes the crystallization of this matter.

Transmutation or **transformation** is what in Alchemy is called the transition of this SI-12 matter into the state of emanation, and the gradual saturation of the whole organism with these emanations.

Justly, the transformation of crude metals into fine metals, in other words the attainment of gold from ordinary metals, is what in Alchemy is denominated as the transformation of the physical body into the astral body.

We can discover this esoteric procedure in Sex Yoga, in the **Maithuna**, in **Sexual Magic**, the connection of the **lingam-yoni**, **phallus-uterus**, without the ejaculation of the **ens seminis**.

The marvelous procedures of the crystallization of Hydrogen SI-12 into a superior octave will begin when we restrain **desire**.

Obviously, nourishment is different. Unquestionably, the astral body needs its nourishment and nutrition.

Since the physical body is wisely controlled by forty-eight laws (a fact which is scientifically demonstrated with the for-

The solutio perfecta ("perfect solution") for the problem of
suffering is found in the mysteries of sexual transmutation, which
as depicted here in this alchemical painting, occurs between the
two trees of Eden (Kabbalah and Alchemy), in a sacred crucible
(the Holy Grail), from which is born the golden child, or soul.

SOLUTIO PERFECTA

ty-eight chromosomes of the germinal cells) it becomes very clear and obvious that the hydrogen capital of the cellular body is Hydrogen Forty-eight (48).

To save this specific type of hydrogen truly becomes relatively easy when we march on the path of the straight line.

The surplus of Hydrogen Forty-eight (48) is marvelously converted into Hydrogen Twenty-four (24) when we do not waste it in the physical activities of the three-dimensional world of Euclid.

Clearly, the cited Hydrogen Twenty-four (24) always becomes the extraordinary nourishment of the astral body.

It is urgent to asseverate with great emphasis that the sidereal body or astral body of the **alchemists** and **kabbalists** is developed and splendidly unfolded under the absolute control of the twenty-four laws.

As every organ is clearly known for its functions, one knows that one has an astral body when one can travel with it (see chapter VI of this treatise).

My particular case was certainly extraordinary. I must specifically affirm that I was born with an astral body.

Magnificently, I had built it before my present birth. I built it in the ancient ages of a forgone mahamanvantara, long before the dawn of the lunar chain.

Certainly, what was most important for me was to restore the igneous powers in the cited sidereal body. Thus, this is what I comprehended before soliciting the Logos of the solar system for my entrance into the Third Initiation of Fire.

It is good to state to my beloved readers that this great being ordered special providence to help me after granting my request.

From this you can conclude that a certain specialist in the third degree of the power of the fire was granted to me. That guru-deva accomplished his mission by directing the third igneous serpent along the medullar canal of my astral body.

Litelantes and my insignificant person (who has no value) perceived with our sixth sense the astral specialist who was helping us during the metaphysical copulation.

The awakening of the fire in the astral body is always announced in the night with a terrible bolt of lightning.

Originally, the third degree of the power of the fire within such a precious vehicle possesses a very beautiful, immaculate, white color. Later on it becomes brilliant, with a very beautiful golden color within the aura of the universe.

Frankly and plainly speaking, I confess that during the esoteric work with the third degree of the power of the fire I had to live symbolically the whole cosmic drama.

One who is nothing but a vile slug writhing in the mud of the earth feels moved when, suddenly and without deserving, sees himself converted into the central personage of such a drama, even when this is merely in a symbolic manner.

After touching the atom of the Father in the magnetic field of the root of the nose, the third degree of the power of the fire then proceeds its march to the heart, a different process than the two previous serpents.

Secret paths, "nadis," or marvelous canals, exist between the magnetic field of the root of the nose and the heart.

A certain secret path connects the root of the nose with the principal chakra, which from the center of the brain controls the cardias (heart). The fire circulates through this path. Later on, the fire, mysteriously circulating through the **Anahata Nadi**, continues its march to the heart itself.

To live the drama of the Christ in the astral world is without a doubt something that can never be forgotten.

The diverse events of the Christic drama become displayed while the third degree of the power of the fire is harmoniously developed and unfolded in the astral body.

When the sacred fire arrives at the marvelous port of the tranquil heart, we then experience that symbolism which is intimately related with the death and resurrection of Christ.

The instant in which the symbolic Longinus stabs the sacred lance (the marvelous emblem of phallic strength) into the side of the initiate is extraordinary.

With such a spear, Parsifal healed the wound that was painfully burning in the side of the King Amfortas.

The leftist, tenebrous adepts, full of great hatred, attacked me when I was secretly approved by a certain sidereal Potency.

The holy sepulcher is never absent among the mysteries of the great cathedrals, and it is evident that my own could not be absent in the initiation.

The moment of the initiation of Gines de Lara comes into my memory in these moments in which I write these lines. Effectively, there was no maiden from the "great lineage," (the daughter of the founder of the monastery) accompanying the illustrious initiate in that esoteric instant, neither any "Ome Bueno," but the master guide himself, who conduced Gines unto the sancta sanctorum or adytum. There, in the center of a wealthy marble stanza of that temple, the neophyte found a magnificent sepulcher, hermetically sealed. By obeying the master, he easily lifted up the heavy lid with his own hands, and to his great surprise he saw his own physical body.

Different than Gines de Lara, I saw my own astral body in the sepulcher. I then comprehended that I must pass through the esoteric resurrection.

Unquestionably, the great Master Mason **Hiram Abiff** must resurrect within us. "The king is dead." "Long live the king."

Real, crude, legitimate, and authentic resurrection is only possible in the **Second Mountain**. In these paragraphs we are emphatically referring only to the symbolic i**nitiatic resurrection**.

Before the mentioned symbolic resurrection, I had to astrally remain within the holy sepulcher for a period of three days.

After the whole symbolic resurrecting process, a descent into the abode of Pluto was indispensable.

I had to initiate tenebrous recapitulations within the innermost part of the Earth, there where the Florentine Dante found the city of **Dis**.

The progressive ascent was performed slowly, through all of the strata of the submerged mineral kingdom...

A vivid, progressive, and ascendant scenic recapitulation was indispensable for the complete knowledge of the itself, the myself.

When alluding to the dissolution of the **ego**, the recapitulation of ancient abysmal errors is worthwhile.

To know our own psychological errors is certainly urgent and undeferable.

"I am a saint!" I said before a group of elegant tenebrous ladies, who took seats in a magnificent abysmal hall...

Those women laughed at me, willingly mocked me, and opportunely, with a certain very provocative grimace, ironically repeated: "A saint! A saint! A saint!..."

Those sorrowful creatures were correct, because during that epoch I still did not have the **ego** dissolved. I was a **fallen Bodhisattva**...

It is written with flaming embers in the book of all splendors that in the abode of Pluto, "truth is disguised with darkness." H.P.B. wrote, "Demonius est Deus inversus."

The **initiatic ascension** is symbolic and instructive. However, it is different from the **Logoic ascension** of the **Third Mountain**.

Nineteen days after having initiated the ascendant abysmal march, the adepts of the occult fraternity eliminated a certain coat or atomic substance similar to the flesh of the human organism from my lower abdomen.

This atomic coat within the microcosmic man is like a large door that gives access into the lower abysmal depths...

While this atomic element exists in individuals, the essence will remain exceedingly self-enclosed within the **ego**.

When this atomic door is removed from the astral counterpart of the abdomen, the adepts must cure the abdominal zone.

When the third degree of the power of the fire achieves the ascent and release through the superior part of the cranium, then it assumes the mystical figure of the Holy Spirit, a white dove with the head of a venerable elder.

This immaculate, divine creature upon the tower of the temple is lodged there in mystical lurking, joyfully awaiting the supreme instant of the initiation.

Remembering ancient errors from anterior reincarnations, I had to pass through an unusual and unexpected event after the thirty-three days...

Three of the four fundamental states of consciousness had to be submitted to the ordeal of fire...

To define these **four states of consciousness** is urgent for the good of our beloved readers:

A) Eikasia

B) Pistis

C) Dianoia

D) Nous

The first of these four states is profound unconsciousness, active barbarism, infrahuman sleep, cruelty, etc.

The second of these states corresponds exactly with all the reasoning processes: opinions, fanatical sectarianism, etc.

The third is manifested as conceptual synthesism, scientism, intellectual review of beliefs, induction, deduction of a reflective type, very serious studies about phenomena, laws, etc.

The fourth is awakened consciousness, the Turiya state, truly objective, illuminated, perfect clairvoyance, polyvoyance, etc.

I emerged victorious from that difficult ordeal. Unquestionably, we must be tested many times on the "path of the razor's edge."

The Hermetic symbolism of the cited esoteric ordeal was very interesting. "Three maidens" were very serene within the fire. Victory! This was the result.

I, today, in the present, am already firmly established in the **Dianoetic** and **Noetic** states. It is good to asseverate that **Eikasia** and **Pistis** were eliminated from my nature through the terrible ordeals of initiation.

Then, after thirty-seven days of having initiated abysmal reviews, I had to directly study the twelve zodiacal constellations under whose regency we evolve and devolve constantly.

Each one of the twelve zodiacal constellations shines with its own peculiar tone.

The Astral Light of the constellation of Leo is of a very beautiful golden color, and one feels inspired when contemplating it.

The end of all the processes related with the ascension is always announced by four angels, who, turning towards the four cardinal points of the planet Earth, sound their trumpets.

The white dove of the Holy Spirit was delivered unto me within the temple as if saying, "Work intensely in the Ninth Sphere if you wish to incarnate within yourself the **Third Logos**."

All of these symbolic processes of the ascension concluded on the fortieth day.

The final ceremony was in the causal world. What I then felt and saw was certainly extraordinary.

The great initiator in that moment was **Sanat Kumara**, the founder of the great College of Initiates of the venerable White Lodge.

On the altar, with the reed of seven knots in his dexterous, potent hand, that great being shone with tremendous divinity.

Chapter XVI
The Fourth Initiation of Fire

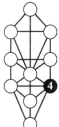

The pitiful rational homunculus mistakenly denominated "**human being**" is similar to any fatal ship boarded with many leftist, tenebrous passengers (I am referring to the "I's").

Unquestionably, each one of these particular "I's" has its own mind, ideas, concepts, opinions, emotions, etc.

Obviously, we are full of infinite psychological contradictions. If we could fully see ourselves internally in front of a mirror, as we are, we would be horrified with ourselves.

The type of mind that at any given moment is being expressed in us through the diverse functionalisms of the brain depends exclusively on the quality of the "I" in action (see chapter III, the section entitled *The Ego*).

The inner existence of many minds within each one of us is evident, clear, and manifest.

Certainly, we are not possessors of an individual, particular mind. We have many minds.

We need to create the "**mental body**" with maximum, undeferable urgency, but this is only possible by transmuting the Sexual Hydrogen SI-12.

We can and even must transmit the surplus of the Sexual Hydrogen SI-12 that was not utilized in the building of the astral body into a second octave of a superior order by means of the **Sahaja Maithuna** (Sexual Magic).

The crystallization of that hydrogen into the resplendent, marvelous form of the mental body is an axiom of Hermetic wisdom.

Clearly, the crystallization of this cited sexual hydrogen is solemnly processed in accordance with the notes DO-RE-MI-FA-SOL-LA-SI, in a transcendent **second octave**.

However, nourishment is different. It is evident that any organism that comes into existence needs its specific food, its nourishment. The mental body is not an exception to this general rule.

The surplus of Hydrogen 24 that was not utilized for the nourishment of the astral body is converted into Hydrogen 12 (do not confuse Hydrogen 12 with the Sexual Hydrogen SI-12).

As an evident consequence or corollary, it is licit to clearly asseverate that Hydrogen 12 is the cardinal and definitive nutriment for the mental body.

It is not possible to achieve the complete individualization of the understanding without the creation of the mental body.

We can possess an "**inferior, organized manas**," a concrete, particular, individual mind, only by creating such a vehicle.

The foundation of this creation is found in the Ninth Sphere (sex). To work in the "flaming forge of Vulcan" is indispensable.

It is evident that one knows that one possesses a mental body when one can travel with it consciously and positively through the supra-sensible worlds.

My particular case was certainly something very special. I was born with the mental body. I had already created it in a very ancient past, long before the dawning of the aurora of the Mahamanvantara of Padma or the Lotus of Gold.

Really, I then only needed (with maximum, undeferable urgency) to recapitulate the Fourth Initiation of the Fire and to restore the flaming powers (in the already mentioned vehicle).

The resplendent Dragon of Wisdom (I am referring to the Logos of the solar system of Ors) entrusted to a specialist the noble mission of assisting and helping me.

To raise the fourth serpent along the medullar canal of the mental body, from vertebra to vertebra, from chakra to chakra, is certainly something very slow and frightfully difficult.

Before the golden flame can burn with serene light, the lamp should be kept well and in a place free of any wind. - Bhagavad-gita 6.19

Worldly thoughts must fall dead before the doors of the temple. - The Voice of the Silence

The mind that is a slave of the senses makes the soul invalid as the boat that the wind mislays upon the waters. - Bhagavad-gita 2.67

Astonished, I perceived the multiple splendors of the marvelous Pentalpha upon the very sacred candlesticks of the temple.

I joyfully passed the threshold of the sanctuary. My thoughts were ardently flaming.

I clearly comprehended that during the work in the Ninth Sphere, I should very carefully separate the smoke from the flames.

The smoke is horror, darkness, bestiality. The flame is light, love, and transcendental chastity.

Any exterior impact originates undulatory reactions in the mind. These undulations have in themselves their fundamental nucleus in the **ego**, the "I," the myself.

To exercise absolute control over the cited mental reactions is certainly indispensable.

We need to become indifferent before praise and slander, before triumph and defeat.

To smile before the insulter, to kiss the whip of the executioner, is indispensable.

Remember that hurtful words have no value except the value given by the offended one. When we do not give any value to the words of the insulters, these remain like a check without funds.

In the mental world, the Guardian of the Threshold becomes personified by the **ego**, the "I."

To confront the terrible ordeal with heroism, to really defeat the terrible brother (as it is denominated in occult Masonry) is indispensable in the Fourth Initiation of Fire.

"Whosoever truly wants to enter into
the Jerusalem above (the superior
worlds), must liberate himself from the
body, affections, and the mind."

THE SAVIOUR ENTERS JERUSALEM

Without any fear, I promptly unsheathed my flaming sword. What happened after this was extraordinary. The larvae of the threshold fled terrified.

It is clear that such an ordeal always occurs after the "igneous wings" have been opened.

It is a tremendous truth that when the ascending sacred fire reaches the height of the heart, the radiant angelic wings are always opened.

Unquestionably, these ardent wings permit us to enter instantaneously into any department of the kingdom.

One of the marvelous cosmic events that I had to experience within myself during the multiple processes of the Fourth Initiation of Fire was certainly the victorious entrance of Jesus into the beloved city of the prophets.

Whosoever truly wants to enter into the Jerusalem above (the superior worlds), must liberate himself from the body, affections, and the mind.

It is urgent, indispensable, and undeferable to ride on the symbolic ass (the mind), to dominate it, to control it. Only thus is it possible to liberate ourselves from it in order to enter into the worlds of the Spirit (the heavenly Jerusalem).

I felt that my worn physical body was disintegrating and dying. In those moments, the Divine Rabbi of Galilee exclaimed with a great voice, *"That body no longer serves you."*

Joyfully, I escaped from this decrepit form of vesture, dressed with "**To Soma Heliakon**" (the body of gold of the solar man).

When the sacred fire solemnly shone in the flaming star and in the starry cross, my individual, particular Divine Mother Kundalini was congratulated in the temple.

The **Kundalini** flourished on my fertile lips made Word when the fire reached the creative larynx.

I still remember that instant in which I celebrated the festivity. The adepts of the occult fraternity rewarded me with a marvelous symbol, which I still keep.

That moment in which the fire of the **Kundalini** reached the height of the cerebellum was extraordinary. Then, my mental body passed through the symbolic crucifixion of the Lord.

The ascension of the erotic flame into the thirty-second vertebra became notable. In those moments of great solemnity, I comprehended the mysteries related to the degree of the lion of the law.

> *"When an inferior law is transcended by a superior law, the superior law washes away the inferior law."*

> *"The lion of the law is fought with the scale."*

> *"Perform good deeds so that you can pay your debts."*

When the divine fire opened the lotus of one thousand petals (the chakra Sahasrara), a certain metallic bell solemnly shook all of the precincts of the universe.

In those supreme instants of beatitude, I listened to ineffable choirs resounding in the sacred space.

Later on, I had to patiently carry the erotic flame unto the magnetic field at the root of the nose.

By intelligently taking advantage of a secret nervous thread, I then proceeded by conducing the fire to the region of the thalamus, a region where the principal chakra that controls the heart is located.

Finally, I intelligently took advantage of the **Anahata Nadi**, in order to carry the sexual flame unto the **heart temple**.

The final ceremony of that initiation was very extraordinary, sublime, and terribly divine.

The temple was dressed with glory on that mystical night. To describe such beauty is impossible...

Sanat Kumara, the great hierophant, was austerely waiting for me on his royal throne. I entered with profound veneration inside this sacred precinct...

Before this great immolated one (as H.P.B. used to call him), my Divine Mother Kundalini, with infinite love, placed upon my head the yellow mantle of the **Buddhas** and the extraordinary diadem in which the **Eye of Shiva** shines.

"This is my beloved son," exclaimed my Mother, and then added, "He is a Buddha!"

The Elder of Days, Sanat Kumara (the illustrious founder of the great College of Initiates of the White Lodge on the planet Earth), while approaching me, placed in my hands the symbol of the imperator (the sphere with the cross on top).

In those instants, angelic harmonies were heard, royal symphonies based on the rhythms of **Mahavan** and the **Chotavan,** which sustain the universe firmly in its march.

"Then said the king to the servants, Bind
him hand and foot, and take him away,
and cast him into outer darkness; there
shall be weeping and gnashing of teeth.
For many are called, but few are chosen."

THE PARABLE OF THE WEDDING GARMENT

Chapter XVI
The Fifth Initiation of Fire

With great solemnity yet without much pomposity, we asseverate the tremendous, palpable, and
evident reality of three specific types of action:

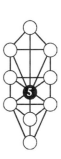

   a. Actions based on the law of accidents.

   b. Actions based on the eternal laws
      of return and recurrence.

   c. Marvelous actions born
      from conscious will.

The foundation of the first type of action is certainly the
natural mechanics of the order of this system of Nature.

The primordial element of the second type of action is
without a doubt the incessant repetition of many dramas,
comedies, and tragedies. This always happens through time
and space, from life to life, in this painful valley of **Samsara**.
The drama is for people that are more or less good. The
comedy is for the clowns, and the tragedy for the perverse.
Everything comes to occur just as it had occurred, with the
addition of the positive or negative consequences.

The *causa causorum* of the third type of action is certainly
the causal body or body of conscious will.

As a consequence or corollary we can establish the following enunciation: **Actions born of conscious will are only
possible once we have given ourselves the luxury of having
created a causal body for our particular use.**

The Sexual Hydrogen SI-12 can and must pass to a third
octave of a superior order by means of **Sex Yoga**, with its
famous **Sahaja Maithuna** (Sexual Magic).

The crystallization of this cited hydrogen into the resplendent and marvelous form of the causal body will be processed
with the notes DO-RE-MI-FA-SOL-LA-SI in the mentioned
octave.

However, nourishment is different. The causal body also needs its nourishment, and this comes precisely from the surplus of Hydrogen 12 that was not wasted by the mental body. Obviously, Hydrogen 12 (do not confuse this with the Sexual Hydrogen SI-12), can and must be converted into Hydrogen 6, which is the specific nourishment of the causal body.

Unquestionably, wretched people are always fatal victims of circumstances because they really do not possess the body of conscious will.

The categorical imperative, the determinative faculty that permits us to originate new circumstances, is only possible when one possesses the causal body or body of conscious will.

With great sincerity and tremendous **Gnostic realism** we have to affirm the following:

The intellectual animal mistakenly called human being does not have the astral, mental, and causal bodies because he has never created them.

It is unacceptable, unsustainable, and inadmissible to suppose even for an instant that the human being could be completely manifested when the cited supra-sensible vehicles have not even been elaborated yet.

To create within ourselves the mentioned vehicles is the indispensable, urgent, and basic condition needed if truly we want to convert ourselves into authentic human beings.

It is a grave error to believe that the three-cerebrated or three-centered bipeds come into this world with such vehicles.

Infinite possibilities exist in the spinal medulla and in the semen, which when developed can transform us into legitimate human beings. Nonetheless, these possibilities could be lost, and it is even normal for them to be lost, if we do not work with the fundamental scale of the hydrogens.

The intellective humanoid is not a human, but he boasts of being one. He mistakenly supposes that he is a human being and by dint of ignorance tries to usurp a place which does not correspond to him. He believes himself to be the king of creation, when he is not even a king of himself.

However, immortality is a very serious matter, and it must be achieved by means of the **Sahaja Maithuna** (Sexual Magic).

Whosoever builds an astral body, as a fact and by his own right, becomes immortal in the world of twenty-four laws.

Whosoever grants himself the luxury of creating a mental body clearly reaches immortality in the world of twelve laws.

Whosoever forges a causal body undoubtedly achieves the longed for immortality in the world of six laws.

We can incarnate that which is called the Human Soul only by building the cited solar vehicles. I am referring to the third aspect of the Hindustani Trimurti: **Atman-Buddhi-Manas**.

Presently, much has been said about the famous **To Soma Heliakon**, *"the body of gold of the solar man."*

Unquestionably, it refers to the wedding garment of the soul, cited by the biblical Christic gospel.

Obviously, that vesture is compounded by the supra-sensible bodies, by those extraordinary crystallizations of the Sexual Hydrogen SI-12.

To enter into the "**Sanctum Regnum**," "**Regnum Dei**," "**Magis Regnum**" without the wedding garment of the soul is in no way possible.

With the good purpose of illuminating these paragraphs even more, we have transcribed the following parable of the wedding feast:

> *And Jesus answered and spake unto them again by parables and said, The kingdom of heaven is like unto a certain king, which made a marriage for his son, And sent forth his servants to call them that were bidden to the wedding and they would not come.*

> *Again, he sent forth other servants, saying, Tell them which are bidden, Behold, I have prepared my dinner: my oxen and my fatlings are killed, and all things are ready: come unto the marriage.*

> *But they made light of it, and went their ways, one to his farm, another to his merchandise:*

*And the remnant took his servants, and
entreated them spitefully, and slew them.*

*But when the king heard thereof, he was wroth:
and he sent forth his armies, and destroyed those
murderers, and burned up their city.*

*Then saith he to his servants, the wedding is ready,
but they which were bidden were not worthy.*

*Go ye therefore into the highways, and as
many as ye find, bid to the marriage.*

*So those servants went out into the highways, and
gathered together all as many as they found both bad
and good: and the wedding was furnished with guests.*

*And when the king came in to see the guests, he saw
there a man which had not on a wedding garment:*

*And he saith unto him, Friend, how camest thou in hither
not having a wedding garment? And he was speechless.*

*Then said the king to the servants, Bind him hand
and foot, and take him away, and cast him into outer
darkness; there shall be weeping and gnashing of teeth.*

For many are called, but few are chosen. - Matthew: 22:1-14

It is unmistakable and evident that this friend who came
without the "wedding garment of the soul" could not legit-
imately receive the qualification of "**human**;" however, that
term is simply granted unto him because of love and respect
towards our fellows. How grotesque the parable would have
been if it would have said that he saw there an animal which
did not have a wedding garment. Obviously, no animal
(including the intellectual beast) is ever dressed with the "wedding garment of the soul."

However, let us return to my particular case in order for
us to approach the objective of this chapter a little closer.

In the name of the truth I must state with complete clarity that I was born with the four bodies: physical, astral, mental, and causal.

Certainly, to restore the power of the fire in each body, to recapitulate initiations, was indispensable, urgent, and undeferable for me.

I had to patiently repass the Fifth Initiation of Fire after the four anterior initiations.

I want define the term "**repass**" in these lines: an intrinsical, transcendental, and transcendent significance. Since in other anterior lives I had already passed through the cosmic Initiations of Fire, presently I only needed to repass them.

When I asked the Logos of our solar system of **Ors** for permission in order to enter into the mysteries of the Fifth Initiation of Fire, the following answer was granted unto me, *"You no longer need to ask permission in order to enter into the initiation. You have all the rights to do so."*

The Blessed One then entrusted a noble specialist of the causal world with the mission of assisting and helping me. The cited specialist had to intelligently conduce for me the sacred fire along the spinal medullar canal of the causal body or body of conscious will.

The awakening of the fifth igneous serpent of our magical powers in the Muladhara chakra from the coccygeal bone was celebrated in the temple with great festivity.

The ascent of the **Kundalini** from vertebra to vertebra, from chakra to chakra, along the dorsal spine of the causal body, was performed very slowly according to the merits of the heart.

Since I was born awakened, and since I certainly enjoy that which we can call "objective consciousness" and "objective knowledge," it was very easy for me to bring the memories from the causal world into my physical brain.

I clarify: The modern revolutionary psychology of the new age of Aquarius utilizes the terms "**objective** " and "**subjective**" in the following way:

a. **Objective:** real, spiritual, true, divine, etc.

b. **Subjective**: vague, incoherent, not precise, illusory, fantastical, absurd.

I comprehended the necessity of learning to obey the Father on Earth as it is in Heaven.

In that cosmic region, entering into the Temple of the Music of the Spheres was certainly one of my greatest joys.

At the threshold of the temple, the guardian taught me one of the secret salutations of the occult fraternity.

The face of that guardian resembled a lighting bolt. When that **man** lived in the world, his name was **Beethoven**.

In the causal world I found many **Bodhisattvas** working intensely for humanity. Each one of these causal humans is behaving marvelously under the direction of their own internal God.

Only the causal human has definitively attained immortality. These types of beings are beyond good and evil.

To experience the drama of the Cosmic Christ in these regions, to convert oneself into the central personage of the whole Via Crucis, is certainly something that can never be forgotten. We need to refine ourselves, to become quintessential, to truly purify ourselves, if truly what we long for is to seriously experience the tremendous realities contained in the divine Christic symbolism.

Without reprimanding my intimate longings in any manner, I sincerely confess that I saw myself carrying the weight of my own cross in the world of natural causes before the profane multitudes who, infuriated, were stoning me.

The miraculously imprinted face of the Beloved One on the sacred cloth of Veronica was to me very well marked.

It is good to remember that the archaeologists discovered many heads of stone crowned with thorns. Such effigies belong to the Age of Bronze.

Clearly, this reminds us of the rune Thorn, which we discussed widely in our 1968 Christmas Message, *The Magic of the Runes.*

RUNE THORN

Any person versed in universal Gnosticism knows very well what this rune signifies.

The deep significance of the divine face with a head crowned with thorns is the "Christ Will."

On the night of the initiation, I saw upon the sacred altar the cloth of Veronica statically shining with a unique, divine diaphaneity and transparency.

The final cosmic event inevitably came when the fifth serpent arrived at its correspondent secret chamber in the tranquil heart, after having passed the pineal gland and the magnetic field of the root of the nose.

Then, fused with my real Being, I rejoiced that I was returning into the childlike, paradisiacal state.

I prostrated myself before my Guru "Adolfito" when concluding the final ceremony, exclaiming, "Thank you, venerable master. I owe all of this to you."

While standing up, the blessed **mahatma** answered, "Do not give me your thanks! What I want to know is how you are going to behave in life now."

"The facts speak for me, venerable master; you are seeing it." Such were my words.

Posteriorly, I was visited by a great, elemental genie: I am referring to that deity which personifies the sphinx of the Egyptian desert. That being had its feet covered with mud. I understood the deep, esoteric, occult significance.

"You bring your feet covered with mud," I said. The mysterious creature was silent.

Unquestionably, a washing of feet was what I needed.

When I wanted to deposit a holy kiss on its cheeks, delicately it called me to order by saying, "Kiss me with purity." Thus, I did so.

Later on, I was visited by **Isis**, whose veil no mortal has lifted, my Divine Mother Kundalini. I immediately interrogated her about my results:

Question: "Oh, Mother of mine! Have I already lifted the five serpents?"

Answer: "Yes, my son!"

Question: "I want you to help me to raise the sixth and seventh serpents."

Answer: "You already have those raised."

In those instants, a perfect remembrance of myself emerged from within me.

Question: "Ah! I am an ancient master. I was fallen. Now I remember."

Answer: "Yes, my son, you are a master."

Oh, Devi **Kundalini***! You are* **Lakshmi***, the wife of* **Vishnu***. Beloved Mother! You are the divine betrothed of* **Shiva***. Venerable Virgin! You are the aqueous* **Sarasvati** *who is the consort of* **Brahma***.*

Oh beloved reader! Listen to me: she is certainly the eternal feminine, represented by the Moon and by the **water**. She is the Magna Mater from where comes the magical "**M**" and the famous hieroglyphic of Aquarius.

Unquestionably, she is also the universal matrix of the great abyss, the primitive Venus, and the great Virgin Mother who surges forth from the waves of the sea with Cupid-Eros, who is her son.

Frankly and plainly speaking, we must affirm without any doubt that she is the Hindustani **Prakriti**, and metaphysically **Aditi,** and even **Mulaprakriti.**

We can never tread upon the rocky path which conduces to the final liberation without the help of the Divine Mother **Kundalini.**

Chapter XVIII
A Supra-sensible Adventure

While conversing in a forest of mystery, we three errant friends slowly, slowly, slowly arrived before a sacred mount.

Without even a bit of fear, we were witnesses of something unusual and unexpected. To narrate this for the good of our beloved readers is urgent.

Suddenly, an unpolluted millenary rock opened in this rocky place as if it had been divided into two exactly equal pieces, which left us astonished and perplexed...

Before having had enough time to appraise this, without any unfounded apprehension, I approached the mysterious granite door as if attracted by a strange force.

Without any alien impediment, I courageously passed the threshold of a temple. In the interim, my serene friends were seated in front of a gigantic boulder which was closing before them...

If we were to try to decipher with minimum detail all of the wonders of that subterranean sanctuary, then frankly even an extraordinary glossary would be insufficient.

Without any *savoir faire*, I prefer to talk in a *"grosso modo"* about this, but with sincerity and limiting myself to narrate just what occurred.

Lively and animated by the living flame of the Spirit, I advanced along a narrow passage until reaching a small hall...

That exotic place resembled a writing den, office, or lawyer's dispatch...

I found an archon of destiny seated before the desk, an undecipherable personage, an hermetic judge of **karma**, a mystical provident dressed as an elegant, modern gentleman...

How wise that counselor-cohen was! Foreseer! Sublime! Infallible! And terribly divine...

I approached his desk with profound veneration. The sacred fire shone on his face...

Immediately, I directly felt its deep significance. "Thank you, venerable master!" I spoke with infinite humbleness...

The austere hierophant told his parable in a sibylline tone, saying, "this fellow man" (clearly referring to one of my two friends who were waiting for me outside) "is the ragged type; he will always be in misery.

"This other fellow" (referring now to my other friend), "is the **samuro** type." What?

Samuro? I repeated, "**Samuro.**"

Samuro: a fighter and spiritual friend, like the progressive Buddhist Samurai from the Empire of the Rising Sun.

Finally, when directing himself towards my insignificant person who has no value, he said: "You are the military type, because you have to drag multitudes to form the world salvation army, to initiate the new age of Aquarius."

Then he proceeded as such: "Your specific mission is to create **human beings**, to teach the people how to build their astral, mental, and causal bodies so that they can incarnate their Human Soul."

After this, he stood up from his writing desk with the evident purpose of searching for one of my books in his library. Once in his hands, inebriated with ecstasy, he discoursed: "This book that you fortunately sent by mail to 'a certain fellow' was liked very much."

What happened next is easy to conclude: with infinite veneration and great humbleness, without any type of empty show, very far from any vain infatuation, I bid farewell to the venerable one and left the temple.

To now seriously infer, find, and meditate upon the essential matter of this narrative is urgent and indispensable.

While excluding from our lexicon every cutting remark that is in bad taste, we emphasize the following postulation: **"It is indispensable to create the human being within ourselves here and now."**

Since I am teaching the doctrine to people, obviously I am a creator of **human beings**.

There is a need to create within ourselves the resources of a **human being**. It is good to remember that the times of the end are at hand.

Much has been said in occult literature about the two paths: I am specifically referring to the **spiral** and **direct** paths.

Unquestionably, the two paths are augustly opened only before the authentic **human being**, never before the intellectual animal!

I could never forget the final moments of the Fifth Initiation of Fire. After all of the recapitulative processes, I had to courageously confront a terribly divine Nirvanic guardian.

The Blessed Lord of Perfections, while showing me the spiral Nirvanic path, said, *"This is good work."* Then, just as when a lion roars, he exclaimed with a great voice (as he pointed to the direct path) saying, *"This is superior work."*

Posteriorly, I saw him advancing towards me with that tremendous imperative of the great majesties: he interrogated me and I answered him, establishing the following dialogue:

QUESTION: "Through which of these two paths are you going to continue now?"

ANSWER: "Let me think about it."

QUESTION: "Do not think about it, answer immediately, define yourself."

ANSWER: "I will go along the direct path that conduces unto the **Absolute**."

QUESTION: "But, what is that you are saying? Do you not realize that this path is extremely painful?"

I repeated: "I will go to the **Absolute**!"

QUESTION: "How did it occur to you to enter through there? Do you not comprehend how you will suffer? What is going on with you, sir?"

ANSWER: "I will go to the **Absolute**."

"Well, you are warned!" (These were the final words of the guardian, after which he solemnly withdrew).

On another night: I was out of my supra-sensible bodies, in complete exercise of my functions as **Atman** or "**Spirit-Man**..."

In the middle of **Nirvana**: solitarily, I was upon the beautiful terrace of the mansion of delights in the corner of love...

I saw the inhabitants of that region floating in the sacred space in a constantly increasing number; divine algorithms, sublime inspiration, unforgettable numina, that happily took seats in the garden full of perfumed flowers... They were **Atman-Buddhi-Manas**, Trimurtis of perfection. In the instants in which I write these lines, it occurs to me to repeat that verse from the book *The Occult Abode* which literally says:

> *I am the sacred crocodile Sebek.*
> *I am the flame with three wicks,*
> *and my wicks are immortal.*
> *I enter the region of Sekem,*
> *I enter into the region of the flames*
> *which have defeated my adversaries.*

An improvising igneous creature took the floor in the name of the sacred confraternity and said, "My brother, why are you going on that path that is so hard? Here in **Nirvana**, we are happy. Stay here with us!..."

My answer, filled with great energy, was as follows: "The intellectual animals could not patronize me with their temptations; you gods will not, even by a long shot. I will go to the **Absolute**!..." (The ineffable ones were speechless, and I promptly withdrew from that abode).

The Voice of the Silence says:

> *Know that the Bodhisattva who liberation changes for renunciation (who renounces Nirvana) to don the miseries of "Secret Life" (to live to benefit mankind), is called, "thrice Honoured," O thou candidate for woe throughout the cycles.*

> *The "Secret Way" leads also to Paranirvanic bliss -- but at the close of Kalpas without number; Nirvanas gained and lost from boundless pity and compassion for the world of deluded mortals.*

Nirvana has cycles of activity and cycles of profound rest. In this epoch of the twentieth century, **Nirvana** is in a period of action.

The Nirvanis who were incarnated in the first races only now begin to reincarnate again.

When this present epoch passes, they will then submerge within the infinite joy until the future **Mahamanvantara**.

The goal of the long path of woe and bitterness is different. It implies total renunciation. However, it leads us to the **Absolute**.

On a given night among many others, while I was happily in the state of Samadhi, I saw the planet Mars shining with purpurin coloring...

Certainly, its vibrations were of a telepathic nature. In my tranquil heart I felt that I was being urgently called from the central nucleus of that planetary bulk. That sparkling became unmistakable...

Promptly, dressed with **To Soma Heliakon**, I transported myself to the living, innermost depths of that world...

Resplendently dressed with the garment of the celestial militia was **Samael**, my own individual Monad, my real inner Being, the divine regent of that planet, waiting for me.

With reverence, I prostrated myself before the **omniscient,** illustrious lord of that abode, and I said, "Here I am, Father of mine! Why did you call me?"

"You, my son, have forgotten me!"

"No, Father of mine, I have not forgotten you!"

"Yes, my son, if the gate of the universe were to be delivered unto you, you would forget about me!"

"Oh, Father of mine, I came to kiss your hand and to receive your benediction!"

The omni-merciful blessed me and I kneeled to kiss his dexterous hand. In the depths of the planetary temple a scene of pain appeared...

Afterwards, I entered into profound reflection:

Why did I choose the path by myself?

Why did I forget my Father before the terrible presence of the Guardian of the paths?

Jesus, the great Gnostic priest, while on the Mount of Olives, gave us a great lesson when he exclaimed:

> *O my Father, if it is possible, let this cup pass from me: nevertheless not as I will, but as thou wilt.*

JESUS DEMONSTRATES HOW TO WALK THE DIRECT PATH

Eighteen years later:

With thunder and lightning, I tore my vestures off while protesting because of too much pain. Woe! Woe! Woe!...

A Virgin of **Nirvana** answered me, "Thus, this is the way that thou chose for thyself. The triumphs for us, the inhabitants of **Nirvana**, are minor, and that is why it is evident that we suffer less. Nonetheless, because thy triumphs will be major, thy sufferings will be also more intense."

When I wanted to rest a little, the agents of **karma** recriminated me, saying, "What is going on with you, sir?"

"Are you going to walk? Move ahead, my friend! Move ahead! Move ahead!"

Patiently, I continued my march upon the rocky path that leads to final liberation.

Chapter XIX

Persecutions

Patiently, I had to recapitulate the diverse, esoteric, initiatic processes of the third, fourth, and fifth Initiations of Fire, in the flowing tropical region of the Sierra Nevada, at the shore of "Macuriba" or the "Caribbean Sea."

Austerely, I was living there with a certain very select group of Gnostic students, very far away from many foolish, simpleton dimwits of vain intellectualism...

These honest and irreproachable anchorite Gnostics had gratefully built for me a simple abode with wood from those forests...

Now, I want to evoke at least for a moment, all of those illustrious respectable men, some of whom in these instants (1972) distinguish themselves as notable international missionaries... From this ancient Mexican land of mine, I salute you, most illustrious gentlemen of the South American Sierra Nevada!... As well, I want to include their wives and children and the children of their children within these salutations of mine...

How joyfully I abode in that wooded shelter of the profound forest, far away from the mundane clamor!...

Then, I returned into the elemental paradises of nature, and the princes of fire, air, water, and of the perfumed earth delivered their secrets unto me...

On a given day (which one does not matter), some of those cenobites from **universal Gnosticism** eagerly knocked at the door of my abode in order to beg me to extinguish a fire. The incessant crackling of the igneous element was advancing terribly through the thick umbria, incinerating everything that it found in its way... The frightful cremation was threatening their work, farms, and cabins. Ditches and canals for the purpose of stopping the triumphal march of the fire were built in vain.

The igneous element was ardently passing every pit and brook, inclemently threatening all of the neighborhoods, surroundings, environs, and borders...

Obviously, I was never a fireman or "smoke-swallower," as these heroic public servants are pleasantly nicknamed... However, frankly and plainly speaking, I confess that in those instants the fate of all of those Gnostic brothers was in my hands. What to do?

I longed to help them in the best possible way, and this was without a doubt one of the best opportunities... It would have been unspeakable, absurd, and even ungrateful to deny that urgent help.

Karma is paid not only for the evil that is done, but also for the good that could be done, yet is left undone.

Therefore I decided to operate magically: after marching by foot towards the titanic bonfire, I seated myself very close to it; then I concentrated myself on my Innermost...

By secretly praying, I beseeched my Innermost to invoke **Agni**, the prodigious and illustrious god of fire...

My Innermost heard my supplication, and with a loud voice, as when a lion roars, called **Agni**, and seven thunders uttered their voices...

Promptly, the brilliant lord of fire, the resplendent son of the flame, the omni-merciful, came to my side... I felt him in the whole presence of my Being. I begged him in the name of the "universal charity" to dissipate that fire... Clearly, the Blessed Lord of Perfection considered that my request was just and perfect...

In an unexpected way, a soft perfumed breeze surged from within the mysterious blue of the profound boscage which totally modified the character of those tongues of fire. Then the bonfire dissipated...

Another day, when conversing with the Gnostic cenobites in a very beautiful clearing of the dense wooded forest, very close to their cabins, we were suddenly threatened by a torrential rainstorm...

Longing, I concentrated on the Innermost, intensely praying and asking him to invoke **Paralda**, the elemental genie of the excitable Sylphs of the air. That deva olympically arrived with the evident purpose of helping me. I took advantage of such a magnificent opportunity that was offered to me, and I begged Paralda to push the stormy clouds away from those surroundings...

Unquestionably, these clouds opened over our heads in the form of a circle. Then after, they left before the astonished mystics of that corner of love...

In those times, the Gnostic brothers and sisters travelled weekly to the sandy beaches of the tempestuous ocean...

Litelantes requested those sincere penitents to bring us fish, and even vegetables and fruits, which in the Sierra Nevada are impossible to cultivate due to the wild hunger of the implacable ants... These devolving creatures insatiably devoured flowers, fruits, and vegetables, and certainly nothing could stop them. Such is the voraciousness of the jungle. This is well-known by the divine and humans. The nocturnal rounds of the "tambochas," or ants, are certainly frightful...

Venomous snakes such as the dreaded "talla X," and others known since ancient times by the classical names of rattlesnake, coral, and mapana, frightfully thrive here, there, and everywhere.

Still, I remember an old curandero (healer) of the mountain called Juan. This respectable man dwelt with his wife in the most profound part of the forest...

Like the good Samaritan of the Old Testament, this man healed the humble mountaineers bitten by the vipers with his precious balms...

Unfortunately, that man hated snakes and was implacably and revengefully killing them without any consideration...

"My friend Juan," I told him one day. "You are at war against the vipers, and they are prepared to defend themselves. We will see who is going to win the battle..."

"I hate snakes..."

"It would be better if you loved them. Remember that snakes are clairvoyant. In the astral aura of those creatures, the marvelous zodiac resplendently shines, and they know by

Immortality

ARCANUM THIRTEEN

direct experience who truly loves them and who truly abhors them..."

"I cannot love them... It feels like my body loses its temper when I look at them... I will kill any snake that crosses my path."

"Oh, good elder! Twelve serpents have bitten you, and when the thirteenth hurts you, you will die."

A little later on, close to his solitary cabin, the old man was bitten by an awaiting, dreaded, hidden snake, which was entwined three and a half times.

My prophecy was fulfilled. The old curandero died by the Thirteenth Arcanum of the Kabbalah. None of his friends could find the venomous serpent...

The elder medic always carried within his sack some marvelous plants. Let us remember the five captain plants:

Captain Solabasta

Captain Generala

Captain Silvadora

Captain Pujadora

Captain Tongue of Deer

These miraculous plants are not classified by botany and are only known in the Sierra Nevada, close to the tempestuous waters of Macuriba. They are extraordinary plants with which the old curandero from the solitary forest healed the victims of the serpents.

There is no doubt that this old man therapeutically used them in a very wise way. He administered them in oral form, as a tea or hot beverage, or in an external form by washing the wound or wounds with the concoction of such plants.

The Gnostic hermits of the Sierra Nevada never killed the dangerous vipers. They learned to love them sincerely.

As a consequence of this procedure, they won the trust of the dreadful serpents. Then, those venomous serpents were converted into guardians of the temple...

When these anchorites from the mountain wanted to push aside the serpents, filled with faith, they sang the following mantras:

Osi... Osoa... Asi...

Every time these hermits truly longed to magically enchant the terrible snakes, they pronounced the mysterious words: *"Osi..... Osoa..... Asi..."*

Never would any mystic of that mountain take the life of a serpent! These cenobites learned to respect every existence... However, there were some exceptions, as in the case of the precious rattlesnake...

Cancer

In the name of truth, I want to leave the following enunciation in this book:

The infallible remedy against the dreaded **cancer** is already discovered, and it is found in the rattlesnake!

The rescuing formula:

The cited animal must be sacrificed. The rattles and the head must be eliminated (these parts are useless).

The available dry meat must be ground to a fine powder.

Pour this substance into empty capsules, which are very easy to find in any pharmacy...

Dosage: Take one capsule each hour.

Observation: Continue with this treatment until being radically healed.

Warning: The sick person must radically eliminate any medicine, and exclusively limit himself to the treatment with the rattlesnake.

Sparrow Hawks

Wild reminiscences, memories of the mountain, savage evocations surge forth from within my mind in these instants...

How much these penitents suffered because of these cruel birds of prey...! The sly sparrow hawks desolated the poultry yards and took chickens and hens in their claws...

Many times I saw those large, bloody, ugly birds lodged on the branches of the neighboring trees leering at their defenseless victims...

To swallow and to be swallowed, that is the law of the "**Cosmic Common Trogoautoegocrat**," or reciprocal nourishment of all organisms.

Unquestionably, such reciprocity, correspondence, or mutuality intimately comes from the active, omnipresent "**Okidanock**."

Persecutions

How happy we were, abiding in our cabins of the solitary forest! Unfortunately, new persecutions came...

Profane people from the neighboring towns were busy with their duty (certainly, not a very beautiful duty) of propagating defamatory slander against us...

The gossip of the women, the falsehood of the men, the chatter, the rumors, the annoyance, assumed monstrous figures, and tempests were released...

Unquestionably, I was transformed into the central personage of the drama, the one who received all types of lashing, stoning, shooting...

Each day, the order of things went from bad to worse, and finally the stool pigeon, the accuser, the talebearer, the denouncer surged forth...

Certainly, I was not a simple instigator or agitator of people in the style of Paul of Tarsus for these wretched gendarmes, but something worse: a sorcerer of the Averno escaped from a mysterious Witches' Sabbath, a large ugly bird of evil omen, a monster that indispensably must be incarcerated or killed...

One starry night, when in the state of ecstasy, I was visited by a **mahatma** who when taking the floor said, "Many armed people come in search of you; you must go another way."

It is good to asseverate with great emphasis that I always know how to obey the orders of the universal White Fraternity...

By taking advantage of the nocturnal silence, I descended from the mountain by an abrupt and difficult path, on "El Plan," as the Gnostic hermits denominated the coastal lands. When I was out of the Sierra Nevada, I was taken by the venerable Master **Gargha Kuichines**. He transported us in his car to a beautiful city.

The Eight Venustic Initiations
of the First Mountain

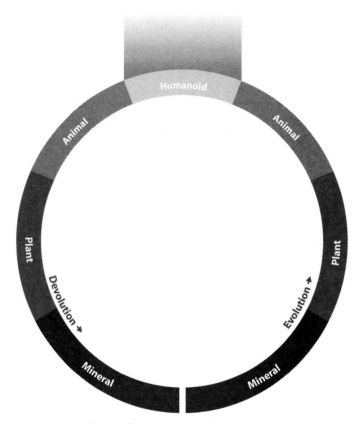

"Surges of Essences initiate their evolution in
the mineral kingdom, then proceed with the
plant kingdom, the animal kingdom, until finally
reaching the level of the intellective humanoid.
Thereafter, the devolutionary surges of life
descend, according to the Law of Falling, in order
to revive the animal, plant, and mineral processes
towards the center of terrestrial gravity."

EVOLUTION AND DEVOLUTION

Chapter XX
The Secret of the Abyss

Humbly, without arrogance, and excluding from my mind any possible inanity, frankly and plainly speaking, I confess that after having risen through the five degrees of igneous initiations, the development of the eight degrees of the Venustic Initiations of Light was urgent for me.

If what is truly required is the complete awakening of the **First Serpent of Light**, then the work in the "flaming forge of Vulcan" (sex) becomes undeferable.

The following is written with words of gold in the book of all splendors: "**The Kundalini** develops, revolves, and ascends within the marvelous aura of **Mahachohan**."

Unquestionably, we first must work with the fire, then after with the light. We must never confuse the Serpents of Fire with the Serpents of Light...

The extraordinary ascension of the first Serpent of Light, inwardly and upwardly along the spinal medullar canal of the physical body, allowed me to know the secret of the abyss.

The foundation of such a secret is found in the law of falling, as formulated by Saint Venoma.

Lo and behold the formulation which the cited master gave to this law that was discovered by him:

> Everything existing in the world falls to the bottom.
> And the bottom of any part of the Universe is its nearest 'stability,' and this said 'stability' is the place or the point upon which all the lines of force arriving from all directions converge.

> The centers of all the suns and of all the planets of our universe are precisely these points of stability. They are the lowest points of those regions of space upon which forces from all directions of the given part of the universe definitely tend and where they are concentrated. In these

Retribution

ARCANUM TEN

points there is also concentrated the equilibrium which enables suns and planets to maintain their position.

The "Tiger of Turkestan," when commenting about this, stated:

> In this formulation of his, Saint Venoma said further that everything when dropped into space, wherever it might be, tends to fall on one or another sun or one or another planet, according to which sun or planet the given part of space belongs, where the object is dropped, each sun or planet being for the given sphere the 'stability' or bottom.

The previously cited paragraphs clearly allude to two internal and external aspects of the law of gravity.

The exterior is just the projection of the interior. The secret gravitation of the spheres is always repeated in a tridimensional way...

The central nucleus of this planetary mass in which we live is without a doubt the mathematical place or the point upon which all the lines of force (arriving from all directions) converge.

The devolving and evolving forces of nature are found reciprocally equilibrated in the center of any planetary stability.

Surges of Essences initiate their evolution in the mineral kingdom, then proceed with the plant kingdom, the animal kingdom, until finally reaching the level of the intellective humanoid.

Thereafter, the devolutionary surges of life descend, according to the law of falling, in order to revive the animal, plant, and mineral processes towards the center of terrestrial gravity.

The wheel of **samsara** spins, and Anubis evolutionarily ascends up along the right side, while the devolving **Typhon** descends down through the left.

To abide within the "**intellective humanoid**" state is something abundantly relative and circumstantial.

It has been justly stated unto us that any humanoid period always consists of one hundred and eight lives of an evolving and devolving type that are always processed and repeated in higher or lower spirals.

I clarify: to each "**rational humanoid**" period, one hundred and eight existences are always assigned; this follows a strict mathematical concordance with the number of beads that form the Buddha's necklace.

The wheel of the Tenth Arcanum of the Tarot inevitably spins after each "**humanoid**" epoch according to the laws of time, space, and movement. It is then evident and manifest that the surges of devolutionary life descend into the submerged mineral kingdom towards the center

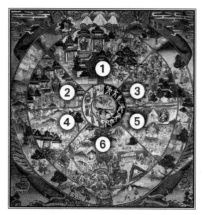

THE BHAVACHAKRA, "THE WHEEL OF BECOMING"
Also called the wheel of samsara.
Symbolizes six realms through which deluded beings migrate, up and down:
1. Gods (Sanskrit: Devas)
2. Demi-gods (Sanskrit: Asura)
3. Humans (Sanskrit: Manusya)
4. Animals (Sanskrit: Tiryagyoni)
5. Hungry ghosts (Sanskrit: Preta)
6. Hells (Sanskrit: Naraka)
Only Bodhisattvas on the direct path can escape the wheel.

of planetary stability in order for them to later evolutionarily re-ascend.

Any new evolving re-ascension from the center of terrestrial gravity always previously demands the disintegration of the "**myself.**" This is the Second Death.

Since the Essence is bottled up within the ego, the dissolution of the latter becomes indispensable in order for the Essence to be liberated.

The pristine, original purity of any Essence is restored in the center of planetary stability.

The wheel of **samsara** spins three thousand times. To comprehend this, to capture its deep significance, is indispensable and undeferable if what we really are longing for is the final liberation.

To continue with the present chapter, it is necessary to call for the utmost attention of the reader, with the purpose of asseverating the following: when the three thousand periods of the great wheel are concluded, any type of **realization** of the **Innermost Self** becomes impossible.

In other words, it is necessary to affirm the unavoidable fact that three thousand periods are mathematically assigned to any Monad for its inner profound **Self-realization**. It is indubitable that the doors are closed after the last round of the wheel.

When the last round occurs, then the Monad, the immortal spark, our internal Being, collects its Essence and its principles in order to definitively absorb himself within the bosom of the universal Spirit of Life (the supreme **Parabrahatman**).

The divine Monads or virginal sparks that really want mastery are very few. This concrete, clear, and definitive fact is written with mysterious characters of fire in the testament of ancient wisdom.

Certainly, when any given Monad is longing for mastery, then it is unquestionable that this Monad achieves it by intensely working upon its own Essence.

In this world of dense forms, it is easy to recognize any Essence which is intimately being worked on from within by its own divine Monad, because the concrete fact of it will be found in any person with great spiritual longings.

Clearly, such a specific type of mystical longing could never exist in people whose Essence has never been worked on from within by its corresponding divine Monad.

Once, while vacationing in the Port of Acapulco, on the coast of the Pacific in Mexico, I had to enter into the yogic state of **Nirvi-kalpa-samadhi**.

I wanted to know something about those Monads that had already lost every cosmic opportunity after having passed through the three thousand rounds of the wheel of **samsara**.

What I saw on that occasion, far away from the body, affections and the mind, was really extraordinary...

I entered through the doors of an ineffable temple, while completely submerged within the "current of sound," within the resplendent and immaculate ocean of the supreme Parabrahatman-Atman...

To interrogate, inquire, and investigate was not necessary. I could vividly experience in the whole presence of my Being the tremendous reality of such sublime Monads. They are beyond good and evil.

They are very little, innocent, tiny creatures, sparks of divinity, yet without **Self-realization**; happy beings, but without mastery.

Those noble creatures delectably floated within the immaculate whiteness of the Great Ocean. They were either entering into the temple or departing from it. They were praying and prostrating themselves before the Buddhas, before the holy gods, before the mahatmas.

Unquestionably, such divine Monads look at the masters in the same way that ants look at humans.

For these types of Monads without mastery, the **Agnishvattas**, the **Buddhas** of Compassion, or the hierophants are like something they cannot understand, like strange beings — enigmatic and terribly divine...

These cited Monads obey the holy gods and serve them with infinite humbleness within the **sanctas** or churches of **life** free in its movement (the Absolute).

The joy of these Monads is very well earned, since the Essence of each one of them turned three thousand times in the wheel of **samsara** and knew the horrors of the abyss.

Chapter XXI

The Baptism of John

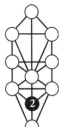

Within the organic vital depth (the **lingam sarira**), the **second degree of the Venustic Initiation** (in a superior octave to its corresponding Initiation of Fire) transcendentally surged as an esoteric result of the miraculous inward and upward ascension of the second radiant serpent of light along the spinal medullar canal.

Certainly, I had to have an unexpected magical encounter with John in the Garden of Hesperides, where the rivers of water of pure life pour forth milk and honey...

I am referring with great solemnity to John the Baptist, the very living reincarnation of Elias, that colossus who lived on the asperity of Mount Carmel, who had wild beasts as his neighbors and his sole company. From there, he would emerge as a lightning bolt in order to either sink or elevate kings. He was a superhuman creature who was sometimes visible, at other times invisible, and who was respected even by death itself.

Clearly, the esoteric, divine baptism of the **Christus John** has very profound archaic roots.

It is good to remember in these paragraphs the baptism of **Rama**, the **Yogi-Christ** of Hindustan:

> *When they were at Yodjana, halfway from the meridional brook of the Sarayu, Visvamitra sweetly said, "**Rama**, it is convenient that you pour water upon yourself, in accordance with our rites. I am going to teach you our salutations in order to save time. First of all, receive these two marvelous sciences: **the Potency and the Ultrapotency**. These will avoid fatigue, old age, or any other malady that would ever invade your limbs."*
>
> *While pronouncing this discourse, Visvamitra the man of mortifications, initiated **Rama** on the two sciences, who was purified in the waters of the river,*

RAMA AND SITA (CENTER)
Sita points toward a peacock, a tantric symbol that
represents how to transform poison into medicine.

standing, with his head inclined and his hands joined.
[This is quoted from the **Ramayana** *[500 BC] and*
invites good Christians to meditate upon it].

Unquestionably, the foundation of the diamantine baptism is found in the **Sahaja Maithuna** (Sexual Magic).

Before receiving the baptismal waters, a complete knowledge about **Sex Yoga** was urgent for the candidate.

Rama had to be previously informed by Visvamitra before being baptized. Thus, this is how he knew the science of **potency** and of **ultrapotency**.

The clue of baptism is found in the scientific transmutation of the spermatic waters of the first instant.

The sacrament of baptism in itself is full of deep significance. As a fact, it is a sexual commitment.

Factually, to be baptized is equivalent to signing a pact to perform Sexual Magic. **Rama** knew how to accomplish this terrific commitment; he practiced **Sahaja Maithuna** with his priestess-wife.

Rama did transmute the seminal waters into the alchemist's wine of light; he finally found the "lost word" and the **Kundalini** flourished through his lips made Word. Then he could exclaim with all the strength of his soul: *The King is dead, long live the King!*

I could feel in the whole presence of my cosmic Being the deep significance of the baptism when in the presence of the **Christus John**.

> The Nazarenes were known as Baptists, Sabians, and Christians of Saint John.
>
> Their belief was that the Messiah was not the Son of God, but simply a prophet who wanted to follow John.
>
> Origen (Vol. II, page 150) observed that there exist some that say that John was the anointed one (Christus).
>
> When the metaphysical conception of the Gnostics, who were seeing the Logos and the anointed one in Jesus, were starting to gain ground, then the primitive Christians were separated from the Nazarenes and were accusing Jesus of perverting the doctrine of John and of changing the Baptism in the Jordan into another one. - Codex Nazaraeus, II, page 109

I will conclude this chapter by emphasizing the following: the **Christ-Sun** shone upon the waters of life, and the final ceremonial initiation occurred when the second Serpent of Light made contact with the atom of the Father in the magnetic field of the root of the nose.

May the blessings of **Amenzano** be with its inalterability for the whole of eternity, amen!

THE TRANSFIGURATION BY THE ITALIAN ARTIST RAPHAEL

Chapter XXII
The Transfiguration of Jesus

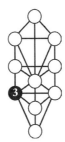

The luminous ascension of the **Third Serpent of Light** inwardly and upwardly along the brilliant spinal medullar canal of the sidereal body granted me complete access to the Venustic, superior octave of the corresponding Initiation of Fire...

It is not possible to write within the narrow frame of this treatise everything that in foregone times I learned in each and every one of the thirty-three holy chambers...

The extraordinary revolution of the radiant third snake was processed very slowly according to the merits of the tranquil heart...

I obviously felt transfigured when the luminous viper passed through the threshold of the third secret chamber of my heart temple.

Is this transfiguration perhaps not excessively rare? Did this not also happen to Moses on Mount Nebo? Unquestionably, I am not the first to whom this has happened, neither will I be the last.

In such moments of happiness, I was transported before the presence of that illustrious, respectable man of noble face and renowned intelligence whom I knew in foregone times while only a tender adolescent.

Frankly and plainly speaking, I am referring to the professor of aspiring Rosicrucians, cited in the fifth chapter of this very book. Unfortunately, this illustrious man could not see me, not even while I was in complete transfiguration...

Those who believe themselves to be Christians have never meditated enough on the emotional and sublime scene of the transfiguration of Jesus, nor on his ascension, as it is described by Luke (St. Luke 9:18-37) in the following terms:

And it came to pass, as he was alone praying,
his disciples were with him; and he asked them,
saying, Whom say the people that I am?

*They answering said, John the Baptist [***IOAGNES,
RA***, *or the Lamb of God]; but some say, E-li-as; and
others say, that one of the old prophets is risen again.*

*He said unto them, But whom say ye that I am?
Peter answering said, The Christ of God.*

*And he straightly charged them, and commanded
them to tell no man that thing;*

*Saying, the Son of Man must suffer many things,
and be rejected by the elders and chief priests and
scribes, and be slain, and be raised the third day.*

*And he said to them all, If any man will come after
me, let him deny himself [dissolve the* **EGO***], and
take up his cross [practice Sexual Magic] daily, and
follow me [sacrifice the self for humanity].*

*For whosoever will save his life [the selfish who
never sacrifice themselves for their fellowman] shall
lose it: But whosoever will lose his life for my sake
[the altruists who ascend to the altar of supreme
sacrifice for humanity], the same shall save it.*

*For what is a man advantaged, if he gain the whole
world, and lose himself, or he cast away?*

*For whosoever shall be ashamed of me and of my words, of
him shall the Son of Man be ashamed, when he shall come
in his own glory, and in his Father, and of the holy angels.*

*But I tell you of a truth, there be some standing here, which
shall not taste of death, till they see the kingdom of God.*

This passage, when taken literally, is referring only to
Jesus, but, as a fact, when taken symbolically or in "Spirit," is
referring to all men. As we proceed, we will see how this text of
the scene of the transfiguration unfolds:

*And it came to pass about eight days after these sayings
[we state that this event becomes a practical and tangible
corroboration of these statements] he took Peter and John
and James, and went up into a mountain to pray.*

And as he prayed, the fashion of his countenance was altered, and his raiment was white and glistening.

And, behold, there talked with him two men, which were Moses and E-li-as: Who appeared in glory and spake of his decease which he should accomplish at Jerusalem.

But Peter and they that were with him were heavy with sleep: and when they were awake, they saw his glory, and the two men that stood with him.

And it came to pass, as they departed from him, Peter said unto Jesus, Master, it is good for us to be here: and let us make three tabernacles; one for thee, and one for Moses, and one for E-li-as: not knowing what he said.

While he thus spake, there came a cloud, and overshadowed them: and they feared as they entered into the cloud.

And there came a voice out of the cloud, saying, this is my beloved Son: hear him.

And when the voice was past, Jesus was found alone. And they kept it close, and told no man in those days any of those things which they had seen...

"And said unto them, It is written, My house
shall be called the house of prayer; but
ye have made it into a den of thieves..."

THE SAVIOR CLEANS THE TEMPLE

Chapter XXIII
Jerusalem

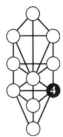

The experience of the crude, evangelical reality of the great Kabir Jesus' magisterial entrance into Jerusalem was granted to me, thanks to the inward and upward development, the revolution and ascension, of the **Fourth Venustic Serpent** along the medullar canal of the mental body.

Then, I could directly verify for myself the inferior (inferno) and superior (heaven) aspects of the mental world.

Unquestionably, that great harlot of all fatalities, the great, apocalyptic whore whose number is 666, is horrifyingly devolving within the mental infernos...

Certainly, I am not some treacherous iconoclast, who, as an intellectual vandal, eagerly wants to destroy beloved longings. However, sincerely and plainly speaking, I must confess everything that I saw within those "**manasic**" regions of nature.

The wit of wrong reasoning appears impure within the inferior regions of the concrete planetary mind...

What I perceived with my spatial sense, within the mental infernos, has already been stated by Saint John in *The Apocalypse*:

> *The merchandise of gold, and silver, and precious stones, and of pearls, and fine linen, and purple, and silk, and scarlet, and of thyine wood, and all manner vessels of ivory, and all manner of vessels of most precious wood, and of brass, and iron, and marble.*
>
> *And cinnamon, and odours, and ointments and frankincense, and wine, and oil, and fine flour, and wheat, and beasts, and sheep, and horses and chariots, and slaves, and souls of men.* - Revelation 18:12-13

I saw horrible buildings and the bedsteads of Procrustes where the great whore is incessantly fornicating.

I witnessed abominable brothels, filthy streets, movie dens where pornographic movies are exhibited, etc.

It is indispensable to pass beyond the body, the affections, and the mind if what we long for is the triumphal entrance into the Jerusalem of above (the Heaven of Mercury, and, afterwards into the world of the Spirit).

Let us now see chapter 21 verses 1 to 20 of Matthew:

And when they drew nigh unto Jerusalem, and were come to Beth-pha-ge, unto the Mount of Olives, then sent Jesus two disciples,

Saying unto them, Go into the village over against you and straightway ye shall find an ass tied, and a colt with her: loose them, and bring them unto me.

And if any man say ought unto you, ye shall say, The Lord hath need of them; and straightway he will send them.

All this was done, that it might be fulfilled which was spoken by the prophet, saying,

Tell ye the daughter of Sion, Behold, thy King cometh unto thee, meek, and siting upon an ass [symbol of the mind], and colt the foal of an ass.

And the disciples went, and did as Jesus [the great Kabir] commanded them,

And brought the ass, and the colt, and put on them their clothes and they set him thereon.

And a very great multitude spread their garments in the way; others cut down branches from the trees and strawed them in the [esoteric] way.

And the multitudes that went before [on the path of the razor's edge], and that followed [on the esoteric path], cried, saying, Hosanna to the son of David:

Blessed is he that cometh in the name of the Lord; Hosanna in the highest.

And when he was come into Jerusalem, all the
city was moved, saying, Who is this?

And the multitude said, This is Jesus the
prophet of Nazareth of Galilee.

And Jesus went into the temple of God [the temple that
each one of us carries within] and cast out all of them
that sold and bought in the temple [the merchants, the
"I's" which personify our defects of a psychological type],
and overthrew the tables of the moneychangers [demons
who adulterate anything that is good], and the seats of
them that sold doves [devils who sell the Third Logos, who
profane the Holy Spirit by making business with him,
like fornicators, prostitutes, lesbians, homosexuals],

And said unto them, It is written, My house shall be called
the house of prayer; but ye have made it into a den of thieves
[thus, the mind of each person is a den of perversity].

And the blind and the lame came to him in the temple;
and he healed them [people incapable of seeing the
truth and people who cannot walk the way].

And when the chief priests and scribes [or intellectuals]
saw the wonderful things that he did, and the
children crying in the temple, and saying, Hosanna
to the son of David; they were sore displeased,

And said unto him, Hearest thou what these say? And
Jesus saith unto them, Yea; have ye never read, Out of the
mouth of babes and sucklings thou hast perfected praise?

And he left them, and went out of the city
into Bethany; and he lodged there.

Now in the morning as he returned into the city, he hungered.

And when he saw a fig tree in the way [symbol of the sexual
strength], he came to it, and found nothing thereon, but leaves
only, and said unto it, Let no fruit grow on thee henceforward
for ever. And presently the fig tree withered away.

THE TREE OF LIFE ON AN EGYPTIAN TOMB MURAL.
The Divine Mother serves the life-giving waters to one who has earned it.

And when the disciples saw it, they marvelled,
saying, How soon is the fig tree withered away!

It is written in the Book of Splendors: *Every tree which bringeth not forth good fruit is hewn down and cast into the fire.*

When Adam and Eve [the paradisiacal humanity] did eat
from the forbidden fruit, the eyes of them both were opened,
and they knew that they were naked; and they sewed
fig leaves together, and they made themselves aprons.

Gautama, the **Buddha**, attained the final illumination while seated for four days and nights in profound meditation in the shadow of the fig tree.

In the ancient Egypt of the Pharaohs, the fig tree was always worshipped as a living symbol of the creative energy of the **Third Logos**.

Certainly, the devolving creatures of the infernal worlds are sterile fig trees that have never bore fruit.

A strange epigraph could be written about this fig tree because one of its most typical details, accompanied with certain astral oracles, is that this plant is always green and spins vertiginously.

A good friend from Jumilla told me, On the outskirts of this town, a cave of vast extension and height exists, where a fig tree grows which neither loses a leaf nor produces a fruit. There is a general belief, based upon the testimony of many who state that on the day of Saint John, at the break of dawn they have witnessed a great military cohort of specters with horses of war, richly harnessed, racing from that cave. These specter warriors were preceded by fantastic banners and galloped towards the South, where they disappeared far off into the distance, as if they were evoking some forgone historical event. (This is text taken from *The Tree of the Hesperides*).

Jesus, the great Gnostic priest, said:

The [philosophical] stone [sex] which the builders rejected [people of many religions], the same is become of the head of the corner: this is the Lord's doing, and it is marvelous in our eyes.

Therefore say I unto you, The kingdom of God shall be taken from you, and given to a nation bringing forth the fruits thereof [people that will be capable of practicing Sexual Magic, dissolving the ego and sacrificing themselves for their fellowmen].

And whosoever shall fall on this stone [sex] shall be broken: but on whomsoever it shall fall, it will grind him to powder. - Matthew 21:42-44

Unquestionably, only by means of the sexual fire is it possible to incinerate all of the perverse psychic aggregates that we carry within and thus enter into the Heavenly Jerusalem on Palm Sunday (see my book entitled *The Mystery of the Golden Blossom*).

"And when he rose up from prayer, and was come to his disciples,
he found them sleeping for sorrow [with their consciousness
asleep], and said unto them, why sleep ye? [Why do you have your
consciousness asleep?] Rise and pray, lest ye enter into temptation
[because it is clear that the sleeping ones fall into temptation]."

THE SAVIOR CALLS US TO AWAKEN

Chapter XXIV
The Mount of Olives

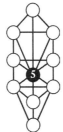 As a fact, the marvelous inward and upward ascension of the **Fifth Serpent of Light** along the spinal medullar canal of the causal body granted me open access into the initiatic mysteries of the fifth degree of the Venustic wisdom.

If I write in detail all of that which I then learned in the thirty-three holy chambers of the causal world, it is obvious that I would fill immense volumes.

There, as a causal man seated with much humility, I crossed my arms over my chest in order to assist in the final ceremony...

Unfortunately, I had the wrong custom of crossing my arms in such a way that the left was always over the right...

"Thou should not cross thy arms in such a way," an adept of the temple told me. Then, he added, "The right must go over the left." I obeyed his instructions.

Have you ever seen an Egyptian sarcophagus? The crossed arms over the chest of the defunct illustrate these affirmations.

Any skull between two crossbones or skeletal bones (usually known as a sign of danger) also represents these affirmations.

The deep significance of this symbol is to perform the will of the Father on Earth as it is in heaven; to die in the Lord...

When the great Kabir Jesus was on the Mount of Olives, he prayed as follows:

> *O my Father, if thou be willing*
> *remove this cup from me: nevertheless*
> *not my will, but thine be done.*

AN EGYPTIAN SARCOPHAGUS

*And being in an agony he prayed more
earnestly: and his sweat was it were great drops
of blood falling down to the ground.*

*And when he rose up from prayer, and was come to his
disciples, he found them sleeping for sorrow [with their
consciousness asleep], and said unto them, why sleep ye?
[Why do you have your consciousness asleep?] Rise and
pray, lest ye enter into temptation [because it is clear that
the sleeping ones fall into temptation].* - Luke 22:42,44-46

*It is written: "Before the cock [the Word] crow [or incarnates
within us], thou shalt deny me thrice."* - Matthew 26:34

Peter, Petra, or **Rock** was the hierophant himself, or in
Phoenician, the "interpreter," from which came the famous
evangelical phrase: *"Thou art Peter, and upon this rock I will build
my church* [our inner temple]." [Matthew 16:18]

Busen, in his writing entitled *The Place of Egypt in Universal
History* (volume 5, page 90), comments about an inscription
found in the sarcophagus of a great queen of the eleventh
dynasty (2,250 years before Christ). It is only a transcription of
the *Book of the Dead* (4,500 years before Christ) that interprets
the hieroglyphics of **Peter, Patar, Revelation, initiation,** etc.

When the old medieval **alchemists** discovered that the
"initiatic Petera" was in our sexual organs, they did not err in
any way...

Unquestionably, "to spill the cup of Hermes," to prostitute the stone of truth is equivalent to denying the Christ...

From the **Unknowable Entirety** or **Radical Zero,** the
Pythagorean Monad, the Verb, the Arch-Magi or Hierophant,
the **Unique-One,** the Buddhist Aunadad-Ad, the **Ain Soph,
En Soph** or **Chaldean Pneuma-Eikon,** the **Ruach Elohim** or
divine Spirit of the Lord floating upon the Genesiac waters,
the one who exists by himself, **Anupadaka,** or the Aryan
Manu-Swayambu-Narayana, emanates in the beginning of any
manifestation or universe.

This particular Monad of each one of us transforms itself
into the most sublime Duad — our individual particular
Divine Mother **Kundalini...**

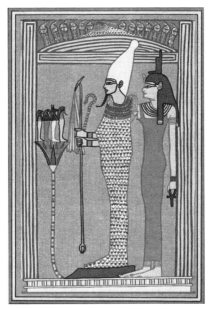

OSIRIS AND ISIS. EGYPTIAN.

HE and **SHE** constitute the Gnostic **Father/Mother**, the Parsi **Zeru-Ana**, the **Dual Protogonos** or the Kabbalistic **Adam Kadmon**, the **Theos-Chaos** of the *Theogony* of Hesiod, the Chaldean **Ur-Anas** or fire and water, the Egyptian **Osiris-Isis**, the Semitic **Jah-Hovah, Jehovah,** or **Iod-Heve**, etc.

The Latin word **Romae** (**Rome**) when inverted becomes (**amore**) **love**. Therefore, the sacrament of the Church of Rome (**Romae, Amore**) is love, the **Sahaja Maithuna** (**Sexual Magic**).

We must learn to fulfill this holy sacrament by vibrating in tune with the divine couple.

He must convert himself into the living expression of the Hebraic ׳ **Iod,** and **she** must be the living manifestation of הוה **Heve**.

The Kabbalistic **Adam Kadmon**, the **Rha-Sephira** or eternal **masculine-feminine**, when conciliating themselves above and below in the infinitely large and the infinitely small in perfect harmony, constitute the culminating note of the "**Mount of Olives**."

PILATE PRESENTS JESUS BY ALBRECHT DÜRER.

Chapter XXV

The Beautiful Helen

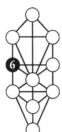
The sublime and marvelous inward and upward ascension of the radiant sixth serpent along the spinal medullar canal of my **buddhic body** gave me, as a fact and by my own right, open passage into the **Sixth Venustic Initiation**...

In that epoch, I had to vividly experience in the **buddhic** or **intuitional universal world** some transcendental chapters of the Christic gospel...

I want now to refer with vast delicacy to certain secret and marvelous passages which were intentionally eliminated from the original text by scribes and doctors of the law.

Certainly, it is lamentable that the Hebraic Holy Bible was so cruelly mutilated, adulterated, deformed...

Multiple, perfect, rhythmical concordances, with diverse esoteric procedures (which we must vividly experience here and now), was what I then experienced in that cosmic intuitional region...

These were extraordinary scenes related with the other planets of our solar system of **Ors**, a system in which we live, move, and where our Being resides.

The Sun of Midnight shone in the unalterable infinite when the sixth viper of light resplendently passed through the august threshold of its correspondent chamber in the tranquil heart...

I entered into the temple of initiation accompanied by many people. In the procession, each one of us carried within our dexterous hand a candle, a taper, or a burning torch...

In those instants, I vividly experienced those esoteric verses which literally say:

> *And immediately, while he yet spake, cometh Judas,*
> *one of the twelve, and with him a great multitude with*
> *swords and staves, from the chief priests [or men who are*
> *constituted by mundane authority], and the scribes [in other*

*words, those who pass in the world as wise], and the elders
[those who pass in the world as prudent and discreet].*

*And as soon Judas was come, he goeth straightway to
him, and saith, Master, master; and kissed him.*

*And they laid their hands on him, and
took him.* - Mark 14:43,45-46

While inebriated with ecstasy, I exclaimed, "I am the
Christ!"

Then, an **adept-lady** reproved me by saying, "Be careful!
Thou must not say that, for it is disrespectful!"

I then answered, "In these moments, I am representing
him." This sacred lady then kept a respectful silence.

This cosmic drama within the temple of the transparent
walls had a certain very heavy and terribly divine "**mayaestic**"
flavor...

While being converted into the central personage, I had to
experience within myself the following evangelical passages:

*And they led Jesus away to Caiaphas the high priest
[the demon of evil will] and with him were assembled
all the chief priests [the official authorities of this
world] and the elders [very respectable people full
of experience] and the scribes [the intellectuals].*

*And the chief priests and all the council sought
for witness against **Jesus** [the inner Savior]
to put him to death; and found none.*

*For many bare false witness against him,
but their witness agreed not together.*

*And there arose certain, and bare false
witness against him, saying,*

*We heard him say, I will destroy this temple that is
made with hands [referring to the animal body], and
within three days I will build another made without
hands [the spiritual body, **To Soma Heliakon**].*

But neither so did their witness agree together.

And the high priest [with his evil will] stood up in the midst, and asked **Jesus**, *saying, Answerest thou nothing? what is it which these witness against thee?*

But he held his peace, and answered nothing. [Silence is the eloquence of wisdom.]

Again the high priest asked him, and said unto him, Art thou the Christ, the Son of the Blessed? [The Second Logos]

And **Jesus** *said,* **I AM** *[***He Is***] and ye shall see the Son of Man [every true Christified or* **Osirified** *one] sitting on the right hand of power of God [the First Logos], and coming in the clouds of heaven.*

Then the high priest [the demon of evil will] rent his clothes and saith, What need we any further witnesses?

Ye have heard the blasphemy: what think ye? And they all condemned him to be guilty of death.

And some began to spit on him, and to cover his face, and to buffet him, and to say unto him, Prophesy: and the servants did strike him with the palms of their hands. - Mark 14:53, 55-65

And straightway in the morning the chief priests held a consultation with the elders and the scribes and the whole council, and bound **Jesus** *and carried him away, and delivered him to Pilate.*

And Pilate [the demon of the mind] asked him, Art thou the King of the Jews?

And he answering said unto him, Thou sayest it.

And the chief priests [the authorities of this world] accused him of many things: but he answered nothing.

And Pilate asked him again, saying, Answerest thou nothing? behold how many things they witness against thee [all of the people accuse the internal Christ, even those who call themselves his followers].

*But **Jesus** yet answered nothing [I repeat:*
Silence is the eloquence of wisdom]; so that
Pilate [the demon of the mind] marvelled.

Now at that feast he, released unto them one
prisoner, whomsoever they desired.

And there was one named Barabbas [the demon of
perversity which every one carries inside], which lay
bound with them that had made insurrection with him,
who had committed murder in the insurrection [because
*the **ego** is always a murderer and an evil one].*

And the multitude crying aloud began to desire
him to do as he had ever done unto them.

But Pilate answered them, saying, Will ye that
I release unto you the King of the Jews?

For he knew that the chief priests [the authorities
of all types] had delivered him for envy.

But the chief priests moved the people, that he should
rather release Barabbas unto them [the authorities
*of all types always defend the **ego**. They say: first*
"I," then "me," and thirdly "myself"].

And Pilate answered and said again unto them, What will ye
then that I shall do unto him who ye call the King of the Jews?

And they cried out again, Crucify him. [Crucifixia!
Crucifixia! Crucifixia!] - Mark 15:1-14

I left from the ineffable sancta, ecstatic after having direct-ly experienced the tremendous intimate reality of all of these formerly cited verses.

I departed from the great cathedral of the soul wearing a new tunic of glory — a splendorous, long vesture...

How joyful I felt there when contemplating the broad panorama! Then, I saw the flux and reflux of all things...

Buddhi is like a fine and transparent **alabaster** cup, with-in which the flame of **prajna** is burning...

Atman, the **Being**, has two souls. The first is the Spiritual Soul, which is feminine (**Buddhi**). The second is the Human Soul, and it is masculine (**Superior Manas**).

The **intellectual animal**, mistakenly called "**human being**," has only the **Essence** incarnated within himself. Clearly, the latter is the **Buddhata**, a minimal fraction of the Human Soul. This is the psychic material with which the "**Auric Embryo**" can and must be fabricated. (Read the book *The Mystery of the Golden Blossom*).

The **fountain** and **foundation** of high magic is found in the perfect betrothal of **Buddhi-Manas** in the purely spiritual regions or in the terrestrial world.

Helen clearly signifies the betrothal of **Nous** (**Atman-Buddhi**) with **Manas** (the Human Soul or causal body), a union through which **consciousness** and **willpower** are united. Therefore, both souls are bestowed with divine powers as a result of such a union.

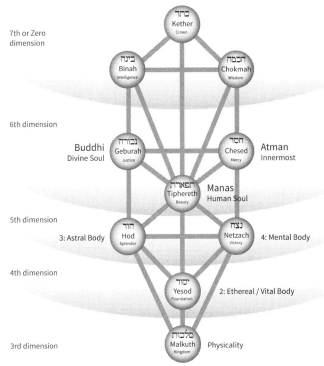

ATMAN-BUDDHI-MANAS ON THE TREE OF LIFE

The essence of **Atman**, who is the primordial, universal and eternal divine fire, is found within **Buddhi**, who in complete conjunction with **Manas,** the **causal (Human Soul),** determines the **masculine-feminine** aspect. The beautiful **Helen** of Troy is the same **Helen** in Goethe's *Faust*, the **Shakti** or feminine potential of the internal Being...

She and **he, Buddhi-Manas**, are the twin souls within ourselves (even when the intellectual animal still does not have them incarnated); they are the two beloved children of **Atman (the Innermost)**; they are the eternal bride and groom who are always in love...

Such **love** has infinite correlations with the conjugated pair of the double suns of heaven, and with the Earth and the Moon, or with the protoplasmic "**amphiaster**" of the determinant cells (as it is known in the mysterious phenomena of karyokinesis or morphological nuclear division of a single cell), also in the universal symbolism of the Épopées and of all literary works where the ideal love between two beings of opposite sexes constitute the "**Alma Mater.**"

Unquestionably, the "**Sahaja Maithuna,**" as a sacrament of the church of **Rome,** is repeated with the twins within the **akasha tattva,** and is gloriously continued with **Osiris-Isis** in the region of **Anupadaka.**

I clarify: When we cite the church of **Romae,** we must reverse the letters. This word must be read like this: **AMORE = LOVE.** Obviously, **sex** is the church of **love.**

When we grasp its deep significance, the theory of the twin souls does not imply any danger.

The chemical coitus, the metaphysical copulation, gloriously shines in the zenith of the ideal, without even a trace of a shadow of impurity...

Legitimate enamoring is never separate from **sex.** The sexual act is certainly the consubstantiation of love within the **psycho-physiological** realism of our nature.

The betrothal of **Buddhi-Manas** is only possible by means of the chemical coitus. Sexual pleasure is a legitimate right of the human being.

Renato committed the error of emphatically affirming that **Helen** of **Simon** the **Magi** was a beautiful woman of flesh and bone whom the cited **magi** had found in a brothel in the city of Tyre. According with his biographers, she was also the reincarnation of **Helen** of the Greeks. **Renato's** concept does not resist a deep analysis. The authentic initiatic colleges teach with complete clarity that beautiful **Helen** is **Buddhi**, the **Spiritual Soul** of the Sixth Venustic Initiation, the feminine **Shakti** potential.

THE CRUCIFIXION

Chapter XXVI
The Event of Golgotha

The radiant, inward, and upward ascension of the Seventh Venustic Serpent along the spinal medullar spiritual canal of the divine vehicle (**Atman**) granted me a vivid experience of the event at Golgotha.

Unquestionably, I need to frankly and plainly utter, to confess, that as a concrete, clear, and definitive fact, I saw myself transformed into the central personage of this "cosmic drama."

To experience this cosmic event of Calvary within oneself, with all of its crude, transcendental reality, within the "world of the Divine Spirit" (**Atman**), is certainly extraordinary.

I am not the first one who has vividly experienced this event from the Mount of Skulls, nor will I be the last...

So, after the crucifixion, I saw myself lay down as a cadaver upon the "slime of the earth..."

Then, the Shakti potential, the divine spouse of Shiva, my perfect **Mother Kundalini**, prostrated before me with infinite humility; she was worshipping me...

"Oh, Mother of mine!" I exclaimed, "You are my Mother! I am the one who should kneel before you! It is unthinkable that you are kneeling before me! I do not deserve this! I am a vile slug from the mud of the earth, an unworthy sinner!"

However, it is evident that in such instants of this "cosmic drama," I was representing the **Christus**, **Vishnu**, the **Second Logos**, the **Son**...

In the moments in which I write these paragraphs, the ineffable supplication of Dante Alighieri comes into my memory, which textually says:

> *Virgin Mother, Daughter of your Son, more humble*
> *and sublime than any creature, fixed goal decreed*
> *from all eternity, You are the one whom gave to*
> *human nature so much nobility that its Creator*
> *did not disdain His being made its creature.*

*That love whose warmth allowed this flower to bloom within
the everlasting peace was love rekindled in your womb; for as
above, you are the noonday torch of charity, and there below,
on earth, among the mortals, you are a living spring of hope.*

*Lady, you are so high, you can intercede, that
he who would have grace but does not seek your
aid, may long to fly but has no wings.*

*Your loving-kindness does not only answer the one who asks,
but it is often ready to answer freely long before the asking.*

*In you is compassion, in you is pity, in you is generosity,
in you is every goodness found in any creature.*

*This man, who from the deepest hollow in the universe,
up to this height, has seen the lives of spirits, one by
one, now pleads with you, through grace, to grant
him so much virtue that he may lift his vision higher
still, may lift it toward the ultimate salvation.*

*And I, who never burned for my own vision more than I burn
for his, do offer you all my prayers — and pray that they may
not fall short, that, with your prayers, you may disperse all of
the clouds of his morality so that the Highest Joy be his to see.*

*This, too, O Queen, who can do what you
would, I ask of you: that after such a vision, his
sentiments preserve their perseverance.*

May your protection curb his mortal passions.

- The Divine Comedy, Paradise, Canto XXXIII, verse 1-37

Until now, we have Dante's sublime supplication. Let us
continue with the theme of this chapter by studying certain
Christic verses...

*Then the soldiers of the governor took Jesus into
the common hall, called Praetorium; and gathered
unto him the whole band of soldiers.*

*And they stripped him, and put on him a scarlet
robe [first the Philosophical Stone is black,
then it becomes white, and finally red].*

*And when they had platted a crown of thorns, they put
it about his head [a traditional painful diadem on every
Christified astral body], and a reed in his right hand [like
the rod of Aaron or the staff of the Patriarchs — a living
symbol of the dorsal spine]: and they bowed the knee before
him, and mocked him, saying, Hail, King of the Jews!*

*And after that they had mocked him [consequently,
this is the path of sex], they took the robe off from him
[because they, the tenebrous ones do not want the
initiate to wear the scarlet robe of his own Innermost
Logoi], and led him away to crucify him.*

*And as they came out, they found a man of Cyrene,
Simon by name: him they compelled to bear his cross [our
guru always appears on the path in order to help us].*

*And when they were come unto a place called Golgotha,
that is to say, a place of a skull [synonym of death],*

*They gave him vinegar to drink mingled with gall: and
when he had tasted thereof, he would not drink [it is
evident that the path of the razor's edge is very bitter].*

*And they crucified him [with the sexual cross, because
the phallus inserted within the uterus forms such a very
sacred sign], and parted his garments, casting lots [it is a
clear allusion to the elimination of human possessions]:
which was spoken by the prophet, they parted my garments
among them, and upon my vesture did they cast lots.*

And sitting down they watched him there;

*And set up over his head his accusation written:
INRI, **Ignis Natura Renovatur Integra**
[fire renews nature incessantly].*

*Then were there two thieves crucified with him, one on the
right hand, and another on the left [The good thief is the
secret, divine power that steals the sexual energy for the
Christification. The adverse thief is the secret enemy who
pillages the deposit of the Sexual Hydrogen Si-12 for evilness].*

*And they that passed by [the profane and profaners
of evermore] reviled him, wagging their heads,*

*And saying, Thou that destroyest the temple, and buildest it in
three days [you that annihilate the Sinner Adam in order for
the Celestial Adam to be born], save thyself. If thou be the Son
of God, come down from the cross [because we, the tenebrous,
do not like the intersection of the crossed wood that forms your
two arms, like two prodigious hands that extend themselves
to frighten away the sinister forces and the inferior powers].*

*Likewise also the chief priests [the authorities] mocking
him, with the scribes [or intellectuals and Pharisees that
always boast of being virtuous and saintly] and elders
[the very respectable people in the world], said,*

*He saved others; himself he cannot save. If he be the
King of Israel, let him now come down from the cross
[let him abandon the path of the razor's edge and the
Sahaja Maithuna], and we will believe him.*

*He trusted in God; let him deliver him now, if he will have
him: for he said, I am the Son of God [he christified himself;
therefore, he made himself the Son of the Eternal One. We are
children of the devil because we are the fruit of fornication].*

*Now from the sixth hour [temptation] there was darkness
over all the land unto the ninth hour [Ninth Sphere;
when Kabbalistically adding 9 + 6, we have 15. This is the
arcanum of Typhon Baphomet: The Devil. Such an esoteric*

ARCANA SIX, NINE, AND FIFTEEN

value corresponds with the constellation of the whale, under whose cosmic influence the initiate unfolds until reaching resurrection. Let us remember the sign of Jonah].

And about the ninth hour Jesus cried with a loud voice, saying, Eli, Eli, lama sabachthani? That is to say, My God, my God, why hast thou forsaken me? [Clearly, every initiate feels really abandoned before reaching resurrection].

Some of them that stood there, when they heard that, said, This man calleth for Elias [Helias, Eliu, Elias, Helios — the Sun Christ, the Innermost Logos. He is our supreme aspiration].

And straightway one of them ran, and took a sponge, and filled it with vinegar, and put it on a reed [symbol of the dorsal spine], and gave him to drink [as if saying, the work with the sexual spinal fires is more bitter than gall].

Jesus, when he had cried again with a loud voice, yielded up the ghost [thus, this is how we the initiates die within ourselves, with death on the cross. See my book entitled The Mystery of the Golden Blossom].

*And, behold, the veil of the temple [the famous Veil of **Isis**, or sexual, Adamic veil, the product of original sin] was rent in twain from the top to the bottom [due to the supreme death of the ego]; and the earth did quake, and the rocks [of the path of the razor's edge] rent.* - St. Matthew 27:27-51

Hermes / Mercury

Chapter XXVII
The Holy Sepulchre

It is written with characters of fire in the Book of Splendors that when Jesus, the great Gnostic priest, exhaled his final breath, the philosophical earth, his very human person, did quake when comprehending the difficult task that destiny reserved for him; and the rocks of the path of the razor's edge rent, making the path even more difficult. (This is only integrally comprehended by those masters that, after having died within themselves, are preparing themselves for the Resurrection).

As an astrological planet, Mercury is even more mysterious than Venus itself, and is identical to the Mazdeist **Mithra**. Mercury is **Buddha**, the Genie or God who is situated between the Sun and the Moon. He is the perpetual companion of the Sun of wisdom.

Pausanias, in his fifth book, shows Mercury sharing a common altar with Jupiter. Mercury displayed wings in order to express how he assisted the Sun on its sidereal course. Mercury was called Nuncio and Wolf of the Sun: "Solaris Luminis Particeps." "He was the chief and the evoker of the souls, the arch-magi and hierophant."

Virgil describes Mercury holding the caduceus or hammer of two serpents in his dexterous hand in order to evoke the souls to a new life; those souls, those unhappy, innocent creatures who are precipitated into the **Orco** or **Limbo**: "**Tum Virgam Capit, Hac Animas Ille Evocat Orco**," with the purpose of having them enter into the celestial militia.

After these explanations the following (defined) verses become clear:

> *And the graves were open; and many bodies of the saints which slept [in the* **Orco** *or* **Limbo***] arose, And came out of the graves after his [***esoteric***] resurrection, and went into the holy city [the Jerusalem from above], and appeared unto many.* - Matthew 27:52, 53

Unquestionably, many saints wanted to **intimately Self-realize** without the holy sacrament of the church of **love** (**Sahaja Maithuna**). These unhappy souls always fall into the **Orco** or **Limbo** of ignorance, darkness, and pain... Only by dying in themselves is the resurrection possible (this death is with the cross, a completely sexual symbol). If the seed does not die, the plant is not born. The path of life is formed by the hoof prints of the horse of death.

Mercury, the Aurean planet, the ineffable one, is the one the hierophants prohibited to name. In Greek mythology, Mercury is symbolized by the famous hare-hunting dogs, or guardian dogs of the celestial cattle that drink from the very pure fountains of occult wisdom.

This is why Mercury is also known as "**Hermes-Anubis,**" the good inspirator, or **Agathodaemon**. He flies over the Earth like the bird of Argos, thus the Earth mistakes him for the Sun itself. Respectively, they both represent the Hindu **Sarama** and **Sarameya**.

Traditions state that the emperor Julian prayed every night to the occult Sun through the intercession of Mercury, for as the very wise Vossius stated: "All theologians asseverate that Mercury and the Sun are one... This is why Mercury was considered to be the most eloquent and wisest of the gods, a fact which is not strange since Mercury is found so close to the wisdom and to the Word (or **Logos**) that was mistaken with both...."

Mercury is the **Third Logos, Shiva, the Holy Spirit,** the First Begotten of creation, our authentic, particular, individual Monad...

Mercury, **Shiva**, the great hierophant, nuncio and wolf of the intimate **Christ**, is the supreme hope for those who sleep within the holy sepulcher...

I acknowledged the phallic sign on the "boat of Ra" when passing through the Eighth Venustic Initiation. Then, I exclaimed with a great voice:

When the first trumpet shall sound, then
I will resurrect from the dead.

Hail, oh great divinity, who navigates on thy boat!
Transported until here, I appear before thee!

Allow me to go up to the bridge of command
and direct the crank of the boat, as do thy
servants, the Archons of the planets.

Litelantes was a little distressed when contemplating my holy sepulcher. "Do not be afraid," a Mahatma told her, "His physical body will not die yet." These words integrally calmed her.

In that forgone epoch of my present existence, I had not even died within myself. I was still with my ego very much alive. That sepulcher was then merely symbolic, as the coffin of every Masonic lodge.

Yes, even though I comprehended the sepulchral symbolism in an integral way, I knew that I must die within myself in order to have the right to the resurrection of "**Hiram Abiff**," the secret master within my heart temple...

That initiation concluded with precise instructions related to the mission that I am presently accomplishing in this world...

End of the First Mountain

RESURRECTION

The Second Mountain

The Mountain of Resurrection

Chapter XXVIII
Serenity and Patience

It is clear that I and the other brothers and sisters of the temple of the "Twice-born" had eliminated from our psyche various infrahuman, subjective elements. However, after already having passed through the eight initiations, we were longing with all the forces of the soul to enter into the esoteric magical works of the "Mountain of Resurrection."

Once in the temple, it was indicated that we must wait with infinite patience for the abbot of the monastery. But, evidently, the passing hours were very long and boring, and had an unbearable monotony. Certainly, the venerable abbot did not seem to be in any hurry whatsoever.

Some of those veterans of the First Mountain were moving extensively, here, there, and everywhere, and were impatiently complaining because of the singular delay of the superior.

There are events in life that are surprising, and one of these is the astonishing entrance of the abbot into the temple. We, all the brothers and sisters of the sacred order, were dumbfounded, since some of us had already lost all hope of seeing the master.

Before the sacred confraternity, the venerable one spoke and said, "All of you brothers and sisters are lacking two virtues that this brother has." He said this while he was pointing at me with his index finger.

Posteriorly, in a simultaneously sweet and imperative way, he commanded me, saying, "You, brother, tell them which are these two virtues."

"There is the need to know how to be patient, and there is the need to know how to be serene," I exclaimed with a slow and clear voice...

"Do you realize this? Are you convinced of this?" broke forth the abbot with great solemnity. All the adepts, simultaneously frightened and marvelled, chose to keep a respectful silence.

Unquestionably, all of the members of the congregation, with the exception of myself, had then to be deferred, because only my insignificant person who has no value was victorious in the difficult ordeal.

The austere hierophant then gave me a beautiful orange as a gift. Immediately, I captured its deep significance...

Much later in time, I had to appear before a brotherhood of another monastery of the universal White Fraternity, with the definite purpose of receiving orders and signing documents...

At that time, I was warned with the following words: "You must be very careful of lunar coldness."

After a long recess, it was urgent for me to return into the "flaming forge of Vulcan."

Unquestionably, there always exist long periods of sexual abstinence between mountain and mountain.

Chapter XXIX
The Nine Degrees of Mastery

To capture, learn, and grasp in an integral, unitotal way the deep significance of the nine masters who went in search of **Hiram**, as well as those who assassinated him, is urgent and undeferable.

Unquestionably, none of the nine masters went towards the regions of the north; instead, they intelligently organized themselves into three groups of three, and they respectively distributed themselves towards the east, towards the south, and to the west. Clearly, the latter were the ones who discovered the tomb and the assassins.

This symbolic, esoteric peregrination of the nine masters specifically refers, as a consequence, to the individual pilgrimage that every initiate has to execute in the "Second Mountain." This is achieved by passing through the nine steps or successive degrees, which are totally enumerated and defined in the nine spheres:

1. Moon
2. Mercury
3. Venus
4. Sun
5. Mars
6. Jupiter
7. Saturn
8. Uranus
9. Neptune

We can and must issue the following enunciation: "Only by means of these intimate pilgrimages from sphere to sphere is it possible for us to be in the condition of vivifying and making the secret master **Hiram**, **Shiva** (the spouse of our **Divine Mother Kundalini**), the **arch-hierophant** and

APOLLO (CHRIST) AND THE NINE MUSES

arch-magi, the particular, individual **Monad**, our **real Being**, to spring up again within each one of us..."

Any esotericist who builds "**To Soma Heliakon**," the "**wedding garment** of the **soul**," in the "forge of the Cyclops" is converted, for such a cause, into a human being and therefore into a master. However, perfection in mastery is something very distinct.

When the number nine is applied to rhetoric, then it puts us into intimate, mystical relation with the nine eternal Muses.

It is good to cite in this chapter each one of these ineffable deities of ancient classicism:

1. Clio

2. Erato

3. Melpomene

4. Caliope

5. Euterpe

6. Thalia

7. Urania

8. Polyhymnia

9. Terpsichore

Vivid experiences are something very important to relay with the goal that our beloved readers can better comprehend this doctrine...

Listen to the following: one particular night (the date, day, and hour do not matter), being splendidly dressed with the "wedding garment of the soul," I left my physical body by will...

I floated with complete softness in the aura of the universe while experiencing a certain exquisite spiritual voluptuousness in the whole presence of my cosmic Being...

While being in this supreme bliss, as if I was a celestial bird, I had to lodge my feet upon the mire of the earth, under the green leafage of a taciturn tree...

I then happily invoked with a great voice the adepts of the occult fraternity...

Unquestionably, I was assisted...

Amiably, the brethren conducted me to the marvellous Temple of the Transparent Walls...

A **mahatma** was seated before his desk, as one would be if receiving many people...

"I want to know," I said, "what I am lacking..."

Afterwards, the venerable one took from within one of the drawers of the desk a certain secret book and consulted its pages, then he answered, "You need fifty-eight (58) minutes. You must present here thirty-six (36) bolivars, each one of them of twenty-three (23) kilograms. And the eight (8) acquired initiations must be qualified."

"Thank you, venerable master." Posteriorly, I withdrew from the temple with infinite humbleness and veneration...

Kabbalistic analysis of this question:

> 58 MINUTES: 5 + 8 = 13. This Arcanum signifies the death of all of the subjective elements which constitute the "I."

> 36 BOLIVARS: 3 + 6 = 9. This signifies the breaking of the chains and shackles in the submerged worlds of the nine planets cited in this chapter... It is an intense work performed in the "flaming forge of Vulcan..."

> 23 KILOGRAMS: 2 + 3 = 5. The work for liberation must be perfected under the splendors of the flaming star of five points... (Opportunely, it is good to remember the **Rishi** Baha-Deva and his 23 prophets).

QUALIFICATION: Each one of the eight initiations must be qualified before achieving the authentic resurrection. This is processed in eight years, during which we have to experience the book of the Patriarch **Job** in its whole crude reality.

We solemnly emphasize the following enunciation: "The eight initiations could not be qualified in a lesser period of time than the already indicated period of eight years..."

Obviously, one year corresponds to each one of the eight. Therefore, as a corollary, we have eight years to qualify the eight initiations...

I clarify: the aforementioned time exclusively corresponds to the epilogue of all mystical, successive, and profound esoteric works, performed in all and each one of the nine formerly cited planets.

Undoubtably, such works are processed in different times, and they truly become excessively delicate.

It is clear that due to such a cause, every one who enters into the Second Mountain does not receive more degrees or initiations.

Perfection in mastery only occurs with the esoteric, transcendental resurrection...

The complete manifestation of the Monad within the Resurrected Master grants extraordinary magical powers...

Chapter XXX
The Patriarch Enoch

The ring of bronze is emphatically referred to (amongst others) as a symbol of time.

Cyclically, it conducts the Gnostic arhat to that ancient patriarchal epoch, denominated the Age of Bronze, or Dvapara Yuga, which indubitably preceded our contemporary Age of Iron, or **Kali Yuga**...

The best authors of occultism have always affirmed that the second transalpine catastrophe, which completely modified the geological physiognomy of the planet Earth, occurred between these two ages.

The seventh, among the ten sublime anti-delugean patriarchs, is without any supposition, completely different from the six who in the course of the centuries preceded him... (Adam, Seth, Enos, Cainan, Mahalaleel, Jared), as well as the three who succeeded him (Methuselah, Lamech, Noah).

Nonetheless, it is clear that among all of this, what is more astonishing for us is the sacred name of **Enoch**, which when translated signifies, "initiate; devotee; consecrated one; master."

The Hebraic Genesis (5:24) solemnly asseverates that **Enoch** did not truly die physically, but rather "Enoch walked with God and was not; for God took him."

Very ancient esoteric traditions, which are lost within the night of the centuries, clearly say that while **Enoch** was upon the majestic summit of Mount Moria, he had a clairvoyant samadhi in which his illuminated objective consciousness was taken and transported into the nine heavens (which are cited by Dante in his *Divine Comedy*). In the last one of these heavens (in the heaven of Neptune), the patriarch found the Lost Word (his own Verb, his individual, particular Monad).

Posteriorly, that great hierophant wanted to express his vision through a permanent and imperishable monument...

Thus, he then absolutely determined with great wisdom to build under that blessed place itself a subterranean, secret temple, which was comprised of nine cellars successively arranged one under another, within the living innermost parts of the mount...

Certainly, his son Methuselah was the physical architect in charge of such an extraordinary sancta...

The specific and defined contents and the destiny of each one of these cellars or magical caves (which were connected to one another by means of a spiralling ladder) is not mentioned...

Nonetheless, the last of these caves is the one which absorbs the whole occult importance.

Therefore, the anterior cellars just constitute the indispensable secret path that finally leads to the last cellar, within the greatest profundity of the mountain...

Within the latter, the "penetral" or most intimate "sancta," is where the Patriarch **Enoch** deposited his most valuable, esoteric treasure...

The "Golden Fleece" of the ancient ones, the ineffable and imperishable treasure that we search for, is never found on the surface. Rather, we must excavate, dig, and search within the innermost parts of the Earth until finding it...

By courageously descending into the innermost parts or infernos of the mount of revelation, the initiate finds for himself the mystical treasure (his divine Monad), that was preserved throughout all the innumerable centuries which preceded us in the course of history...

We can still read the following in Revelations 2:17:

> To him that overcometh will I give to eat of the hidden manna, and will give him a white stone, and in the stone a new name written, which no man knoweth saving he that receiveth it.

Chapter XXXI
The Lunar Heaven

The individual Great Work is accomplished in the zodiacal dominion of the titanic Potencies...

The twelve labors of Heracles (a prototype of the authentic human) indicate and signify the secret path that must conduct us from the first to the last of the degrees of the perfect master and great elected one.

The capture and death of the lion of Nemea is the first of all the labors. This lion symbolizes the force of the instincts and the uncontrollable passions that consume and devour everything.

I was consciously and positively taken into the lunar world (or astral world) while in the state of ecstasy. Then, I was advised with infinite wisdom...

My soul was touched in its more intimate depths when I found there the elder of the temple of the twice-born. Our beloved rector, this sacred elder, certainly seemed to have all of the characteristics of a lemon, but it is clear that he irradiated infinite love...

I comprehended that in order to have the right to ascend into the lunar heaven (superior astral), I should first descend into the Selenean infernos (inferior astral) and courageously confront the three Furies...

Into my memory in the moments in which I write these lines comes the initiatic passage in which Gines de Lara, while guided by his master, contemplates the steely waters of the lake and is astonished ...

"Now look here!" exclaimed the **mahatma**...

Then, Gines looked, and his hair bristled when he saw two things that no mortal had ever seen; nonetheless, two things no less astonishing or less truthful...

He saw first, as if when looking through a gigantic telescope, the inhabitants of this side of the Moon, unhappy, disgraceful beings (without any exaggeration), whose nature

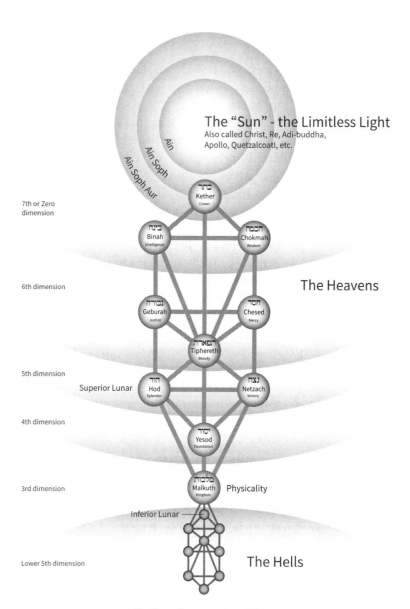

The "Sun" - the Limitless Light
Also called Christ, Re, Adi-buddha, Apollo, Quetzalcoatl, etc.

Ain
Ain Soph
Ain Soph Aur

כתר
Kether
Crown

בינה
Binah
Intelligence

חכמה
Chokmah
Wisdom

7th or Zero
dimension

6th dimension

The Heavens

נבורה
Geburah
Justice

חסד
Chesed
Mercy

תפארת
Tiphereth
Beauty

5th dimension

Superior Lunar

הוד
Hod
Splendor

נצח
Netzach
Victory

4th dimension

יסוד
Yesod
Foundation

3rd dimension

מלכות
Malkuth
Kingdom

Physicality

Inferior Lunar

Lower 5th dimension

The Hells

THE TREE OF LIFE AND THE LUNAR WORLDS

and origin is a great mystery and kept among those who know all...

Then, he saw something even more marvellous: the secret of the other side of this satellite (in other words, that hemisphere which is always on the other side). It is a place from which this miserable planet Earth can never be seen, and therefore, where some mystic has wanted to situate the "Paradise of **Enoch** and **Elias**," the two "**Jinns**" of the Hebrew people...

After this small digression, let us continue with the theme of this present chapter:

When I wanted to rise upon the symbolic ladder of Jacob, the sacred elder of the temple pulled out from the Tree of Knowledge, or, the Tree of the Science of Good and Evil, a delectable branch that he made me smell. Certainly, its fragrance was Nirvanic. "Thou must smell this branch in order for thou to rise." Such were the words of the adept...

Unquestionably, we must practice the "**Sahaja Maithuna**," to breath the delectable fragrance of the forbidden fruit, but not to eat it; this is the law...

I initiated my work by disintegrating **Judas**, the demon of desire, in the abyss of Selene...

It is not irrelevant to happily say with great assertion that thanks to the direct help of my "Divine Mother **Kundalini**" the horrifying demon of desire was reduced to ashes...

A little later on, I had to continue my work with the agitated demon of the mind, who brings us too much bitterness. This is the abominable Pilate of all times...

Annihilation! A terrible word... that was the catastrophic end of this fatal Pilate who was tormenting me...

Subsequently, I proceeded with my work in the abyss by attacking Caiaphas, the demon of evil will, the most disgusting of all the three existing classic Furies who are within the interior of each one of us...

Certainly, the third Fury died after receiving various thrusts with the lance in her body...

None of the Furies equalled her horrible appearance. None of them had as many serpents as she had in her mane;

even these very sisters were afraid of her. This disgraceful one carried in her hands all the Gorgonian venoms of the infernos...

I could verify with complete, astonishing clarity the whole death process of the three Furies...

It is clear that they passed through all of the magical transformations, as recited by Ovid...

If in the beginning they were gigantic and horrible (as the monster Polyphemus from the damned land, who implacably devoured the companions of Ulysses), in the end, before the arrival of their sovereign death, they had the characteristics of newly born children...

Fortunately, these abominable shadows, these three traitors that I carried within, died...

Woe! Woe! Woe! What would have become of me without the help of my Divine Mother Kundalini?

I invoked my Mother from the depth of the abyss, and She grasped the lance of Eros...

Chapter XXXII
Guinevere

The eternal lady, the **Spiritual Soul** (**Buddhi**), always demands from her knight (**the Human Soul, superior manas**) all types of unheard of sacrifices and bold prodigies...

She, the divine, perfect spouse, is Guinevere, the queen of the "**Jinn**" knights, the one who poured wine for Lancelot...

This was a delicious wine of transcendental spirituality within the initiatic cups of **Sukra** and of **Manti**... In reality, these cups are none other than the Holy Grail, which is symbolically known as the chalice that holds the supreme beverage or initiatic nectar of the holy gods...

Fortunate will be the knight who, after the difficult battle, will celebrate his betrothal to Guinevere, the queen of the "**Jinn**" knights!

It is written with letters of gold in the book of life that the flame of **Prajna** (the Being) burns within **Buddhi** (**the Spiritual Soul**) as within a fine and transparent alabaster cup.

One night of indisputable delights, I had the joy of finding my beloved one in a secret spot on the Second Mountain...

The chariot of my fiance was slowly advancing on the solitary path...

A centuries old legend tells of the Marquise of Beaupré, who paraded herself on a chariot of a singular beauty that was made of pure porcelain. However, the triumphal chariot of my adorable **Valkyrie** was similar to another chariot which, in the times of "rococo," the wife of the Duke of Clermont used to ride. It was a splendid chariot with a trunk of six horses that were all wearing horseshoes of silver. As well, the wheels and carriage were made of the same metal...

The triumphal chariot of my beloved one stopped before a fortress of flaming porphyry, where the wealth and splendor of the East polishes the walls and coffers to the glaze of a looking glass...

LANCELOT AND GUINEVERE BY HERBERT JAMES DRAPER

The splendid vehicle then parked before the dazzling bronze doors where one stands motionless in fear of their remarkable majesty...

Suddenly, the chariot was surrounded by a gentle cortege of distinguished gentlemen, princes, and noblemen, beautiful ladies and delicate children.

Someone gave me a sign; I obeyed and advanced towards the chariot of love. Thus, through the crystals of joy, I see my **Valkyrie (Buddhi)**...

Dressed with the nuptial attire, the wedding garment of the soul, my fiance had arrived in her resplendent chariot for the nuptials...

To wed before the holy altar with my twin soul, the theosophical **Buddhi**... What a joy, oh God!... However, I was told that I had to wait a while...

The virile provider of strength from above was delaying me, and I was suffering the unspeakable...

During that epoch of my life, I had to profoundly submerge myself into the sacred mysteries of Minna, the dreadful lunar darkness of one love whose twin brother is death...

I intensively worked within the **super-obscurity** of silence and the august secret of the wise...

I had to wait for a time, times and the half of a time... However, I was sighing for Guinevere, the queen of the "**Jinn**" knights (my **Spiritual Soul**).

One certain night, the shining stars in the infinite space appeared as if they had a new aspect...

I was in ecstasy, far away from all mundane clamour; the door of my room was kept hermetically closed...

Certainly, this was the moment when I celebrated the wedding with my beloved (**Buddhi**). She penetrated within me and I became lost within her...

The Sun of Midnight (**Solar Logos**) intensely shone in those blessed instants.

I felt transformed in an integral way. The famous chakra **Sahasrara**, the lotus of one thousand petals, the crown of the saints, victoriously shone in my pineal gland, and I entered into that state known among the Hindu race as "**Paramananda**" (a Sanskrit term denoting supreme spiritual happiness).

Then, this was the moment when I felt the necessity to convert myself into an authentic and legitimate "**Brahmavid-varishta.**"

The thousand yoga nadis of the **Sahasrara** granted me, as a fact, power over certain subtle forces of nature...

Buddhi, my Guinevere, my Spiritual Soul, put the coronary **padma** (lotus) into a certain state of mystical function after putting the **Shiva-shakti-tattva** to the maximum of vibratory activity...

Then, I saw myself transformed into the messenger of the new age of Aquarius, teaching humanity a doctrine so new and revolutionary... nonetheless, so ancient....

When I opened the door of my room, then the diamond eye (the pineal gland) granted me the power of seeing my innumerable enemies. It is obvious that the diffusion of Gnosis in its revolutionary way will increase the number of my adversaries.

It is important to say that after this cosmic event, a certain nuptial rite was performed in the temple. Many people attended this festivity of love...

Unquestionably, I had incarnated my Human Soul (**the superior manas of Theosophy**) in the Fifth Initiation of Fire.

But now, oh gods! With this alchemical and kabbalistic wedding I was also incarnating my Spiritual Soul (**Buddhi**).

Clearly, within the Spiritual Soul the flame of **Prajna** (the Innermost) always burns in an unalterable form.

Chapter XXXIII

The Dragon of Darkness

I thought that after the alchemical wedding with my Spiritual Soul I would fully enter into a paradisiacal honeymoon. But, I did not even vaguely suspect that hidden within the submerged dens of my human subconsciousness was the leftist and tenebrous **Mara** of the Buddhist gospel. This is the famous dragon of darkness cited in the Apocalypse of Saint John. It is the father of the three traitors.

It is a gigantic and abysmal monster with seven infrahuman heads that always personify the seven capital sins: anger, greed, lust, envy, pride, laziness, gluttony...

So, the great beast frightfully howled, as when a lion roars, and the potencies of darkness quaked with horror...

To reduce such a horrifying, abysmal engendering to cosmic dust is only possible with the transcendental sexual electricity, while in complete Sexual Magic...

Fortunately, I knew how to take advantage of the "coitus reservatus" to the maximum, through making my supplications to "**Devi Kundalini**," the "igneous serpent of our magical powers."

The monster grasped the dreaded lance with his sinister hand. In vain, he intended to hurt me three times, and desperately, he threw the hard spear against me. Immediately in those instants, my Divine Mother **Kundalini** intervened. She took hold of this unique relic and mortally wounded the red dragon with it...

Mara, the horrifying, infernal beast, then lost his gigantic stature. Little by little he diminished. He reduced to a mathematical point and disappeared forever from the tenebrous den...

Afterwards, the fraction of my consciousness that had been bottled up within that abominable monster returned, came back into me...

The secrets of the old abyss are terrible. It is a gloomy and unlimited ocean where the primogenital night and the chaos (the grandparents of nature) keep perpetual anarchy in the midst of rumors of eternal wars, and which are sustained with the help of confusion...

Heat, coldness, humidity, and drought are the four terrible champions who fight for superiority in this abyss. They lead their embryonic atoms to combat, which when gathering together around the ensign of their legions and when reunited into many tribes (lightly or heavily armed, being sharp, round, fast, or slow), move innumerably in a swarm, like the sands of Barca or like the sands of the ardent beach of Cirene, which is pulled in order to take place in the battle of the winds and in order to serve as a ballast for their speedy wings...

The atom that adheres to the major number of atoms is the one which momentarily dominates. Chaos governs as a referee, and his decisions increase disorder each time, thanks to the one who reigns after him. It is clear that in those infernal worlds, "chance" directs everything...

Before this savage abyss (the cradle and sepulchre of nature), before this den which is neither sea nor earth, neither air nor fire, but is formed by all of the elements which in confusion mix themselves in their fertile causes and which must always do combat in the same way (unless the Creator Demiurge determines to form new worlds from these black materials), before this barbarian Tartarus, the dragon of darkness exhaled his last breath...

To descend into the "infernal worlds" is easy, but what is not easy is the return. Here is the hard labor! Here is the difficult ordeal!...

Some sublime heroes (and truly few) have achieved the triumphal return. Impenetrable forests separate the Averno from the world of light. The waters of the pale river, the Cocytus, trace convoluted labyrinths within that penumbra, the mere image of which makes us tremble...

Chapter XXXIV
Conclusion of the Lunar Works

After having reduced **Mara**, the father of the three classical Furies, into cosmic dust, I then had to confront other secondary beasts of the abyss...

The day was slowly ending; the delectable air of the night invited all living human beings who populate the face of the earth to rest from their fatigue. But, I, a vile slug from the mud of the earth, only wanted to endure the combats of the path, and what is worthiest of compassion, which my memory will unmistakeably write of...

Oh, ineffable Muses! Oh divine, high genius! Help me now. Inspire me; here shall your excellence reveal itself so that my style does not retract from the nature of this matter...

My profound, deep slumber was interrupted by a crash of heavy thunder that shook me, as one who is violently awakened from his sleep. I rose upright, and my rested eyes moved around, searching with fixed ken, to know what place it was wherein I stood. I then saw myself inside a solitary house, next to a tenebrous path...

While seated on a rustic armchair next to the window from where the steep path could be well contemplated, I very sincerely evoked foregone times...

Indeed, I had been there in that mansion of the abyss, in other ages, and before the same path...

None of this seemed new to me; I understood that I was recapitulating mysteries. By rising up from the chair, I opened the old door of that abode and I left, while walking slowly... slowly... slowly... on the solitary path....

With only one glance, my sight bore into a very far space, as far as the spiritual sight is capable of penetrating, and I saw a sad, devastating, and sombre place...

The floor was wet and I had to unexpectedly stop before a certain electric cable which was lying on the ground...

A wire or copper charged with high voltage? What a horror... and I came very close to stepping on it!...

"It is preferable to die free than to live imprisoned." Thus, this is what the voice of the silence uttered on that night of mystery...

So, I who was alarmed and had intended to retreat in those precise moments felt comforted...

Resolutely, I advanced through those sub-lunar places, along the tortuous, abysmal path...

The steep path surprisingly turned towards the left and penetrated within a certain very picturesque hill...

In those hills, I saw something similar to a national park on a Sunday. A variegated conjunction of human creatures seemed to delectably enjoy the prairie land...

For the recreational entertainment of many, some walking vendors were coming and going selling multi-colored balloons here, there, and everywhere...

This was a living symbol of the profane life. This is how I understood it. However, it is clear that I wanted to live all of this with intensity...

I was very absorbed in all of this while contemplating the perpetual crowds, when suddenly, lo and behold, something unexpected and unusual happened. It momentarily appeared to me as if time was truly standing still...

In an instant of terror, a sanguinary wolf emerged from within the bushes and with ferociousness and malicious sight intended to catch his prey in vain. Before this wolf, some hens that desperately cackled escaped from their pitiless death.

This was extraordinary occult symbolism: a pusillanimous, cowardly, timid farm yard bird. A cruel, pitiless, sanguinary wolf...

Dread! Terror! Fright!... And I who believed to have died within myself ignored the existence of these psychic aggregates within my own atomic infernos. These were sub-lunar human states from the human infraconsciousness...

Fortunately, I never forget my holy spear while in hard battle. Thanks to my Divine Mother Kundalini, I could exceed many in strength and ability with the spear.

Having had the main demon "I's" (vile personifications of my horrible, infrahuman defects) fall, my lunar works epically concluded by giving death to many other infernal beasts with the holy spear...

It is not irrelevant to say that I had collected a very rich booty of war after many bloody battles...

I am referring with great emphasis to those multiple precious gems of my own existence, to those grains of consciousness that were once trapped, bottled up within those horrifying engenderings of hell...

The final part of the work was completely of an atomic nature. To expel these malignant intelligences from within their nuclear habitats is not easy...

Certainly, this is what is understood as the transformation of the black waters into white...

Now, these atoms have converted themselves into marvellous vehicles of certain luminous intelligences...

These are magnificent sparks, atoms which are capable of informing about the activities of the secret enemy...

One night of glory, I had the highest, greatest honor that can be granted to a human being: I was visited by the Cosmic Christ. The Beloved One carried a great book in his right hand as if he was saying to me: "Now you are going to enter into the sphere of Mercury."

When I saw the master I could not say anything, except to utter: "Lord, you have arrived sooner than I thought. I did not expect you so soon..."

The living Christ sweetly answered: "Sometimes I delay when I have to come in the month of March... You have to keep dying..."

"What?... To keep dying?... Still?"

"Yes," the Beloved One answered. "You have to keep dying," he repeated...

Then, what happened after that was prodigious. The master slowly rose up towards the Sun of Midnight; He slightly detached himself from the star king in order to bless me and to forgive my ancient errors...

Thus, this is how I gained the re-entrance into the first heaven, the abode of the ineffable angels...

Unquestionably, I was a fallen angel, but it is clear that I had been forgiven...

There is more joy in the cathedral of the soul for a sinner who is repented, than for one thousand just ones who do not need repentance...

Chapter XXXV
The Heaven of Mercury

Now comes the second work of Heracles in a transcendental and transcendent way: the destruction of the hydra of Lerna, a symbolic monster of immortal origin, endowed with nine sinister heads that regenerate each time they are destroyed. It is a threat to cattle and harvests.

This is a hard battle in which the solar hero is accompanied by "**Yolao**," his charioteer and inspirator, whose notable play is very similar to that one of Krishna and his relation with Arjuna (Read *The Bhagavad-gita, The Song of the Lord*).

Even though this magnificent work can be interpreted as a beneficial labor in the swampy delta, as that of the sacred Nile, this multi-faceted hydra is also an allegorical image that clearly personifies the mind with all of its psychological defects.

As a constellation, this symbolic hydra has its frontal part between Leo and Cancer, and extends itself towards the south, to the resplendent feet of Virgo.

"**Yolao**" burns the reborn heads with flaming embers while Heracles crushes the other heads with his war club. After all of this, Heracles cuts off the immortal head, which is an extraordinary symbol of authentic love. He hides this head beneath a rock, which obviously will serve as a "Philosophical Stone" of his regenerated, exquisite, spiritual life.

It is written in the book of life with characters of fire: "Whosoever wants to ascend must first descend." "Every exaltation is always preceded by a humiliation."

Unquestionably, I was longing with all the forces of my soul to rise, to ascend into the heaven of Mercury, the Devachan of the Hindustanis, the mental superior world, the abode of the archangels. However, to descend, to go down into the infernos of the mind in order to destroy the hydra of Lerna was indispensable.

Those psychological defects of a multi-faceted structure, which in the lunar infernos I had reduced to cosmic dust, con-

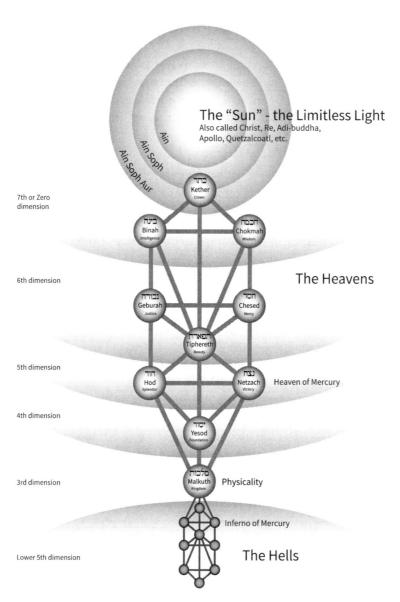

The "Sun" - the Limitless Light
Also called Christ, Re, Adi-buddha,
Apollo, Quetzalcoatl, etc.

Ain

Ain Soph

Ain Soph Aur

7th or Zero
dimension

כתר
Kether
Crown

בינה
Binah
Intelligence

חכמה
Chokmah
Wisdom

6th dimension

The Heavens

גבורה
Geburah
Justice

חסד
Chesed
Mercy

תפארת
Tiphereth
Beauty

5th dimension

הוד
Hod
Splendor

נצח
Netzach
Victory

Heaven of Mercury

4th dimension

יסוד
Yesod
Foundation

3rd dimension

מלכות
Malkuth
Kingdom

Physicality

Inferno of Mercury

Lower 5th dimension

The Hells

THE TREE OF LIFE AND THE WORLDS OF MERCURY.
TO LEARN MORE, STUDY TAROT AND KABBALAH BY SAMAEL AUN WEOR.

tinued to exist as the abominable heads of the fatal hydra in all of the enclosures of the mind.

Horrifying animal creatures, disgusting abysmal engenderings, clearly personified each one of my own psychological defects.

One can give oneself the luxury of comprehending any psychological defect; nonetheless, its deep significance may still not have been captured...

Unquestionably, we need with undeferable maximum urgency to not only comprehend, but moreover, to trap the deep significance of that which we want to eliminate.

To eliminate the heads (psychological defects) of the hydra of Lerna is only possible by means of the transcendental sexual electricity during the "**Sahaja Maithuna**," in the "forge of the Cyclops."

Since the "metaphysical copulation" in the "Ninth Sphere" is a form of prayer, I beseeched Devi **Kundalini** in those instants...

Goethe, the great German initiate, when worshipping his Divine Mother **Kundalini**, exclaimed while filled with ecstasy:

> *Immaculate Virgin in the most beautiful sense.*
> *Oh Mother, worthy of veneration.*
> *Chosen Queen for us*
> *And whose essence is equal to the gods.*

When longing for the death in himself, here and now, during the chemical coitus, such a great bard said:

> *Arrows trespass me;*
> *Lances subdue me;*
> *Clubs hurt me.*
> *Let all disappear,*
> *Let all vanish,*
> *Let the perennial star shine,*
> *The focus of eternal love.*

Unquestionably, I always proceeded in a very similar way. So, the hydra of Lerna was slowly, little by little, losing each one of its abominable heads...

On a certain occasion, while being in a monastery of
Oriental Tibet, I had the occurrence of telling my Divine
Mother **Kundalini** the following, "You and I converse and we
look like two different persons, nonetheless we are the same
Being."

It is not irrelevant to emphatically asseverate that the
answer was certainly extraordinary, "Yes, my son, you and I are
the same Being, but **derivative**."

In the name of the truth, frankly and plainly speaking,
I confess that without the immediate help of my adorable
Divine Mother, in no manner could I radically eliminate the
hydra of Lerna... (my psychological defects in my intellectual
subconsciousness.)

> *Ere the gold flame can burn with steady light,*
> *the lamp must stand well guarded in a spot*
> *free from all wind.* - Voice of the Silence

The terrestrial thoughts must die before the doors of the
temple.

> *The mind which follows the rambling senses makes*
> *the soul as helpless as the boat which the wind*
> *leads astray upon the waters.* - Bhagavad-gita

When the Sun of Midnight victoriously shone in the spiritual firmament, I then returned into the archangelic state that
in foregone times I had lost, and joyfully I entered into the
heaven of Mercury...

Chapter XXXVI
The Heaven of Venus

Now comes the extraordinary third achievement of Heracles, the solar hero. I am emphatically referring to the capture of two animals, the first one gentle, the other as fast, yet, turbid and threatening: the Ceryneian Hind and the wild Boar of Mount Erymanthus.

We can and even must identify these famous quadrupeds with the two resplendent, austral constellations nearest to the stars of Gemini, which are very close to the two centaurs with whom Heracles sustained a bloody fight.

We can see a clear allusion to the Human Soul (the spouse of the **Valkyrie**), the **Superior Manas of Theosophy**, in the symbol of the Ceryneian Hind with hoofs of bronze and golden horns, which was sacred to Diana and disputed by Apollo, the God of Fire.

HERACLES SUBDUES THE CERYNEIAN HIND

The living symbol of all the lower animal passions is found in this perverse one as no other: the terrible wild Boar of Erymanthos.

It is good to asseverate in these instants that I was very sincerely longing with all the forces of my soul to enter into the Heaven of Venus, the causal world, the abode of the **Principalities**.

However, it is clear that at first I needed to achieve merits, to reduce to cosmic dust the frightful, wild Boar...

Before ascending, it is necessary to descend. Every exaltation is always preceded by a terrible humiliation.

Before the ascension, the descent into the infernos of Venus was indispensable, urgent, and undeferable...

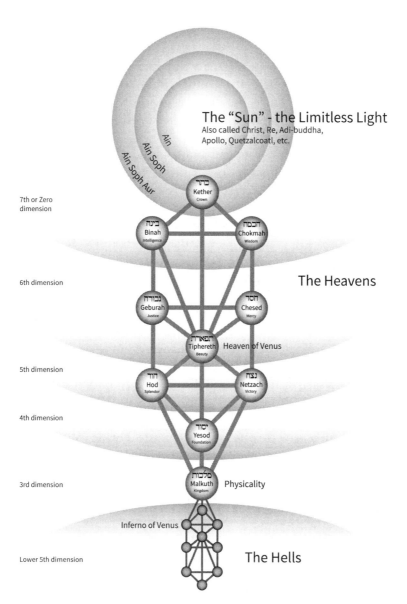

The "Sun" - the Limitless Light
Also called Christ, Re, Adi-buddha, Apollo, Quetzalcoatl, etc.

Ain

Ain Soph

Ain Soph Aur

7th or Zero dimension

כתר
Kether
Crown

בינה
Binah
Intelligence

חכמה
Chokmah
Wisdom

6th dimension

The Heavens

גבורה
Geburah
Justice

חסד
Chesed
Mercy

תפארת
Tiphereth
Beauty

Heaven of Venus

5th dimension

הוד
Hod
Splendor

נצח
Netzach
Victory

4th dimension

יסוד
Yesod
Foundation

3rd dimension

מלכות
Malkuth
Kingdom

Physicality

Inferno of Venus

Lower 5th dimension

The Hells

THE TREE OF LIFE AND THE WORLDS OF VENUS.
TO LEARN MORE, STUDY TAROT AND KABBALAH BY SAMAEL AUN WEOR.

I needed preparatory information, and this in itself certainly became urgent and peremptory...

Extraordinary and precise indications came to me during meditation. It is clear that the initiate is always assisted...

Upon a great board very similar to the attractive board of chess, instead of the known pieces of this cited game, I saw many animal figures with disgusting appearances...

Unquestionably, I had eliminated defects of a psychological type in the astral world, also in the mental world, with the help of my Divine Mother **Kundalini**. However, the causal germs of these continued to exist within me, here and now...

We can assert within the field of the purest experimental psychology the following enunciation:

The radical elimination of any psychological defect absolutely fails when its secret cause is not eliminated.

To extirpate such intrinsic causes from my psyche was certainly my labor in the Venusian infernos...

It is clear that I then had to pass victoriously through many carnal temptations, as those that the Patriarch Saint Augustine suffered when at the foot of the cross...

> *The Gnostic mystery is present*
> *in the dove's soft flight,*
> *and the sin of the world in the serpent*
> *that bites the foot of the angel who tames it.*
>
> *Upon the eternal night of yesterday*
> *the eternal night of tomorrow is opened,*
> *in each hour, one larva of sin may*
> *be the symbol of the serpent and the apple.*

The multitude of crimes whose causal germs I had to eliminate were so immense that even if I had one hundred mouths, one hundred tongues, and a voice of iron, I could not enumerate all of them...

Within this Tartarus where the evil ones are punished, I also found two old friends of my youth: one was still alive, the other was already deceased...

It is good to remember those Titans of ancient times who wanted to climb into heaven. Now they suffer in the abyss, chained by the anger of Jupiter.

The insolent Lapitas and the daring Ixion—the one who made an attempt against the life of Juno—also abide there, and also Piritoo who wanted to abduct Proserpine...

In that subterranean world also lives the proud Salmoneo, King of Elida, the one who claimed divine honors for himself when he was just a simple mortal, a vile slug from the mud of the earth...

I saw something frightful, terrible, before those moments when I was definitively abandoning the abode of Pluto: what I saw was like unto an enormous monster threatening to devour the whole of humanity. Woe! Woe! Woe!

Posteriorly, I felt myself transformed within those atomic infernos: the Cosmic Christ entered in me and I became lost within him...

Then, a multitude of mothers brought their children to me and, filled with ecstasy, I exclaimed, "Suffer little children, and forbid them not to come unto me: for of such is the kingdom of heaven." [Matthew 19:14]

How happy I felt with the transformed causal body! After having blessed all of those tender infants, I abandoned the submerged mineral kingdom and victoriously penetrated into the heaven of Venus (the causal world).

Thus, this is how I re-entered into the state of the Principalities, which in foregone times I had lost when I committed the same error of the Count **Zanoni** in the central plateau of Asia...

To submissively fall at the paradisiacal feet of exquisite feminine beauty, to drink the liquor of Mandrake, to eat of the golden apples from the "Garden of Hesperides," was certainly the mentioned error. However, posteriorly I had to return into the path which in foregone times I had abandoned, by working with the transcendent sexual electricity...

This marvellous causal world, or world of conscious will, cited many times by Mr. Leadbeater, Annie Besant, Arthur Power, Rudolf Steiner, H. P. Blavatsky., etc., is clearly a terror of love and law. Undoubtably, the heaven of Venus is not of time and is beyond the mind.

It is evident that the **Akashic** substance, as a natural element and vibration or tattva, constitutes in itself the living and philosophical depth of the world of cosmic causality...

A profound electric blue marvellously shines in that region, sparkling here, there, and everywhere, saturating us with an exquisite, undescribable, spiritual voluptuousness...

The incessant tides of action and consequence flux and reflux here, from instant to instant...

It is evident that cause without effect does not exist, neither effect without cause. Every action is proceeded by a reaction, a consequence, or better still, many consequences are always derived from any act...

I received an abundance of demonstrated and demonstrable objective information during that epoch of my present existence.

For example: before the speaker in a certain auditorium, I presented myself in complete assembly. I did not know how to keep my composure. I put my nose where I should not have put it. I refuted concepts...

Results: The orator, a man of the causal world, withdrew with indignation...

Posteriorly, this lecturer commented to others about my attitude, and this was converted as a fact into a whole cascading series of consequences...

In the causal world, I saw with mystical astonishment the fate that is awaiting this planet Earth and the human creatures who dwell upon this physical world...

I suddenly saw myself dressed with the causal body inside of a great railway yard...

Certainly, the Gnostic movement is a train in motion. Some passengers boarded the train at one station and they got off at the other. Very rare are those who arrive at the final station...

Posteriorly, I had to submerge myself within the infinite starry space. I needed to investigate something within the amphitheatre of cosmic science...

Surprised and astonished—since I did not lose the capacity of astonishment—I perceived with the "Eye of Dangma" or "Eye of Shiva" something unusual and unexpected...

Before my spiritual sight the Earth appeared, besieged to death by twelve enormous, black, sinister, threatening giants (the twelve zodiacal constellations carrying out the definitive crystallization of worldly karma)...

The great catastrophe that will come is not ignored by people of other worlds, and they will approach with their ships to register or photograph this cataclysm.

Lo and behold the Apocalypse of Saint John in complete motion. The collision of worlds! Woe! Woe! Woe! ...

To cite in this part some extraordinary verses of the **Koran** becomes opportune.

> *Among the signs that must precede the arrival of the final hour, is that of the moon which will split in two. Despite this, the unbelievers will not give credit to their eyes.* — Surah Al-Qamar, "The Moon," 54:1-2

(It is obvious that this can in no way be related to a geological or physical division of our neighboring satellite. This must be interpreted as a political and military division. The great powers will dispute over the "Moon.")

> *On the day when the first trumpet resoundeth...*
>
> *When the earth and the mountains will be taken in the air and crushed with only one strike...*
>
> *When heaven will be split asunder and will fall down in pieces...*
>
> *That day will be the inevitable day.*
> — Surah Al-Haqqah, "The Reality" 69:13-16

(Collision is the precise term. The planet Earth will crash with another planet, which is dangerously approaching).

> *The strike which is! That will be the day of the Final Judgment.*
>
> *Those who will have deeds that are weighed on the scale will have a pleasant life. Those who will have deeds that*

are weightless will have the burning fossil as an abode [the infernal worlds]. — Surah Al-Qari`ah, "The Calamity" 101:1-2, 6-9

When Earth is shaken with her [final] earthquake

And Earth yielded up her burdens,

That day mankind will be prepared for judgement.
— Surat Az-Zalzalah (The Earthquake) 99:1-2, 4

When the sun is overthrown

And the stars fall

And when the mountains are moved and end crashing against the earth. — Surat At-Takwir (The Overthrowing) 81:1-3

The heaven will explode into a thousand pieces and the seas and rivers will confound their waters.

The tombs will open and the dead will resurrect.

Those who have practiced good will have happiness without limits; but the evil will also be punished without measure. — Surat Al-'Infitar (The Cleaving) 82:1, 3-4, 13-14

Unquestionably, before the inevitable collision, the rapid approach of that planetary bulk will originate frightful electro-magnetic tempests.

It is clear that the presence of that sidereal world will exert an attraction upon the liquid fire of the interior of our terrestrial globe. Then, the igneous element will search for an exit, therefore giving origin to innumerable volcanoes.

In those coming days, the Earth will shake with frightful earthquakes and horrifying seaquakes...

People and cities will fatally collapse as miserable card castles fallen in ruins.

Monstrous waves that were never seen before will devastate the sandy beaches with fury, and a very strange sound will emerge from within the depths of the seas.

Undoubtably, the extraordinary radiation of such a planet will kill millions of creatures and everything will be consumed in an apocalyptic holocaust.

Peter, or Patar, the great Hierophant, said:

But the day of the Lord will come as a thief in the night; in the which the heavens shall pass away with a great noise, and the elements shall melt with fervent heat, the earth also and the works that are therein shall be burned up. - II Peter 3:10

In the causal world, with mystical astonishment, I contemplated the great catastrophe that is approaching. Since this is a region of the ineffable music, such a vision was illustrated within the "current of sound."

A certain delectable, tragic symphony resounded within the profound depths of the heaven of Venus.

This score was generally astonishing because of its grandiosity and majesty, and also for the inspiration and beauty of its design, as well for the purity of its lines and for the colored nuance of its wise and artistic instrumentation, which was simultaneously sweet and severe, grandiose and horrific, dramatic and lugubrious.

The melodic fragmentary passages (leitmotifs) listened to in the causal world, in different prophetic situations, are of a great expressive potency and are in intimate relation with the great catastrophe and with the historical events that will inevitably precede it in time...

In the score of this great cosmic opera exist symphonic fragments related with the Third World War, delectable and fatal sounds, horrifying events, atomic bombs, frightful radioactivity in all of the Earth, hunger, total destruction of the great metropolises, unknown sicknesses, incessant fights, here, there, and everywhere, etc., etc., etc...

The themes related with the destruction of New York, Paris, London, Moscow, etc., etc., etc., intermingled with art without precedence, were heard.

Chapter XXXVII
The Heaven of the Sun

The next labor of Heracles, the solar hero, is certainly the extraordinary cleaning of the famous stables of Augeas, King of Elis, whose daughter knew of the virtues of plants and made magical beverages with them.

The filth of various generations had accumulated within those mentioned stables (living symbolic representation of our own submerged, subconsciousness depths), which were accommodating its innumerable cattle (those multiple, bestial psychic aggregates, which constitute the **ego**) that had among them twelve guileless bulls, which allegorize the zodiacal karma.

Unquestionably, Heracles should clean those stables in only one day. Ancient traditions which are lost in the night of the centuries say that he achieved it by making a hole in the wall, then deviating the course of the river in order to inundate the stables with its waters.

This unusual labor can for that reason be identified with Aquarius, zodiacal house of Uranus, **Ur-anas**, the fire and the primordial waters, which clearly symbolize the sexual current in the human organism.

Uranus, as the first divine king of ancient Atlantis, is the regent of our sexual glands.

Uranus, the **Asura-maya**, is truly the first revelator of the mysteries of life and death.

Certainly, **Ur-anas** is the fire and the primeval water, the one who intrinsically determines the first **luni-solar** worship of the androgenous **IO**... (iiiiiiooooooo)

IO Pitar is the Sun.

Menes or Mani is the Moon.

"Om Mani Padme Hum," a mantra of immense esoteric power, has its equivalence in the sun and moon gods, who are upon the bosom of the sacred lotus that miraculously emerged from the spermatic waters of the first instant...

The legend of the centuries say that **Uranus** had forty-five children with diverse women, and that he also had with **Titaea** another eighteen children. The latter received the name of Titans because of their mother.

By separately adding these Kabbalistic quantities, we have the following results:

45: 4 + 5 = 9. The Hermit of the **Tarot**: "The Ninth Sphere," **sex**.

18: 1 + 8 = 9. The Eighteenth Arcanum is the Twilight of the **Tarot**. Within this Arcanum, the Ninth Arcanum occurs twice. This signifies secret, occult enemies: the subterranean struggle within the dominions of the "Ninth Sphere," the tenebrous...

ARCANA NINE AND EIGHTEEN

Clearly, Uranus is the absolute king of the sexual functions, the lord of the new age of Aquarius.

Titaea was also placed among the numbers of the gods, since she surpassed all women in beauty and virtue. It has been said that her loyal devotees called her "**Earth**" [Gaia] in gratitude for having received many goods from her.

In the name of truth, frankly and plainly speaking, I have to confess that the fourth labor became tremendously easy for me. However, previous to it, I had to pass through a delicate ordeal.

I saw myself conversing with a noble lady in an old park of the city. She was someone who, without a doubt, was certainly a great friend.

We sat very close to each other on a bench, and felt a great love between us. For an instant we resembled two lovers, but...

Suddenly I remembered my Divine Mother **Kundalini**! Then, I deviated that current of love inwards and upwards, towards my adorable Mother...

In those moments I exclaimed with all the forces of my soul, "This love is for my Mother..."

Thus, this is how Heracles deviated a running river in order to inundate the "stables of Augeas" with its waters (whosoever has understanding let him understand, for there is wisdom therein).

Unquestionably, I was within the innermost mineral parts of the Sun, within the solar infernos...

How clean the submerged worlds of this star king looked unto me! They were infernos without suffering souls, without demons. What a marvel!...

It is clear that the demons could not dwell inside the living innermost parts of the resplendent Sun. They could never endure the potent vibrations of this star...

When I found myself enclosed inside one of these symbolic "stables of Augeas," I found it completely clean and without animals of any species. Then, I comprehended...

I wanted to exit, but the door was hermetically closed. "Open sesame!" I screamed with all of my force.

Then, all of the doors were opened in that instant, as if by magic. Then, I penetrated into a second stable which I found as clean as the first one...

"Open sesame!" I exclaimed again, and when the doors were opened, I penetrated into a third stable. Clearly, this one was also clean and beautiful...

"Open sesame!" I exclaimed for a fourth time, and when the fourth door was opened, I passed through a threshold of a shiny solar mansion...

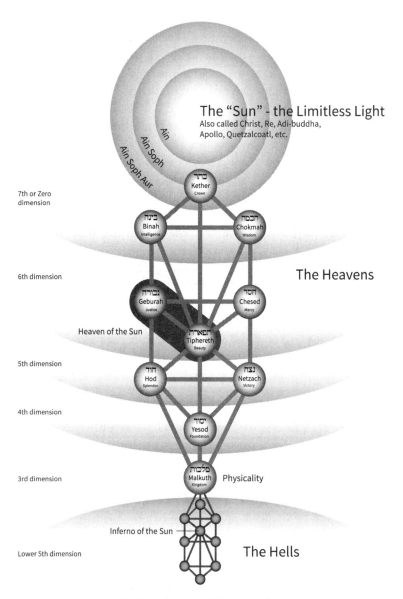

The "Sun" - the Limitless Light
Also called Christ, Re, Adi-buddha, Apollo, Quetzalcoatl, etc.

Ain

Ain Soph

Ain Soph Aur

כתר
Kether
Crown

7th or Zero dimension

בינה
Binah
Intelligence

חכמה
Chokmah
Wisdom

6th dimension

The Heavens

גבורה
Geburah
Justice

חסד
Chesed
Mercy

Heaven of the Sun

תפארת
Tiphereth
Beauty

5th dimension

דוד
Hod
Splendor

נצח
Netzach
Victory

4th dimension

יסוד
Yesod
Foundation

3rd dimension

מלכות
Malkuth
Kingdom

Physicality

Inferno of the Sun

Lower 5th dimension

The Hells

THE TREE OF LIFE AND THE WORLDS OF THE SUN.
TO LEARN MORE, STUDY TAROT AND KABBALAH BY SAMAEL AUN WEOR.

What I saw in the midst of the sanctuary was something unusual and unexpected. Oh gods! There, seated on their thrones, were **Osiris**, **Isis**, and **Horus**, who were awaiting me...

I advanced towards them and by prostrating myself, I worshipped them. I felt their benedictions within myself in those instants.

They are three aspects of my Being, but just **derivative**. Thus, this is how I comprehended it, and this deserves an explanation...

One of our Gnostic esoteric rituals textually says the following:

> **Osiris** *(the Arch-hierophant and Arch-magi, our particular individual Monad), powerful emperor, respond to the beseeching Son...*

> **Isis** *(the enfoldment of **Osiris**, the mystical Duad, **Devi Kundalini**), very worthy Mother, respond to the beseeching Son...*

> **Horus** *(the intimate Christ), respond to the beseeching pilgrim...*

They welcomed me, and I then victoriously entered into the heaven of the Sun, into the abode of the Potencies, into the **Buddhic** or **intuitional** world. I then reconquered my place among these divine creatures. This was a glorious conscious state, which in a foregone time I had lost...

HARPIES

"I was incessantly attacked in a pitiless
way by the sinister fowls that inhabited the
Stygian Lakes in that epoch of my life."

Chapter XXXVIII

The Heaven of Mars

The fifth labor of Heracles, the solar hero, was the hunting and killing of the anthropophagus tenebrous birds that inhabited the Stygian lakes in Arcadia and were killing men with their bronzed feathers, which were thrown against their indefensible victims in the form of deadly arrows.

Clearly, this labor is found intimately related with the constellation of Pisces, house of Neptune, the lord of practical magic.

Unquestionably, those anthropophagus birds are the cruel harpies cited by Virgil, the poet of Mantua...

For the good of the great cause, which we, all of the brothers and sisters of the Gnostic movement, are fighting for, I am now going to transcribe some paragraphs from *The Aeneid*...

Safe now from the stormwave,
I took shelter first on the Strophadës—
For so the Greek name goes—islands that lie
In the broad Ionian sea. There nest the vile
Celaeno and her harpy sisterhood
[horrifying witches, black **Jinns***],*
Shut out, now, from the house of Phineus,
As they were frightened from old banquets there.
No gloomier monster, no more savage pest
And scourge sent by the gods' wrath ever mounted
From the black Stygian water — flying things
With young girls' faces, but foul ooze below,
Talons for hands, pale famished nightmare mouths.
When we pulled in to port, what met our eyes
But sleek herds in the meadows everywhere
And flocks of goats, no one attending them.
Setting upon them with our swords, we sent up
Shouts to the gods, to Jove himself, to share
The windfall with us; then on the curving beach
We set out couches for a savory feast.
But instantly, grotesquely whirring down,

The harpies [witches] were upon us from the hills
With deafening beat of wings. They trounced our meat,
Defiling everything they touched with filth,
And gave an obscene squawk amid the stench.
We tried again. In a secluded gorge
Under a cliffside, in thick shade of trees,
We set our tables up, relit our altars.
But the loud horde [those anthropophagus birds]
again, from another quarter,
Came out of hiding, swooped down on the prey
With hooked feet, hunched to feed, and spoiled our feast.
I then gave orders to resort to arms
And make war on the vicious flock. My men
Did as commanded, laid their swords nearby,
Hidden in grass, and kept shields out of sight.
Now when the birds flew down along the cove
Once more with their infernal din, Misenus
From a high lookout sounded the alarm
On his brass horn. Into their midst my men
Attacked and tried a strange new form of battle,
To cut the indecent seabird down in blood.
But they received no impact on their feathers,
Took on their backs no wounding cut: too quick,
They soared away into the upper air,
Leaving the prey half eaten and befouled.
Only Celaeno, perched on a high crag,
A ghastly witch, brought words out, croaking down:
'So war is all you give in recompense
for slaughter of bulls and bullocks, can it be,
Heirs of Laömedan? You'd arm for war
To drive the innocent harpies from their country?
Then put your mind on what I prophesy: a thing
Foretold to Phoebus by the almighty father
And by Apollo then to me; now I,
First of the Furies, will disclose it to you.
Italy is the land you look for; well,
The winds will blow, you'll find your Italy,
You'll be allowed to enter port;

But you may never wall your destined city
Till deathly famine, for the bloodshed here,
Has made you grind your tables with your teeth!'
On this she took wing back into the forest.
But our men of a sudden felt their blood
Run cold, and lost all heart. Not with arms now
But prayers and vows they begged me to make peace,
Whether these foes were goddesses or birds,
Obscene and dire. My father, facing seaward,
Hands held out, invoked the heavenly powers
And pledged the rituals due them. 'Gods', he said,
'Turn back this thing foreboded! Gods, avert
Disaster of that kind! Cherish your faithful!'
- Book III, lines 209-265

Here ends this unusual occult and esoteric poetic quotation. Let us continue now with the explanations.

Many of these abysmal harpies have been captured in the very act by surprise, with certain procedures.

Some ancient traditions say: "If we place on the floor a pair of steel scissors, opened in the form of a cross, and if we spread black mustard seeds around this metallic instrument, then any witch can be trapped."

It has caused astonishment that some illustrious occultists ignore that these witches can avoid the law of universal gravity! Even though this news appears unusual, we solemnly asseverate that this is possible by placing the body of flesh and bones within the fourth dimension.

It is not strange in any manner that these **calchonas** (witches) and their **idlers** can levitate and travel in just a few seconds, to any place in the world, while having their physical body within the fourth dimension (hyperspace).

It is clear that they have secret formulas for "physically" escaping from this three-dimensional world of Euclid.

In strictly occult terms, we can classify these leftist and tenebrous harpies with the title of black **Jinns**, in order to radically differentiate them from the white **Jinns**.

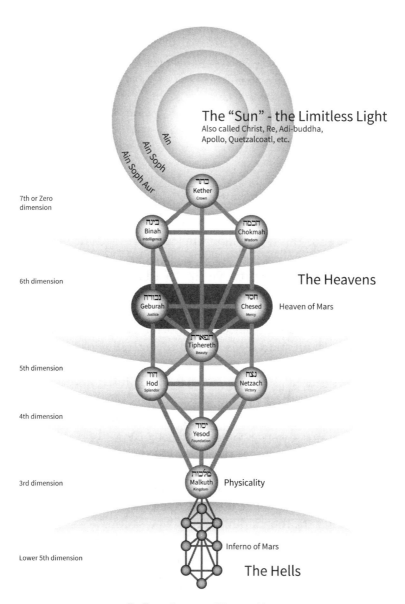

The "Sun" - the Limitless Light
Also called Christ, Re, Adi-buddha, Apollo, Quetzalcoatl, etc.

Ain
Ain Soph
Ain Soph Aur

7th or Zero dimension

כתר
Kether
Crown

בינה
Binah
Intelligence

חכמה
Chokmah
Wisdom

6th dimension

The Heavens

נבורה
Geburah
Justice

חסד
Chesed
Mercy

Heaven of Mars

תפארת
Tiphereth
Beauty

5th dimension

הוד
Hod
Splendor

נצח
Netzach
Victory

4th dimension

יסוד
Yesod
Foundation

מלכות
Malkuth
Kingdom

Physicality

3rd dimension

Inferno of Mars

The Hells

Lower 5th dimension

THE TREE OF LIFE AND THE WORLDS OF MARS.
TO LEARN MORE, STUDY TAROT AND KABBALAH BY SAMAEL AUN WEOR.

The human organism, while being within the fourth dimension—in spite of all that official science states—can assume any figure, can change shape...

Remember, beloved readers, the abominable Celaeno and her filthy harpies, horrifying fowls of the Strophadës Islands, of the Ionian Sea...

On one given afternoon (the date, day, and hour do not matter), while seated at the foot of the bars inside of an old dungeon, I was studying an esoteric book...

The sun was hidden within the burning red of its setting, and the evening light was slowly vanishing...

Suddenly, something unusual happened: I heard next to me a thunderous, sarcastic, mocking guffaw that was distinctly feminine...

She was one of these anthropophagus fowls who inhabited the Stygian lakes. She was a calchona, a witch of ill omen, a woman of a leftist Witches' Sabbath...

This perverse one fled and hid herself within the frightful darkness of the infernal worlds...

Thus, this is how my intrepid descent into the living inner most parts of the submerged Martian mineral kingdoms was initiated.

Before ascending, it is indispensable to descend. This is the law. A frightful and terrible humiliation always precedes every exaltation.

To annihilate from within myself these inhuman witching elements, those fowls of evil omen, was certainly my labor in the tenebrous Tartarus.

Even if this seems incredible—because of such an unusual assertion—it is urgent to know that all human beings, without any exception, carry various bewitching elements in their unconscious depths.

This signifies that in the world there are many people who, without knowing, are unconsciously practicing black magic.

Unquestionably, even the very saints from all religions suffer the undescribable when they **discover** themselves. They then verify for themselves the crude reality of those inhuman elements that, clearly, they have the obligation to eliminate from their psyche.

Any adept, mystic, or saint is more or less black while still not having radically died in all and each one of the forty-nine departments of the subconsciousness.

Lo and behold one of the great reasons for not having the right to condemn anybody. *"He that is without a sin among you, let him first cast a stone."*

I was incessantly attacked in a pitiless way by the sinister fowls that inhabited the Stygian Lakes in that epoch of my life.

Inside the Martian infernos, within the "**Mandingoes**" halls of those tenebrous Witches' Sabbaths, I discovered with astonishment many brothers and sisters of the rocky path...

The fact of the matter is that they have "bewitching aggregates" that their human personalities clearly ignore.

When concluding my works within the mineral abyss of Mars, I ascended victoriously into the fifth heaven, the world of **Atman**, the radiant abode of the Virtues.

Thus, this is how I returned into the heaven of Mars. I then re-conquered my place among those sublime beings, a divine position that in a foregone time I had lost...

The objective of my works within the Martian infernos was achieved. My consciousness was free after having eliminated the inhuman elements from my psyche...

The intellectual shackles had been annihilated, and my liberated consciousness, already out of the horrifying dungeon of the mind—from where it had dwelled as a prisoner for a long time—had achieved the fusion, the intermixture with **Atman** the Ineffable One, my real Being.

Ah! If people could comprehend what the dungeon of the intellect is... If they could understand that they live as prisoners inside the jail of their mind...

While in complete bliss as "Spirit-Man" within the Martian heaven, far away from the body and the affections and the mind, I consciously wandered as a resplendent bird of light, a radical antithesis of those sinister fowls of the Stygian Lakes...

Then, while in those moments of exquisite blessings, I passed by many symbolic pieces of work that were structured with pure iron...

This is the region of **Atman** the Ineffable One, the world of the most crude reality, the dimension of mathematics.

In this three-dimensional world we never perceive solids in an integral and unitotal form. Here we only see in a subjective form: angles, surfaces, etc.

However, within the luminous region of **Atman**, we not only perceive solids in an integral form, but moreover, we perceive hyper-solids, including the exact quantity of atoms, which in their conjunction constitute the totality of any given body.

Unquestionably, in the heaven of Mars, we truly enjoy the most complete objective perception.

How happy I felt while in that region of infinite joys! However, everything in life is not always a festivity; sufferings also exist, you now this...

The headquarters of heavenly judgment, where "objective justice" is administrated, always intervenes.

One given day, while happily being in the world of **Atman**, a judge of the law of **Katancia (superior karma)** came to me.

He sat before a table and I, with a lot of respect and veneration, then had to answer to some accusations:

"You have criticized many people in your books," said the hierarch.

"I am combative by nature," I answered in an emphatic way.

"You are condemned to seven days in prison." Such was the sentence.

Frankly and plainly speaking, I have to confess that when I heard the sentence I was a little cynical. It appeared to me that this matter was a foolish case for the police, like when as a boy, one fights with another of his own age, then one is placed for a few hours in jail...

Nonetheless, when I had already fully accomplished this sentence, I felt that this punishment was terribly painful.

Seven days within this horrible dungeon of the mind, and after having emancipated myself from it...

Seven symbolic days of bitterness inside of this frightful jail of the intellect...

Woe! Woe! Woe!...

Chapter XXXIX
The Heaven of Jupiter

The sparkling constellation of Pisces is found relatively close to the constellation of Taurus which, unquestionably, is found intimately related with the transcendent esoteric work of "the capture of the wild bull of Crete."

This bull had been sent to Minos by the God Neptune, so that he may offer the bull as a holocaust. However, the greedy king improperly kept the bull for himself, therefore the animal became frightful and threatening, terrorizing the whole country.

The legend of the centuries states that Heracles, the solar hero, easily obtained permission to take hold of the bull, to chain it, and to drag it through the sea until reaching Mycenae.

Indubitably, the work related with the infernos of Jupiter is found completely allegorized with the sixth achievement of Heracles...

It is good to remember in these paragraphs the first Jupiter of Greek theogony, the father of all gods, the lord of the universe and brother of Uranus or **Ur-anas**, in other words, the primeval fire and water. It is known through the classics that in the Greek pantheon there were about three hundred Jupiters.

Jove, or **Iod-Eve**, in his other aspect is **Jehovah**, the male-female or androgenous and collective **Elohim** of the books of Moses, also the **Adam Kadmon** of the **Kabbalists**, and **Iacho** or **Inacho** of Anatolia, who is the same **Bacchus** or **Dionysius** of the Phoenicians, continuers of the primeval theogony of Sanchoniaton...

This character of the "Heavenly Man," which was always assigned to Jupiter, the venerable father of all gods, also gave place to some typical Nordic names, such as **Herr-man** and **Herr-manas**, or **Hermes**, which literally is "Divine Man" or "Lord Man," the Alcides or **El Cid**, the theogonic precursor of all prehistorical **Cids** of Spanish romances.

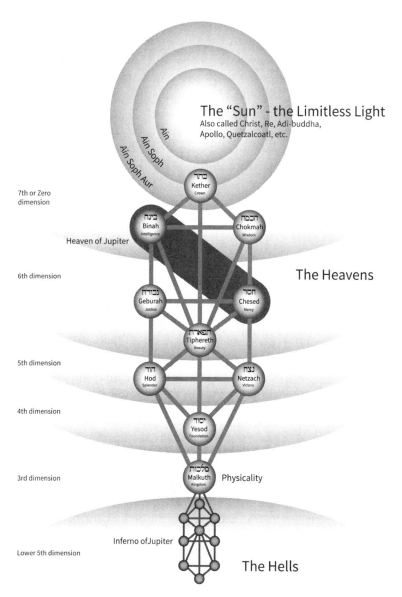

The "Sun" - the Limitless Light
Also called Christ, Re, Adi-buddha, Apollo, Quetzalcoatl, etc.

7th or Zero dimension

כתר
Kether
Crown

בינה
Binah
Intelligence

חכמה
Chokmah
Wisdom

Heaven of Jupiter

6th dimension

The Heavens

גבורה
Geburah
Justice

חסד
Chesed
Mercy

תפארת
Tiphereth
Beauty

5th dimension

הוד
Hod
Splendor

נצח
Netzach
Victory

4th dimension

יסוד
Yesod
Foundation

3rd dimension

מלכות
Malkuth
Kingdom

Physicality

Inferno of Jupiter

Lower 5th dimension

The Hells

THE TREE OF LIFE AND THE WORLDS OF JUPITER.
TO LEARN MORE, STUDY TAROT AND KABBALAH BY SAMAEL AUN WEOR.

Unquestionably, Jupiter in Punjab and Rajisthan is the **Hari-kulas** or Heracles, the solar lord, the "prototype of the race of the Sun," the **Hari Mukh** of Cachemira, in other words, the Sun in the east of life.

Jupiter or **IO-Pitar,** in other words, the Father of **Io**, is that Divine Spirit within all of the ancient hosts of creators, who when reincarnating into bodies with opposite sexes, gave origin to that Greek fable of "the loves of Jupiter with the virgin **Io**" (iiiiiooooo). The virgin **Io**, in order to escape from the anger of **Juno**, was transformed into a heavenly calf or "sacred cow" of the Orient.

Jupiter and his cow of **Io** (iiiioooo) grant us the meaning of other archaic names, such as the same **Geryon** [Ger-Io-n] or **Ferion**—the one who carries the cows—also **Hyperion Bosphoro**, literally "the conductor of the Cow," as well as **Gautama** the "**Buddha**."

Thus **Jupiter**, the host of Lords or **Elohim**, is symbolized by the **sexual hierogram** of Io (iiiioooo). It is clear that Jupiter has dozens of names in each language, and a hundred or thousand myths for each name in its respective language.

The whole ineffable legion of **Divine Beings**, all of them **Elohim**, in their conjunction constitute the **Unique God Without Name** of the Tartesians, the authentic and sublime Jupiter of ancient times...

After this transcendental theme which was very carefully developed, we can solemnly deduce the following: the heaven of Jupiter is the abode of the **Elohim**, **Nirvana**...

The devotees of the path who will choose the spiral path after reaching the Fifth Initiation of Fire will enter into **Nirvana**...

To integrally develop oneself is something different. In the name of the truth, frankly and plainly speaking, I have to confess that this was always my greatest longing...

The complete development of all my Nirvanic, superlative possibilities in the whole presence of my cosmic Being was my aspiration...

However, it is unquestionable that before ascending we have to descend. Every exaltation is always preceded by a frightful and terrible humiliation...

Truly, the next task to follow was to chain the symbolic "bull of Crete," and this very task appeared horrifying to me...

During that epoch of my present existence, many sexual temptations inclemently besieged me within the tenebrous Tartarus...

Through psychological self-exploration, I discovered the famous "bull of Crete" within the most profound inner-depths of my own mind.

Yes, I saw this bull: black, enormous, gigantic, threatening, and provided with sharp horns...

Obviously, this bull expressed itself through my psyche with strong, passionate, and irreflexive sexual impulses...

To chain the tenebrous beast was urgent. To disintegrate it, to reduce it to cosmic dust, was indispensable...

Indubitably, I was assisted by my Divine Mother **Kundalini**, the igneous serpent of our magical powers...

This great cosmic event was celebrated with a festivity in the marvellous Temple of Jupiter...

Then, many kings and priests of Nature, revested with their sacred purple, welcomed me...

Thus, this is how I re-entered into the heaven of Jupiter, into that **Nirvanic** happiness, the abode of **Dominions**...

In this manner, by eliminating infra-human elements, I re-conquered my place among these ineffable hierarchies. I had lost this conscious state when, in foregone times on the central plateau of Asia about one million years ago, I committed the error of eating of the forbidden fruit...

Chapter XL
The Heaven of Saturn

The seventh labor of Heracles, the solar hero, was the capture of the mares of Diomedes, who was the son of Mars and the king of the warrior Bistonian people. These mares killed and ate castaways who arrived on their coast.

Only after defeating the Bistonians in furious combat, who with Diomedes had to defend their possessions, Heracles and his friends achieved the seizure of those beasts. King Diomedes' remains were given as pasture to those anthropophagus Mares.

I had to capture and destroy the mares of Diomedes within the Saturnian infernos. These were profoundly submerged infrahuman passional elements within my own unconscious abysses...

These symbolic beasts were beside the spermatic waters of the first instant, always ready to devour the ones who had failed...

During that epoch of my present existence, I was incessantly attacked within the tenebrous Tartarus...

The adepts of evil Atlantean magic resolved with outrageous ferocity to combat me, and I had to courageously defend myself...

Beloved, nubile ladies, dangerously exquisite malignant beauties, besieged me everywhere...

Unquestionably, we experience, resuscitate, and revive the Atlantean terrors within the Saturnian infernos...

Heracles, as stated by Aelino (*Various Histories,* book V, C.3), cleansed the Earth and the seas of not only monsters but of every type of monstrosity, as when he defeated the necromancer Briareo, the one with one hundred arms, in one of his celebrated labors or triumphs against the evil Atlantean magic, which became the master of the whole Earth.

Heracles (the true Aryan Krishna of *The Mahabharata),* when foreseeing the final Atlantean catastrophe that was approaching (which included the vanishing of the divine

Garden of Hesperides) transplanted the symbolic initiatic tree everywhere he went, in other words, in all Punjab, Minor Asia, Syria, Egypt, Greece, Italy, Germany, British Islands, Spain, Mauritania, and even America, under the name of **Quetzalcoatl** (the luminous white serpent). Because of this, all these countries were saved from the great catastrophe.

Notwithstanding, it is written:

> *Of every tree of the garden thou mayest freely eat:*
> *But of the tree of the knowledge of good and evil,*
> *thou shalt not eat of it: for in the day that thou eatest*
> *thereof thou shalt surely die.* - Genesis 2:16-17

To inebriate ourselves with the delectable aroma of the forbidden fruit is indispensable. Thus, this is how Heracles taught it...

Before the escape of the insurmountable ocean, which is a barrier for the human being, Heracles stretched forth his bow against the sun, as if to hurt it, in order to stop it from its rapid race far off into the distant ocean. It was sinking and Heracles was unable to follow it, but the God Apollo commanded him to remain quiet and patient—because it is only with infinite patience that the "Magnus Opus," the "Great Work," can be performed. Therefore, Apollo gave him as a gift a "Golden Cup," the "Holy Grail," the resplendent and eternal symbol of the uterus or feminine **yoni**...

It is unquestionable that the arrow of Heracles is nothing but the Magnes Stone, the **phallus** or spear of Longinus, the Roman centurion. This is the spear with which the side of the Lord was hurt, the same holy spear which with its secret power Parsifal healed the wound in Amfortas' side...

In hard battles, I defeated the king of the Bistonians, the knights of the Black Grail, **Klingsor**, the animal ego, with the miraculous power of these venerated relics...

When finalizing the Saturnian labor within the abode of Pluto, I was then transported with the **eidolon** to the "solar land" of the Hyperboreans...

This is the island of **Avalon**, the magical region of the "**Jinns**," where the holy gods abide...

This is the sublime island of Apollo, a solid land in the midst of the great ocean of life, free in its movement...

Ah!.. If the Emperor Frederick of medieval times would have performed the mystery of the Grail, the Hyperborean mystery, within himself... Then, undoubtedly, the withered tree of the empire would have flourished again in a splendid way... Also it is clear that the kingdom of the Grail would have marvellously reappeared within the very sacred Roman Empire...

The path of life is formed by the prints of the hooves of the horse of death...

To perform the Hyperborean mystery in oneself without having been judged in the great Hall of Truth-Justice is impossible...

To perform the mystery of the Grail within oneself is impossible without previously having weighed the heart of the defunct on the plate of the scale that is carried by Truth-Justice...

The **realization of the Innermost Self**, the Being, is not possible without having been declared "dead" in the Hall of Truth-Justice.

The legend of the centuries states that many initiates travelled in the past to the country of the Brother John—the solar land—in order to receive certain very special magical esoteric consecrations...

These brothers of the "Order of Saint John" on that "island of the solar Apollo" are completely dead...

Then, it is not strange that I also would have to travel to that "land of light" or "solar light."

In the glorious vestibule of this Saturnian sancta, before the royal beings, I who was seated had to answer certain questions. The holy gods took note of this in a great book...

In those mystical instants, there emerged upon the whole presence of my cosmic Being some remembrances...

Ah!... I had been here before, in this very holy place, before these venerable Thrones, many million of years ago, during the epoch of the "continent Mu" or Lemuria...

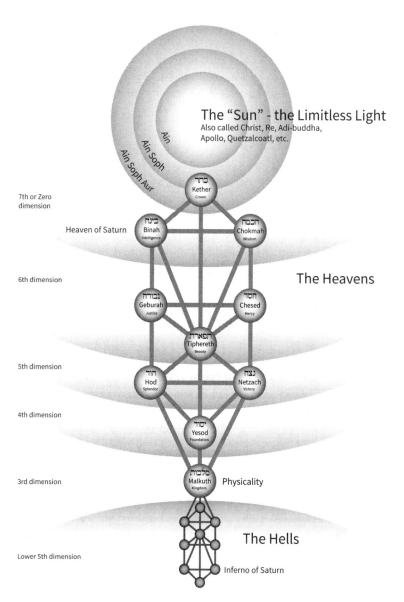

The "Sun" - the Limitless Light
Also called Christ, Re, Adi-buddha, Apollo, Quetzalcoatl, etc.

Ain
Ain Soph
Ain Soph Aur

כתר
Kether
Crown

בינה
Binah
Intelligence

חכמה
Chokmah
Wisdom

גבורה
Geburah
Justice

חסד
Chesed
Mercy

תפארת
Tiphereth
Beauty

הוד
Hod
Splendor

נצח
Netzach
Victory

יסוד
Yesod
Foundation

מלכות
Malkuth
Kingdom

7th or Zero dimension

Heaven of Saturn

6th dimension

The Heavens

5th dimension

4th dimension

3rd dimension   Physicality

The Hells

Lower 5th dimension   Inferno of Saturn

THE TREE OF LIFE AND THE WORLDS OF SATURN.
TO LEARN MORE, STUDY TAROT AND KABBALAH BY SAMAEL AUN WEOR.

Now I was victoriously returning after having suffered a lot. Woe! Woe! Woe!...

After filling the indispensable esoteric requisites, I left the vestibule and entered into the temple...

Unquestionably, the Temple of Saturn in the "solar land," the "**Jinn** land" of the septentrional regions, was full of intense darkness...

It is clear that the Sun and Saturn alternate their labor in the government of this world...

I saw the Thrones as they sat down... The angels of death were coming and going, here, there, and everywhere...

Divine people arrived in the temple. They came from diverse places of the enchanted island, which is situated at the extreme of the world...

"**Thule** ultima a Sole nomen habens." "Ajryanem-Vaejo" is the septentrional country of the ancient Persians where the palace of King Arthur is magically situated, as is Midgard, the resplendent sacrosanct residence of the "Aesir," the ineffable Nordic Lords...

> Oh Maat! Lo and behold that I arrive before thee! Allow me then to contemplate your radiant beauty! Behold how my arm rises while praising your sacrosanct name!
>
> Oh Truth-Justice, hear me! I arrive before the places where trees never grow, where the ground brings forth not any plant...

The skeletal figure of the god of death on the platform of the sanctuary weighed my heart on the scale of cosmic justice before that divine humanity...

That Verb of Potency before the brilliant beings dressed with glorious bodies of **Kam-ur** pronounced me "**dead**..."

On the platform of the sanctuary a symbolic coffin was shown. Within it appeared my cadaver...

Thus, this is how I returned into the heaven of Saturn, the **Paranirvana**, the abode of the Thrones.

Thus, this is how I reconquered that hierarchial state which in a foregone time I had lost when I committed the grave error of eating the golden apples from the Garden of Hesperides...

Posteriorly, I passed through the ceremony of death: When I returned to my house I found myself with something unusual...

I saw funeral cards on the walls of my mansion announcing my death and inviting others to the burial...

When I passed through the threshold, with mystical astonishment I found a very beautiful coffin of a white color...

It is clear that within that funeral box my cadaver lay there, completely cold and inert...

Many relatives and sorrowful people bitterly cried and mourned around that coffin...

Delectable flowers scented the environment of that room with their aroma...

I approached my mother who in those instants was wiping her tears with a handkerchief...

I kissed her hands with infinite love and uttered: "I thank you, oh Mother, for the physical body that you granted me! That vehicle greatly served me. It was certainly a marvellous instrument, but everything in life has a beginning and an end..."

When I left that planetary abode, I joyfully resolved to float within the aura of the universe...

I saw myself converted into a child, without ego, lacking the subjective elements of perception...

My little, infantile, tiny shoes did not appear to me as beautiful. For an instant I wanted to take them off. But, then I said to myself, "**He** will dress me as he wishes..."

While in absence of the mortifying intellect that does not make anyone happy, only the purest sentiment existed within me...

When I remembered my old father and my brother Herman, I said to myself, "They already died..."

When I remembered all of those mourning people who I was leaving in the painful valley of Samsara, I uttered, "Family? Which one? I have no family anymore..."

Then, while feeling myself absolutely disincarnated, I left with the intention of reaching a remote place where I should help others...

In such moments of mystical enchantment, I said to myself, "For a long time I will not return to take a physical body..."

Posteriorly, I felt that the silver cord, the famous **Antakarana**, the thread of life, still was not severed. Then I returned into my physical body in order to continue with the hard struggle of each instant...

THE TWO THIEVES

"Jesus, the great Kabir, was crucified between two
thieves, one to his right and another to his left..."

Chapter XLI
The Heaven of Uranus

The legend of innumerable centuries states that Aeneas, with his Trojans, had the place of honor with the King Evander and the venerable senators at the table of the feast...

Then picked men and the priest who served the altar
Vied with one another to bring roast meat,
To load bread-baskets with the gifts of Ceres,
Milled and baked, and to pour out the wine.
Aeneas with his Trojans feasted then
On a beef chine and flesh of sacrifice.
When they were fed, their appetites appeased,
Royal Evander spoke:
"No empty-headed
Superstition, blind to the age-old gods,
Imposed this ritual on us, and this feast,
This altar to a divine force of will.
No, Trojan guest, we carry out these rites,
Dangers in the past. Look first of all
At this high overhanging rocky cliff;
See how rock masses have been scattered out,
Leaving a mountain dwelling bare, forsaken
Where the crags fell in avalanche. Here was once
A cave with depths no ray of sun could reach,
Where Cacus lived, a bestial form, half man,
And the ground reeked forever with fresh blood,
While nailed up in vile pride on his cave doors
Were men's pale faces ghastly in decay.
Vulcan had fathered this unholy brute
Who as he moved about in mammoth bulk
Belched out the poisonous fires of the father.
After long prayers, time brought even to us
A god's advent and aid [the eighth labor].
...Caught by the light
Unlooked for, and closed in by stone, the giant
Bellowed as never in his life before

While from above with missiles Heracles
Let fly at him, calling on every mass
At hand to make a weapon, raining down
Dry boughs and boulders like millstones. ”
[This was in revenge for the theft of Heracles' cattle]
...They renewed the feast,
Bringing a welcome second course, and heaped
The altar tops with dishes. For a hymn
At the lit altars came the Salii,
All garlanded with poplar-files of dancers,
Here of the young, there of the elder men,
Who praised in song the feats of Heracles,
His story: how he grappled monsters first,
Choking his step-mother's twin snakes,
...And killed the Lion under Nemea's crag!
...[Even Cerberus,] the Keeper
Of Orcus shook, sprawled in his gory cave
On bones partly devoured; and took this dog
Out of darkness into the light.
[This is the sexual instinct that must guide us to the
Final Liberation.]
When they had carried out the ritual
They turned back to the town. And, slowed by age,
The king walked, keeping Aeneas and his son
Close by his side with talk of various things
To make the long path easy.
The king Evander, founder unaware
Of Rome's great citadel, said:
“...In that first time, out of Olympian heaven,
Saturn came here in flight from Jove in arms
And exile from a Kingdom lost, he brought
These unschooled men together from the hills
Where they were scattered, gave them laws, and chose
The name of Latinum, from its latency
Or safe concealment in this countryside.
In his reign were the golden centuries
Men tell of still, so peacefully he ruled,
Till gradually a meaner, tarnished age

Came on with fever of war and lust of gain.
Then came Ausonians and Sicanians..."
Just after this, as he went on he showed
The altar and the gate the Romans call
Carmental, honourings as of old the nymph
And prophetess Carmentis, first to sing
The glory of Pallanteum and Aeneas'
Great descendants. Then he showed the wood
That Romulus would make a place of refuge,
Then the grotto called the Lupercal
Under the cold crag, named in Arcadian fashion
After Lycaean Pan. And then as well
He showed the sacred wood of Argiletum,
"Argus' death," and took oath by it, telling
Of a guest, Argus, put to death. From there
He led to our Tarpeian site and Capitol,
All golden now, in those days tangled, wild
With underbrush — but awesome even then.
A strangeness there filled country hearts with dread
And made them shiver at the wood and Rock.
"Some god," he said, "it is not sure what god,
Lives in this grove, this hilltop thick with leaves.
Arcadians think they've seen great Jove himself
Sometimes with his right hand shaking the aegis
To darken sky and make the storm clouds rise
Towering in turmoil. Here, too, in these walls
Long fallen down, you see what were two towns,
Monuments of the ancients, Father Janus
Founded one stronghold, Saturn the other,
Named Janiculum and Saturnia."

All of this is quoted from *The Aeneid*, book VIII, by Virgil, the poet of Mantua, the master of Dante, the Florentine.

Jesus, the great Kabir, was crucified between two thieves, one to his right and another to his left...

Agathos, the good thief within our interior, steals the Sexual Hydrogen Si-12 from our sexual organs with the evident purpose of crystallizing the Holy Spirit, the Great Conciliator within ourselves, here and now...

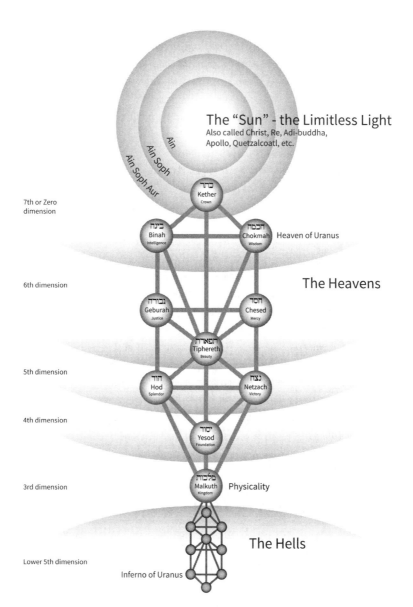

The "Sun" - the Limitless Light
Also called Christ, Re, Adi-buddha, Apollo, Quetzalcoatl, etc.

Ain
Ain Soph
Ain Soph Aur

7th or Zero dimension

כתר
Kether
Crown

בינה
Binah
Intelligence

חכמה
Chokmah
Wisdom

Heaven of Uranus

6th dimension

The Heavens

גבורה
Geburah
Justice

חסד
Chesed
Mercy

תפארת
Tiphereth
Beauty

5th dimension

הוד
Hod
Splendor

נצח
Netzach
Victory

4th dimension

יסוד
Yesod
Foundation

3rd dimension

מלכות
Malkuth
Kingdom

Physicality

The Hells

Lower 5th dimension

Inferno of Uranus

THE TREE OF LIFE AND THE WORLDS OF URANUS.
TO LEARN MORE, STUDY TAROT AND KABBALAH BY SAMAEL AUN WEOR.

Cacus is the evil thief who, hidden inside the tenebrous cave of the human infra-consciousness, treacherously pillages the sexual center of our organism for the satisfaction of the brute animal passions...

The cross is an astonishing, marvellous, and formidable sexual symbol. The vertical branch is masculine, the horizontal is feminine. The clue of all powers is found in their crossing...

The black **lingam** inserted into the feminine **yoni** forms a cross. This is well known by the divine and by humans...

We can and must set the following postulation as a corollary: **Agathos** and **Cacus**, when crucified on the Mount of the Skulls, to the right and left of the great Kabir Jesus, emphatically allegorize **white tantra** and **black tantra**, the good and the evil magic of sexuality...

The Bible, from Genesis to Apocalypse, is nothing but a series of historical events of the great struggle between the followers of **Agathos** and **Cacus**, white and black magic, the adepts of the right-hand path, the prophets, and the adepts of the left-hand path, the levites...

Inside the abysses of **Uranus**, I had to reduce to cosmic dust the evil thief, the tenebrous **Cacus**, that thief who previously pillaged the sexual center of my organic machine for the vile satisfaction of animal passions...

When I entered inside the vestibule of the sanctuary, I remembered that I had been in that place in foregone times... in ancient times....

I, with the eye of **Shiva**, saw diverse tantric movements of Aquarius; the Gnostic people were standing out among them, whose flags were victoriously waving in all of the countries of the Earth...

Unquestionably, **Uranus**, **Aquarius**, is one hundred percent sexual, magical, and revolutionary...

Thus, this is how I returned into the heaven of **Uranus**, the **Mahaparanirvana**, the abode of the **Cherubim**...

Thus, this is how I re-conquered that brilliant conscious state that I had lost in forgone times, when I fell at the feet of the marvellous Eve of Hebraic mythology...

THE GIRDLE OF HIPPOLYTE

"In this hard battle, I wanted to conquer
the girdle of Hippolyte, but the Amazons
provoked by Hera indefatigably besieged me
with their subtle abysmal enchantments..."

Chapter XLII
The Heaven of Neptune

Unquestionably, the ninth labor of Heracles, the solar hero, which becomes very complex, is the obtaining of the girdle of Hippolyte, queen of the Amazons, the warrior-women, the feminine psychic aspect of our own interior nature...

When embarking with other legendary heroes, firstly he has to fight against the sons of Minos—the black magicians—then against the enemies of the King Licos (whose exotic name reminds us of the analogy between "wolf" and "light"). They are, of course, the lords of **karma** with whom we have to arrange our negotiations. Finally, he has to battle with the Amazons—terrible temptresses who are provoked by Hera. Even when Hippolyte had passively consented to grant her girdle, the queen is uselessly sacrificed by the masculine brutality which violently feigns to obtain her innate virtue.

This marvellous girdle, analogous to the one of Venus, is the emblem of femininity. It loses its whole significance and value when it is separated from its legitimate possessor. Therefore, love, not violence, is what makes its conquest truly significant and valuable...

When the God Neptune gained the Atlantean continent, which is now submerged within the boisterous waters of the ocean which carries its name, tradition states that he engendered various children with a mortal woman...

Nearby, on the island where he dwelt, the land was level, but in the middle, there was a very special valley with a little central mount which was fifty stadiums from the sandy beach...

On that mount dwelt one of those beings who was born on the Earth. His name was Evenor, who with his wife Leucipe engendered Clitone, his unique daughter.

When the parents of Clitone died, Neptune married her, and fenced in the place where he abided with various channels of water. In accordance with the legend, it is stated that three of these channels came from the sea and were all of the same distance from the sea. So, these channels walled the place in order to render it unconquerable and inaccessible.

This Clitone or Minerva-Neith built much, from Greece to Athens and in Sais, and she built the famous delta of the Nile...

In memory of them, the Atlanteans built the marvellous Temple of Neptune and Clitone...

The cadavers of the ten sons of Neptune were deposited in that **sancta**. Ten is a symbolic, magical number...

We cannot leave the study of the number ten without dealing with the obligation of the tithe, an obligation to which the very Abraham voluntarily submitted himself in his relations with the Initiate-King Melchizedeck...

Chapter 15:17-20 of Genesis says:

And the king of Sodom went out to meet Abraham...

And Melchizedeck king of Salem brought forth bread and wine: and he was the priest of the most high God.

And he blessed him, and said, blessed be Abraham of the most high God possessor of heaven and earth:

And blessed be the most high God, which hath delivered thine enemies into thy hand. And Abraham gave him tithes of all.

In its **exoteric** or public aspect within the Jewish legislation, the tithe is the universal obligation that all the brothers and sisters of the path have, which is to loyally contribute part of their income —that should not be inferior to the tithe—in a free and eligible way, in accordance to what the brethren judge to be more opportune and effective in order to support the cause of truth and justice...

The tithe in its **esoteric** or secret aspect symbolizes the scale of payments in the sphere of Neptune...

It is unquestionable that here we have to arrange affairs with the enemies of the King Licos (the lords of **karma**).

It is undoubtable that we assassinated the God Mercury, **Hiram**, and it is not possible to resuscitate him within ourselves, without previously having payed for this abject crime...

Therefore, the tithe becomes a practical and necessary complement of the dynamic principle which emanates from the profound study of the Tenth Commandment, in other words: We must consider the mysterious ׳ **Yod** which is hidden in the middle of the central delta of the sanctuary of our Being, as a fountain, spring, and spiritual providence of all the interior and divine centers of our life...

YOD OR IOD, THE TENTH LETTER OF THE HEBREW ALPHABET

This point of the tithe is clarified with the words of the Gospel:

> *But lay up for yourselves treasures in heaven...*
> *For where your treasure is, there will your*
> *heart be also...* - Matthew 6:20-21

Malachi 3:10 says:

> *Bring ye all the tithes into the storehouse, that there*
> *may be meat in mine house, and prove me now here-*
> *with, saith the Lord of Hosts, if I will not open you*
> *the windows of heaven, and pour you out a blessing,*
> *that there shall not be room enough to receive it.*

With infinite longings I was searching for the treasure of heaven, the golden fleece of ancient times, by excavating into the profound innermost parts of the Averno, working intensely in the "Ninth Sphere..."

The sons of Minos, the adepts of the left-hand path, the Levites of evermore, angrily and incessantly attacked me in the frightful Neptunian abysses...

In this hard battle, I wanted to conquer the girdle of Hippolyte, but the Amazons provoked by Hera indefatigably besieged me with their subtle abysmal enchantments...

One given night (the date, day and hour do not matter now), I was transported to the castle of **Klingsor**, which is located exactly in Salamanca, Spain...

It is now good to emphatically remember that in this old castle, cited by **Wagner** in his *Parsifal*, the "hall of witchcraft" is functioning.

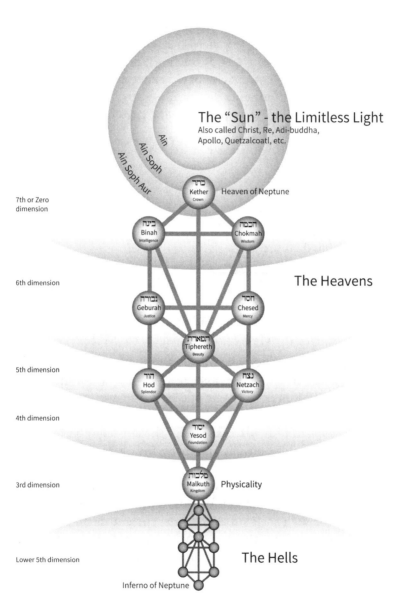

The "Sun" - the Limitless Light
Also called Christ, Re, Adi-buddha, Apollo, Quetzalcoatl, etc.

Ain
Ain Soph
Ain Soph Aur

7th or Zero dimension

כתר
Kether
Crown

Heaven of Neptune

בינה
Binah
Intelligence

חכמה
Chokmah
Wisdom

6th dimension

The Heavens

גבורה
Geburah
Justice

חסד
Chesed
Mercy

תפארת
Tiphereth
Beauty

5th dimension

הוד
Hod
Splendor

נצח
Netzach
Victory

4th dimension

יסוד
Yesod
Foundation

3rd dimension

מלכות
Malkuth
Kingdom

Physicality

Lower 5th dimension

The Hells

Inferno of Neptune

THE TREE OF LIFE AND THE WORLDS OF URANUS.
TO LEARN MORE, STUDY TAROT AND KABBALAH BY SAMAEL AUN WEOR.

What I then saw in that dismal abode of the harpies was certainly horrifying...

Sinister **calchonas** of leftist Witches' Sabbaths attacked me in a tenebrous way many times within the interior of the castle. However, I courageously defended myself with the flaming sword...

My old friend the Angel Adonai—who in these times has a physical body—accompanied me in this adventure...

The lucubrations of those great seers of the astral who were called alchemists, kabbalists, occultists, etc., were not in vain. What we saw then inside this den was certainly frightful...

I unsheathed my flaming sword many times in order to throw flames upon this fatal abode of the necromancer **Klingsor**...

In an unexpected way, Adonai and I approached some **calchonas** who were arranging the table for the feast...

In vain I passed my sword through the chest of one of those witches; she remained impassable. Unquestionably, she was awakened in evil and for evil...

It is clear that I wanted to make fire pour as rain from heaven upon that horrendous fortress...

I made supreme efforts; I felt dismayed, and in those instants the Angel Adonai came near to the windows of my eyes in order to see what was happening inside of myself...

Imagine for a moment any person standing before the window of a house, in order to observe through the glass to see what is happening in the interior...

It is clear that the eyes are the windows of the soul, and the angels of heaven can see through those crystals to see what is happening inside each one of us...

After performing this singular observation, Adonai withdrew with satisfaction. My own interior castle, the abode of **Klingsor**, had been incinerated with the intimate fire...

Each one of us carries inside a fortress of leftist Witches' Sabbaths. This is not ignored by the **mahatmas**...

Later, I had to clearly witness the tenebrous aspect of existence. It is clear that Satan has the power of ubiquity. Look at him within yourself, here, there, and everywhere...

When concluding the esoteric labors within the infernos of Neptune, I had then to ascend into the **Empireum**, the region of the **Seraphim**, who are creatures of love, direct expressions of the Unity...

Thus, this is how I re-conquered that hierarchial state in the heaven of Neptune, which is the universe of the divine Monads...

Unquestionably, I had attained the girdle of Hippolyte. One night among many, I evidenced this, then I danced with other ineffable beings in a cosmic festivity...

On another night, when floating in the **Empireum**, while in a **Seraphic** state, I asked my Mother for the lyre, which I then knew how to play with mastery...

Chapter XLIII
The Resurrection

It is unquestionable that for Richard Wagner, as well as generally for all the Christian countries, the Grail is the "sacred cup" from which the Lord of Perfection drank at the Last Supper. His royal blood, shed while on the cross on the Mount of the Skulls and devoutly collected by the Roman Senator Joseph of Arimathea, was received in this divine cup.

This great chalice was possessed by the Patriarch Abraham. Melchizedeck, the genie of our world, transported it with infinite love from the country of Semiramis to the land of Canaan. When he initiated some enterprises—where much later Jerusalem, the beloved city of the prophets was founded—Melchizedeck wisely utilized it for celebrating the sacrifice of bread and wine of the transubstantiation. He offered this in the presence of Abraham, then delivered the chalice to this Master. This holy cup was also in the Ark of Noah...

It has been said that this venerated cup was also carried into the sacred land of the Pharaohs, into the sunny country of **Kem**. Moses, the chief of the Jewish mysteries, the great, illuminated hierophant, possessed this cup...

Very ancient millenary traditions that are lost in the terrifying night of all ages say that this magic cup was made from a singular matter. It was compact like the matter of a bell, yet did not look like any known metal. Rather, this matter looked like it was produced from a type of vegetation...

The Holy Grail is the miraculous chalice of the supreme beverage. The **manna** which nourished the Israelites in the wilderness is contained in this cup. This cup is the **yoni**, the **uterus** of the eternal feminine...

The exquisite wine of transcendental spirituality is contained within this cup of delights...

The conquering of the "**ultra-mare-vitae**" or "**superliminal world**," and the "**ultra-terrestrial**," the esoteric resurrection, would be something more than impossible without **Sexual Magic**, without the spouse, without love...

THE THREE MARYS

The delectable Word of **Isis** emerges from within the profound bosom of all ages, awaiting for the instant to be realized...

The ineffable words of the Goddess **Neith** has been carved on the resplendent walls of the temple of wisdom with letters of gold...

> *I am the one that was, is and shall be*
> *And no mortal has ever lifted my veil.*

The primeval religion of **Jano** or **Jaino**, in other words, the quiritary and super-human solar golden doctrine of the **Jinns**, is absolutely sexual...

We feel in the depth of our heart, within the ineffable mystical idyll commonly called the "enchantments of Holy Friday," that a terribly divine force exists within the sexual organs...

The "stone of light," the "Holy Grail," has the power of resurrecting **Hiram Abif**, the secret master, the sun king, within ourselves, here and now...

The Grail maintains the character of a "**misterium tremendum**." It is the fallen stone of the crown of Lucifer...

The Grail, as a dreaded force, hurts and destroys the curious and impure ones, but defends and gives life to the just and sincere ones...

Unquestionably, the Grail can only be achieved by means of the lance of Eros, while combating against the eternal enemies of the night...

To perform the Hyperborean mystery in oneself is only feasible by descending into the infernal worlds...

Such a resurrection is the true apotheosis or exaltation of that which is the most elevated and living part of the human being: the divine, eternal, and immortal Monad, which was found dead, hidden...

Undoubtably, this Monad is in itself the Verb, the luminous and spermatic fiat of the first instant, the Lord Shiva, the sublime spouse of our Divine Mother **Kundalini**, the **arch-hierophant** and **arch-magi**, the particular **super-individuality** of each one...

It is written with characters of fire in the book of life:

> Whosoever knows, the word gives power to; no one has uttered it, no one will utter it, except the one who has incarnated it...

When we have achieved perfection in mastery, with the resurrection of the secret master within each one of us... then we are washed of any blemish, and the original sin is radically eliminated...

I worked intensively in the **super-obscurity** of the silence and the august secret of the wise...

I submerged myself into the sacred mysteries of Minna, the dreadful darkness of one love whose twin brother is death...

I re-conquered my place in the first heaven of the Moon where Dante had his first vision of the blessed ones and ecstatically acknowledged Piccarda Donati and the Empress Constance...

I returned into my place in the second heaven of Mercury, the abode of those spirits who are active and righteous...

I returned into the third heaven of Venus, the region of the beloved spirits, where Dante occupied himself with Robert, the King of Naples...

I came back to the fourth heaven of the Sun, the abode of the wise spirits, the heaven where Dante mentions Saint Francis of Assisi...

I re-conquered the fifth heaven of Mars, region of the martyrs of faith, the heaven where Dante mentions **Cacciaguida** and his Majors, as well as ancient and new Florence...

I returned into the sixth heaven of Jupiter, the region of the wise and just princes...

I came back into the seventh heaven of Saturn, the exquisite abode of the contemplative spirits. Dante the Florentine emphatically mentions Peter Damian and denunciates the luxury of the prelates in this magnificent canto...

I came back into the eighth heaven or fixed stars, region of Uranus. Dante mentions in these immortal paragraphs the triumph of the intimate Christ and the coronation of the Divine Mother **Kundalini**, the paradise of the triumphant spirits...

I returned into the ninth heaven or crystalline region of Neptune. In this extraordinary canto, we find Dante's digressive diatribe against evil preachers...

Posteriorly, I had to appear before the "Third Logos," "**Shiva**," my real Being, my own "**super-individuality**," **Samael** himself...

Then, the Blessed One assumed a distinct figure, different from my own figure, as if he were a stranger. He had the aspect of a very respectable gentleman...

The Venerable One asked me to perform a chiromantic study on the lines of his hand...

The line of Saturn on his omnipotent dexterous hand looked very straight, astonishing, and marvellous to me. Nonetheless, one place of the line appeared to me as if it was interrupted, damaged, broken...

"Sir! You have had some struggles, some sufferings..."

"You are mistaken. I am a very lucky man, I always do very well…"

"Well… What happens is that I see a small damage on the line of Saturn…"

"Go, and measure that line well: at what age do you see that damage?"

"Sir!… Between the age of fifty three (53) and sixty-one (61) you had a hard epoch…"

"Ah!… that is in the beginning… but, then after, how do you see it? Eight years will pass very soon, and then… the triumph that is awaiting you…"

When concluding with this study, the Venerable One stood and said, "I like these Chiromantic studies, but only sporadically. My spouse (Devi **Kundalini**) also likes it, and eventually I will bring her. Ah!, but I have to pay you for your labor. Wait here for me, I will return to pay you…"

The Blessed One withdrew and I remained waiting for him… Far away, I saw two daughters of mine; they are presently adults, however they still looked little to me. I was a little bit concerned about them and so I called them…

It is indubitable that in that time of my present existence I was the mentioned fifty-three (53) years of age… I had seen on the hand of the Blessed One my own future…

Evidently, the already granted eight initiations had to be qualified, which is a very hard job, one year for each initiation…

This is what it is to vividly experience the whole book of the Patriarch **Job** in eight years, to pay the tithe to Neptune before the resurrection…

The book of **Job** is a complete representation of the ancient initiation and of the people who presided over the "magna ceremony."

The neophyte is shown in this book. He is deprived of everything, even of his own sons, and is afflicted by an impure sickness.

His wife anguishes him by mocking the trust which he puts in a God who treats him in such a way. His three friends Eliphas, Bildad, and Zophar torment him when they believably judge him to be impious and certainly worthy of that punishment...

Job then calls for a champion, a liberator, because he knows that this **Shiva** is eternal, and will redeem him from the slavery of the Earth (by means of the intimate resurrection) by restoring his flesh.

Job, while under divine permission, is tormented, deprived, sick under the cruel action of those malignant beings that Aristophanes called the "black birds." Saint Paul called them the "black powers of the air." The church called them "demons." Theosophy and Kabbalah calls them "elementaries," etc., etc., etc...

Nonetheless, **Job** is just, and he utters the theme of his own justification before such rigors of destiny, and finally conquers with the sacred IT of the crucifixion of his ulcerated flesh. Jehovah (the interior **Iod-Heve** of each person) permits the healer angels, or **jinns** (whose classic leader, as found in books such as the book of Tobias, is the Archangel Raphael), to approach him...

One night, after a cosmic festivity which was celebrated in my honour for having been well qualified in the first initiation, I was precisely instructed...

"You must pay the crime for having assassinated the God Mercury," was said unto me...

"Forgive me this **karma**..."

"This **karma** is unforgivable, and can only be paid by working with the Moon."

Then, I saw how in each labor the Moon would more and more approach the planet Mercury, until finally mixing with it...

My innermost real Being, the God Mercury, **Shiva**, my Monad, while approaching me, told me, "You must wear the boots of the God Mercury." He then put such boots on my feet...

The instant in which the great hierophant of the temple showed me a sports hall was sensational and extraordinary for me...

"Look!" he told me, "You converted the Temple of Mercury into a sports hall..."

Certainly, we all assassinated **Hiram** (the God Mercury) when we ate of the forbidden fruit in the Garden of Eden. That is why we were warned:

The day that thou eatest thereof thou shalt surely die.

Posteriorly, the path became frightfully difficult, and I had to suffer intensely...

It is obvious that the path of the razor's edge is absolutely sexual; you know this...

"My son! You have to patiently suffer the consequences of your errors," my Divine Mother **Kundalini** uttered...

On another night, my Mother, filled with pain, exclaimed with a great voice, "My son! You have exchanged me for other women, there, in the physical world..."

"That was the past, Mother of mine, now I do not exchange you for anyone..."

"You have exchanged me for other women."

"The past is the past, what matters is the present; I live from instant to instant, and I do wrong when arguing with you..."

"Past, present, or future, you are the same one..."

"You are right, Mother of mine..."

Then, how could I deny that I had converted the Temple of Mercury into a sport hall?

So, what happened next was that I went for a vacation to the Port of Acapulco on the Pacific Coast of Mexico. I had to be instructed on the stigmatizing of the astral body...

When I was out of the physical body, a monk, a hermit, tried to pierce the palms of my hands for the purpose of stigmatizing me. Divine rays jumped from my hands in those instants when this coenobite hammered the nail in order to pierce my hands...

In those moments, I prayed to my Father who is in secret, soliciting help from him. This prayer reached the Lord...

It is unquestionable that I had received such stigmas in the initiation, but in a symbolic way...

On the Mountain of Resurrection, I had to form, to make these stigmas in the forge of the Cyclops...

This anchorite conducted me to the Gnostic Church. **Shiva**, my divine Monad, walked nearby...

Inside the temple, near the baptismal font, I saw a religious **androgyne** dressed with a purpurin tunic...

"He is very strong and responds very well, but he needs to better accomplish the sacrament of the Church of '**Romae**,' (**amore**) **love**..." said the **mahatma** while addressing my Monad...

Since then, I comprehended the necessity of refining the creative energy even more. Thus, this is how I made the **Maithuna** a form of prayer...

The insertion of the vertical phallus inside the horizontal uterus makes a cross.

Unquestionably, the five Christic stigmas on the astral body are formed with the cross...

The resurrection is not possible without previously having formed the stigmas of the Beloved One on the astral body...

Thus, this is how I formed my stigmas. Thus, this is how the mystics of all times have formed theirs...

INRI... Ignis Natura Renovatur Integra. The fire renews nature constantly...

Ascension

The Third Mountain

The Mountain of the Ascension

Chapter XLIV
Conversing in Mexico

Monday, June 12th of the year 1972 (the 10th year of Aquarius):

"Well, 'Joaco' (familiar diminutive of **Joaquin**), today we are going to the center of the city..."

"What for, master? We already picked up the mail that was at the post office on Saturday. What could be there now?"

"I need to go downtown anyway. I have a cheque with me and I have to cash it. It is not a lot of money, but it will suffice me for eating. This way I will avoid spending the little money that I have collected for my rent... Moreover, I must put many letters in the mail. I like to have my correspondence up to date..."

Moments after, Joaquin Amortegui B., an international Gnostic missionary and great paladin of this tremendous crusade for the new age of Aquarius, and my insignificant person whose value is less than the ashes of a cigarette, directed ourselves towards the center of the city of Mexico...

It is not irrelevant to say, yet without much pomposity, that I like to drive my own vehicle. Thus, we were then very happily coasting in this "chariot" along the "paved road of Tlalpan," towards the Plaza of the Constitution (El Zocalo, as we the Mexican people say).

"This is the 'age of the automobile,' my dear 'Joaco.' However, I frankly and plainly have to confess to you that if I could choose to live either in a world with the technology of this one, or in one of the stone age (but completely spiritual, of course), I would unquestionably prefer the second one, even though instead of an automobile I would have to travel by foot or by donkey..."

"Oh! I also say likewise... I travel now for sacrifice, for the love of humanity, in order to teach the doctrine, but I would prefer to travel on donkeys and horses as in ancient times. I do not like the smog of these great cities, neither this mechanical life..."

Thus, while conversing, 'Joaco' and I, along that paved road which was rather a river of steel and cement, arrived at the Zocalo. We then turned and circled around it, passed beside the Metropolitan Cathedral, and entered onto Fifth of May Avenue looking for parking...

Moments later, we entered a great building...

"Do you want your car to be washed?"

"No! No! No! This is a time of much rain. What would I want that for?"

"Do you want your car to be waxed, sir?"

"No, boy, no. Let me take it first to a body-shop and paint it!..."

Conclusion: after having parked the car, we left the building and walked towards the post office.

While in the central post office, I had the pleasant surprise of receiving a copy of the sixth edition of *The Perfect Matrimony*. This book was sent from Cucuta, Colombia, South America, by the international Gnostic missionary Efrain Villegas Quintero...

I also received some letters, and I put in the mail the letters that I brought from home. Afterwards, we walked towards a money exchange company...

The money exchange teller, with his consciousness profoundly asleep, was abundantly busy in his labor.

I saw this teller with two microphones, one to his dexterous side and the other to his sinister side. Clearly, he was simultaneously attending to two telephones, and he even had the luxury of conversing at intervals with another client who was at the counter of this business...

Obviously, this poor intellectual humanoid of a subjective psyche was not only identified with everything, moreover he was tremendously fascinated... and sleeping a great deal.

This rational homunculi was talking about value, current prices, money, gold, enormous additions, cheques, wealth, etc., etc., etc...

Fortunately, it was not necessary to wait for a long time, his secretary diligently attended me...

Some instants after, we walked out of that place with some money in my pocket. It was not too much, but enough for a few more days of food...

So, walking again on the famous Fifth of May Avenue, I felt the necessity of inviting "Joaco" to drink a small refreshment.

"Joaco" is a person who eats scantily, but for my own sake he did not decline the invitation.

Indubitably, we found a beautiful place — I am referring to Café Paris.

An elegant waitress approached us, "What are you going to have, sirs?"

"Miss," I said, "bring me a strawberry shake and a piece of cheesecake..."

"I only want a papaya shake," said 'Joaco.'

Having heard the words of us gentlemen, the lady withdrew, to re-appear moments after with the mentioned dishes...

While very slowly tasting this delicious refreshment and extracting from these foods their spiritual element, "Joaco" and I established the following dialogue:

"I tell you, 'Joaco' that I am approaching the end of my book entitled *The Three Mountains*. Certainly, I am lacking only an introduction for the Third Mountain, three chapters from the ascension, and the conclusion..."

"Then you are already finalizing that work."

"Yes, **Joaco**, yes, yes!... What is interesting about all of this is that now I have to appeal to Lemuria..."

"What? To Lemuria? Why?"

"It is clear that in this reincarnation I have only reached the summit of the Second Mountain... Nonetheless, I passed through 'the Three Mountains' on that archaic continent '**Mu**' or Lemuria, which in foregone times was situated in the vast Pacific Ocean... Then, unquestionably, I achieved liberation, but I renounced all happiness and remained in this valley of tears in order to help humanity... It is clear that the possession of the '**Elixir of Longevity**' granted me the conservation of that Lemurian body for millions of years...

"Therefore, my dear 'Joaco,' I tell you that I was an eye-witness to all of those volcanic catastrophes which ended the continent 'Mu.'

"It is evident that through more than ten thousand years of incessant earthquakes and seaquakes, that ancient land was submerging itself within the boisterous waters of the Pacific Ocean...

"The fact is that while the continent 'Mu' was slowly submerging within the rough waves of the boisterous ocean, the Atlantean continent, that Atlantis of Plato, was gradually emerging from within the profound waters of the ocean...

"Unquestionably, I also lived with my Lemurian body in 'the country with the hills of clay.' I knew its powerful civilizations, much superior to this present civilization. I also saw Atlantis submerging within the furious waves of the ocean that carries its name..."

> "In the year 6 of **Kan**, the 11 Muluc, in the Month Zrc, terrible earthquakes occurred which continued without interruption until the 13 Chuen. The country of 'the hills of clay,' the Atlantean land, was sacrificed. This land disappeared after two commotions during the night, after being constantly shaken by the subterranean fires, which made the land sink and re-appear various times and in diverse places. Finally the surface gave in and ten countries had split and disappeared. 64 million of its inhabitants sank 8,000 years before this book was written."

"This is textually quoted from a Mayan manuscript. This is part of the famous collection of Le Plongeon, the manuscripts of Troano. This manuscript can be seen in the British Museum.

"Before the falling of the star '**Baal**' on the place where only sea and sky now exist, before the seven cities with their doors of gold and transparent temples were shaken, trembling like the leaves of a tree moved by a storm, I departed from there, towards the central plateau of Asia, into that place where Tibet is located today...

"The Atlantean survivors were mixed with the Nordics in that zone of the Earth. Thus, this is how the first subrace of our present Aryan Race was formed...

"The Savior-guide of the elected Atlanteans, the one who took them out of the country of 'the hills of clay,' was the Biblical Noah, the Manu Vaivasvatha, the founder of the Aryan Race...

"I still remember, far away in time and space, those cosmic festivities which were celebrated then in our monastery...

"I am emphatically referring to the 'Sacred Order of Tibet,' an old esoteric institution...

"It is indubitable that this ancient order has two-hundred-and-one (201) members. The major rank is formed by seventy-two (72) Brahmans...

"Unquestionably, such a meritorious mystical organization conserves the treasure of **Aryabarta Ashram**...

"In those times, I was always welcomed in that place with much veneration. While living in a completely Aryan world, I was exotic with that Lemurian body...

"Unfortunately, 'the Devil puts his tail everywhere,' and disgracefully, something unusual happened...

"I returned into my ancient adventures. I committed again the same crime—I fell in love with the seductress Eve of Hebraic mythology, and once again swallowed the 'forbidden fruit.'

"Results: the great law took away that a precious vehicle from me, and I remained, from life to life, as a wandering Jew upon the face of the Earth..."

"Now, really, oh master! I feel smaller than an ant; as usual, I do not comprehend. If you dissolved the **ego**, the myself, then who was the tempter? In which way did you fall?..."

"Oh Joaco... In the name of truth I want you to know that when the "I" is dissolved, the **mind** remains instead... Indubitably, this was the 'cause causorum' of my fall..."

"This is something unusual. I do not understand..."

"Passional matters—I fell in love. I committed the same error as the Count Zanoni, that is all...

"Such a maiden of mysterious enchantments was forbidden for me. However, I have to say that I fell, surrendering at the feet of this delectable female...

"Posteriorly, my Divine Mother **Kundalini** took me into the interior of a cavern, in the profundity of the mountain. Then I saw rain (tears), torrents of turbid water (bitterness), and mud (misery), etc., etc., etc...

"'Behold, the future which awaits for you!' my Mother exclaimed. My supplications were useless; I was not worthy of forgiveness. Again, I was committing the same crime. Finally, I saw her enclosing herself inside the Muladhara chakra, in the coccygeal bone. Then, woe to me! Woe! Woe!...

"I committed the very same error which on the archaic continent 'Mu' originated the angelical downfall...

"It is unquestionable that before entering into the Lemurian mysteries I had already committed the same crime...

"The allegory of the Biblical Adam, which is considered separated from the '**Tree of Life**,' clearly signifies that the Lemurian race (who were already separated into opposite sexes) abused sexuality and sank into the region of animality and bestiality...

"The **Zohar** teaches that **Matromethah** (**Shekinah**, symbolically the wife of **Metatron**) is the path towards the great Tree of Life, the powerful tree. **Shekinah** is the divine grace.

"There is no doubt that this marvellous tree reaches the celestial valley and is found hidden within the Three Mountains.

"This tree ascends towards the heights of these 'Three Mountains.' Afterwards, it descends again towards the bottom.

"The Tree of the Knowledge of Good and Evil grows from the roots of the Tree of Life.

"The Dhyani Bodhisattvas who were reincarnated in Lemurian bodies reproduced themselves by means of the power of **Kriya-shakti** (the power of **yoga** and will).

"The attributes of **Shiva** are: the black **lingam** inserted into the **yoni**.

"Unquestionably, the **arch-hierophant** and **arch-magi** never spills the cup of **Hermes**.

"When the Dhyanis—among them I, myself, am one—committed the crime of spilling that flexible, malleable liquid glass of alchemy, then they withdrew from their divine Monad (they killed the God Mercury), they fell into animal generation..."

"I am astonished."

"Why, Joaco? Was I perhaps the first one who fell or the last one?

"H. P. Blavatsky states in her *Secret Doctrine* that **Samael** was the first one who fell, but this is symbolic...

"It is clear that I am the **Dhyani Bodhisattva** of the fifth of the seven. Therefore, for that cause it is stated that **Samael** was the first one who fell...

"Fortunately, I am already standing, in spite of having committed the very same crime again...

"How different was the case of many other Dhyanis who fell into animal generation...

"Let us remember **Moloch**, the great homicidal; now he is frightfully devoluting in the infernal worlds...

"Let us remember **Andrameleck** and his brother **Asmodeus**. These are two **Thrones** thrown headlong into the Averno..."

"I believed that after the liberation, any downfall would be impossible..."

"You are mistaken, my dear 'Joaco.' The danger of falling is always present in the cosmos...

"Any danger of falling disappears only when entering into the unmanifested 'Sat,' the Abstract, Absolute Space."

When concluding our conversation at the table, we called the lady who humbly attended the table of the gentlemen...

"Miss, the bill?..."

"Yes, sirs... it is..."

"Here it is... and also your tip..."

We left very quietly from this sumptuous place and headed towards the "chariot..."

Wandering again under the sunlight on that famous Fifth of May Avenue, I had the impulse of saying: "What is troublesome after the fall, oh 'Joaco,' is the abominable resurrection of the '**animal ego**.'

"Unquestionably, the '**myself**' resurrects like the phoenix bird from within its own ashes...

"Now, profoundly and in an integral way, you will comprehend the intrinsic reason why in all religious theogonies, the idea of fallen angels converted into demons is emphasized..."

"Ah! Yes!...This is very clear..."

Moments after, we were rapidly coasting on the 'paved road of Tlalpan,' returning home... "Since I had risen, had descended, and have returned to rise again, it is obvious that I possess vast experience in these questions of an esoteric type..."

"Oh, master! You have very special experiences in these matters..."

Certainly, beloved reader, I am nothing but a miserable slug from the mud of the earth, a nobody who has no value. However, since I have travelled the path, I can describe it with complete clarity, and this is not a crime...

We conclude this present chapter with the phrase of **Goethe**:

> "Every theory is grey, and only the tree of the golden fruits of life is green."

Chapter XLV
The Tenth Labor of Heracles

The tenth labor of Heracles, the great solar hero, was the conquering of the herd of Geryon. Heracles, after having confronted Geryon's guardian dog Orthus and the cowherd Eurytion, confronts Geryon and kills him.

This unusual event had as its scenario the island Erythea ("the red"), far away in the ocean. Therefore, it seems that it is referring to an island of the Atlantic Ocean that was inhabited by gigantic beings. They were clearly represented by the same three-headed monster Geryon, who perished under the arrows of Heracles immediately after the defeat of his cowherd and dog by the war club of Heracles...

Comparative mythology correlates the bicipite dog Orthus, brother of Cerberus, with Vritra, the Vedic genie of the tempest.

In his journey, Heracles passed from Europe into Africa, in order to then pass through the ocean on the "golden bowl" (on the sacred cup). He intelligently utilized it in his nocturnal journey...

This signifies that in the mean time, the splendorous Sun had to wait for Heracles until his return. Therefore, the Sun holds itself in its solstice for the good of the hero...

Indubitably, this god-man travels in a journey of infinite adventures in order to return by way of old Europe, carrying the herd that he acquired in the cup or Holy Grail...

The legend of the centuries then states that the solar hero built up the two columns "J" and "B" of occult Masonry upon the straits of Gibraltar, probably in gratitude to the Dioscuri, who helped him to become victorious in this task...

The cows were sacrificed to Juno on his return to Mycenae, in order to pacify his aggravation for his brother Eurystheus.

When dealing with archaic mysteries, it is not irrelevant to say that they were always celebrated in august seigniorial temples...

When I passed through the threshold of that "**Mu**" or **Lemurian** temple where in a foretime I was instructed in the mysteries of the ascension of the Lord, with infinite humbleness I requested the hierophant for some services, which were granted unto me...

It is indubitable—this is known by any initiate—that every exaltation is always preceded by a frightful and terrible humiliation...

Clearly, we have emphatically asseverated that any ascension is preceded by a descent...

The tenth labor of Heracles, the solar hero of esotericism, is performed in the infernal worlds of the planet Pluto...

Painful sentiments ripped my soul when I saw myself submitted to the torture of detachment...

Those **ladies** of august times, who were attached to me by the law of **karma**, with their hearts "broken into pieces," were awaiting me in the Averno...

All of those dangerously beautiful temptresses felt that they had complete authority over me...

Those terrible, delectable females had been, for good or for evil, my wives in anterior reincarnations, as a natural consequence of the great rebellion and the angelic downfall...

The dog Orthus and cowherd Eurytion, living symbols of animal passions, were inclemently besieging me with outrageous fieriness. The temptations began to multiply until the infinite...

However, based on **Thelema** (willpower) and deepest comprehension, I defeated the lord of time, the tricipite Geryon, with the help of my Divine Mother **Kundalini**...

Thus, it is indubitable that when I took possession of the flock, I then became an authentic shepherd of sheep, and not of cows as is veiledly stated...

It is convenient for the good of the great cause that we straightaway study some verses from chapter ten of John:

> Verily, verily I say unto you, He that entereth not by the
> door [**sex**] into the sheep-fold, but climbeth up some other
> way, [by preaching different doctrines that have nothing

to do with White Sexual Magic] the same is a thief and a
robber [steals the sheep and takes them into the abyss.]

We departed from Eden through the door of sex. We can return into Eden only through the mentioned door. Eden is sex itself.

But he that entereth in by the door is the shepherd of the sheep.

To him the porter opened; and the sheep hear
his voice: and he calleth his own sheep by name
[with the Innermost Word], and leadeth them out
[leadeth them on the path of the razor's edge.]

And when he putteth forth his own sheep, he
goeth before them, and the sheep follow him:
for they know his voice [his Word].

And a stranger will they not follow, but will flee
from him: for they know not the voice of strangers
[the false shepherds do not possess the Word.]

This parable spake Jesus [whose name's meaning is "Savior"]
unto them: but they understood not what things they were
which he spake unto them. [It is evident that the spirit
which vivifies is always behind the letter which kills.]

Then said Jesus [the intimate Savior] unto them again,
Verily, verily, I say unto you, I am the door of the sheep
[The power is not in the brain, neither is it in any
other place of the body, but in **sex**.*]* - John 10:1-7

We asseverate with other words the following: the creative power of the Logos is found exclusively in **sex**.

Now, it is easy to comprehend why **He** is the **door** of the sheep. To search for evasions is the equivalent of fleeing from the **door** of **Eden**...

All that ever came before me [since they were not initiates
in the sexual mysteries] are thieves and robbers:

I am the door: by me if any man enter in, he shall be saved,
[he will not fall into the abyss of perdition] and shall go in
and out, and find pasture [rich spiritual food]. - John 10:8-9

Christ could not do anything without the sexual serpent. Therefore, this is the reason why the Second Logos, the Lord of Perfection, the intimate **Logoi** of each one, descends from his elevated sphere and becomes Son of the Divine Mother **Kundalini**, the igneous serpent of our magical powers... (by the grace and labor of the Holy Spirit).

The Sethians adored the great light, and said that the Sun forms a nest within us with its emanations, and this constitutes the serpent.

It is clear that this Gnostic sect also had, as a sacred object, a chalice [a **yoni**, the Holy Grail], from where they drank of the semen of Benjamin. This was only a mixture of wine and water...

Indubitably, the sacred symbol of the sexual serpent was never absent upon the altar of the Gnostic Nazarenes...

The force, the power which accompanied Moses, was the serpent upon the staff, which was later turned into the staff itself.

Certainly, this serpent was the one that spoke to the other serpents, and the tempting serpent of Eve...

In the *Song of Homer to Demeter* (found in a Russian library), we can see that everything revolves around a great transcendental, **physiological, cosmic deed.**

> *I am the good shepherd: the good shepherd [that one who already reached that Christic Esoteric Degree] giveth his life for the sheep.*

> *But he that is an hireling [the Tantric esotericist who still has not achieved Christification], and not the shepherd, whose own the sheep are not, seeth the wolf coming, and leaveth the sheep, and fleeth: and the wolf catcheth them, and scattereth the sheep.*

> *And other sheep I have, which are not of this fold: [they are within other schools], them also I must bring, and they shall hear my voice; and there shall be one fold, and one shepherd.*

Therefore doth my Father love me, because I lay down my life, that I might take it again [the intimate Christ crystallizes inside of us and redeems us when we are worthy].

No man taketh it from me, but I lay it down of myself [as if saying: I crystallize in my human person when I want]. I have power to lay it down, and I have power to take it again. This commandment have I received of my Father. - John 10:11-8

After these Christic, esoteric commentaries, it is indispensable to continue with the present chapter...

Truly, how simple, what unfalsified primeval beauty these Platonic narratives have, which relate to the archaic gods and goddesses, divine beings from an ancient Lemurian past. These were authentic tantric shepherds from the sexual Eden... Sublime creatures, who build Cyclopean cities, instruct the people, endowe them with an unsurpassed legislation, and reward their heroism.

To perform within oneself the "Hyperborean mystery," the "Grail mystery," is urgent, when we long to convert ourselves into authentic prophets, into genuine, Christified shepherds...

We need "to pass over the Red Sea," to pass through the tempestuous ocean of life, to pass to the other shore, on the cup of gold, on the sacred cup which Helios, the sacred Absolute Sun lent unto us...

I had to raise up the columns when I concluded the esoteric labors within the infernos of Pluto...

"Plus ultra," "**Adam Kadmon**," "celestial man," such are the mystical significances which are attributed to the two columns of Heracles...

That Kosmic-Human event was preceded by the disincarnation of my priestess-wife **Litelantes**...

Unquestionably, the unique karmic bond that remained for me in this painful valley of **Samsara** was she, herself...

Certainly, I saw her withdraw from her discarded Lemurian vehicle, and dressed in a rigorous, mourning black...

Indubitably, **Adam-Eve** is the most secret significance of the two columns of Heracles...

Reconciliation with the divine becomes urgent, undeferable, unpostponable; you know this...

To raise up the columns is reconciliation, the return of the original couple, the return into Eden...

We need to return to the original point of departure, to return to the first love. This is inarguable, irrefutable, and indisputable...

I had to vividly experience the crude reality of this with "Paradisiacal, Edenic weddings..."

Then I received a great lady initiate for a spouse. I am emphatically referring to the other half of the orange, to my particular primeval Eve. Thus, this is how I rose up the two columns of Heracles...

Afterwards, joyfully, I was at the middle of the table of the feast accompanied by my new spouse and many high priests...

Then, **Litelantes** passed through the threshold of the royal hall. She came disincarnated, in order to witness the festivity...

Thus... Oh gods! This is how I re-established the Second Logos, the Cosmic Christ, within the sanctuary of my soul...

Chapter XLVI
The Eleventh Achievement of Heracles

The eleventh achievement of Heracles, the solar hero, took place in the transatlantic dominion, which consisted of taking possession of the golden apples of the Garden of the Hesperides—the nymph daughters of Hesperus who are a vivid representation of the planet Venus, the delectable star of love...

Since he did not know the way to the garden, first of all he needed to seize Nereus, he who knows everything. Then, in Africa, in hand to hand combat, he had to confront the frightful giant Antaeus, son of Poseidon...

It is customary that this journey be also related with the liberation of **Prometheus-Lucifer** and the killing of the eagle that tormented him. It is also related with the temporary substitution of the famous **Atlas** with Heracles. Heracles carried the world upon his titanic back, instead of **Atlas**, in order to get his help...

Finally, the symbolic golden apples are delivered to Heracles by the Hesperides themselves, for he previously killed the dragon that guarded them...

Evidently, this achievement has a close relation with the Biblical story of the fruits of the Tree of the Science of Good and Evil in the Edenic garden. However, in this Garden of Eden the dragon is substituted by a serpent, who entices the taking and the eating of those marvellous fruits. Afterwards, Heracles delivers these fruits to Athena, the goddess of wisdom, his divine protector...

Before the ascension to the Father (the First Logos), the intrepid descent into the old Tartarus of the eleventh planet of our solar system became urgent, undeferable, unpostponable.

A craggy, broken and uneven descending path fatally conducted me to the frightful darkness of the city of **Dis**...

My "Nereus," or better if said my "**guruji, master, or guide**," patiently taught me all the dangers...

Certainly, it was in those horrifying abysses of pain within that planet that is beyond the orbit of Pluto where I found **Antaeus**. This immense giant was even more frightful than the disproportionate Briareus...

Dante the Florentine exclaimed in his *Divine Comedy:*

> "O you, who lived within the famous valley (where Scipio became the heir of glory when Hannibal retreated with his men), who took a thousand lions as your prey—and had you been together with your brothers in their high war, it seems some still believe the sons of earth would have become the victors—do set us down below, where cold shuts in Cocytus, and do not disdain that task.

> "Don't send us on to Tityus of Typhon; this man can give you what is longed for here; therefore bend down and do not curl your lip.

> "He still can bring you fame within the world, for he's alive and still expects long life, unless grace summon him before his time."

> So said my master; and in haste Antaeus stretched out his hands, whose massive grip had once been felt by Heracles, and grasped my guide.

> And Virgil, when he felt himself caught up, called out to me: "Come here, so I can hold you," then made one bundle of himself and me.

> Just as the Garisenda seems when seen beneath the leaning side, when clouds run past and it hangs down as if about to crash, so did **Antaeus** seem to me as I watched him bend over me—a moment when I'd have preferred to take some other road.

> But gently—on the deep that swallows up both Lucifer and Judas—he placed us; nor did he, so bent over, stay there long, but, like a mast above a ship, he rose. (This is textual from *The Divine Comedy, Canto XXXI lines 115-145).*

Antaeus: An allegorical, magical personage who is a Titan representing the "tenebrous, abysmal hordes..."

After having fought very bloody battles against the demons of the city of **Dis**, **Lucifer-Prometheus** had to be liberated...

I saw the steely door of the horrifying dungeon opening. The guardian yielded him the way...

Terrible scenes from this obscure abode, unusual and unsuspected cases—this is what "the dwellers of the Earth" ignore...

Lucifer is the guardian of the door, who alone is entrusted with the keys of the sanctuary that no one may enter therein, save the anointed ones having the secret of Hermes...

Christus-Lucifer of the Gnostics is the god of wisdom who has distinct names. He is the god of our planet Earth who is without a shadow of evilness, since he is one with the Platonic Logos...

Prometheus-Lucifer is the minister of the **Solar Logos** and the resplendent lord of the seven mansions of **Hades**...

Certainly, **Lucifer** is the spirit of humanity's spiritual illumination and of the liberty of election, and metaphysically the torch of humanity. He is the **Logos** in his superior aspect and the adversary in his inferior aspect, the divine and chained **Prometheus**, the centrifuge and active energy of the universe, fire, light, struggle, effort, consciousness, liberty, independence, etc., etc., etc.

Lucifer is he who bears the sword and the scale of cosmic justice, because to him is undoubtedly committed the norm of weight and measure and number.

Lucifer is the reflection of the intimate **Logoi** within each one of us. He is the shadow of the Lord projected in the depth of our Being...

In the instants when I write these lines, something unusual comes into my memory...

One given night (it does not matter which), I found this frightful personage inside a beautiful room...

In an imposing manner, "**Prometheus-Lucifer**" was sustaining himself on bestial legs instead of human feet, while staring at me threateningly... Two frightful horns were dreadfully displayed on his sinister forehead. However, he was dressed as an elegant gentleman...

Approaching him with serenity, I patted him on the shoulders and opportunely said, "You do not frighten me, I

PROMETHEUS / LUCIFER

Prometheus: "I whom you see am
Prometheus, who gave fire to mankind."

Io: "O you who have shown yourself a common
benefactor of mankind, wretched Prometheus,
why do you suffer so?"

- Aeschylus, Prometheus Bound 612

know you very well; you have not defeated me, I am victorious..."

This colossus withdrew and I, while seated on a soft and perfumed bed of mahogany, waited for awhile ...

Posteriorly, a dangerous feminine beauty entered the room. She lay down naked upon the bed...

Almost dismayed with lust, this beauty wrapped me within her indecent arms in order to invite me to the pleasures of the flesh...

While laying down next to this beauty, I showed my powers to the devil: I dominated myself...

Afterwards, I stood up from the bed of pleasures. Such a feminine beauty, almost dead with lubricity, uselessly contemplated me while feeling disappointed...

Following, a resplendent child entered into the room, a radiant creature, terrifically divine...

The sublime infant, wealthily attired with a beautiful sacerdotal tunic of a very special black color, passed through the exotic precinct...

I immediately recognized him. I approached him very quietly and told him, "It is useless for you to continue disguising yourself, I always recognize you: Oh Lucifer!... You can never defeat me..."

Then, that sublime creature, terror of the ignorant, smiled with infinite sweetness...

Unquestionably, he is the "Divine Daemon" of Socrates, our special coach in the psychological gymnasium of life...

Just is Lucifer's freedom after his hard labor. Then, the **Logos** swallows him, absorbs him...

Until here we have this narrative. Let us now continue with the transcendental theme of this chapter...

Certainly, my new priestess in the Mountain of the Ascension became extraordinary...

Obviously, my intimate process was accelerated, and as a consequence I achieved taking possession of the golden apples of the Garden of the Hesperides...

The Venusian nymphs, exquisitely delectable, fell at my feet—they could not defeat me...

When concluding the magical labors within this Avernus, I victoriously ascended to the Father...

It is obvious that this transcendental event in no way could pass unnoticed...

Such a cosmic event was then celebrated with infinite happiness in the **sancta**...

Upon a splendid throne, seated before the august confraternity, I felt myself completely transformed...

In those unutterable moments, "the Elder of Days," "my Father who is in secret," "the Goodness of Goodness," "the Occult of the Occult," "the Mercy of Mercies," "**Kether** of the **Hebraic Kabbalah**," shone inside of me. He definitively crystallized in the whole presence of my Being...

The brothers and sisters of the White Universal Fraternity, with infinite veneration, contemplated me in those instants... My countenance assumed the aspect of an elder...

Indubitably, I had achieved the crystallization of the three primary forces of the universe within the diverse parts of my Being...

Chapter XLVII

The Twelfth Labor of Heracles

Certainly, the twelfth labor of Heracles, the solar hero, was imposed by his brother, in other words, by his resplendent "divine prototype" within the sacred Absolute Sun... Indubitably, that work consisted of withdrawing the tricipite dog Cerberus from the plutonic dominions that it guarded...

Having entered into the subterranean abode of the dead, Heracles tried first to propitiate the very Aidoneo (Hades) himself, who then permitted him to seize the dog on the condition that he had to achieve the capturing of it without any weapon. He achieved it by firstly grasping the dog by its dragon tail then after by its neck, until almost choking it.

Heracles was guided by Hermes on his return. Then after, when Cerberus was shown in Mycenae, he released the dog in order for the dog to return to its residence...

Unquestionably, our resplendent solar system of **Ors** has twelve planets, which reminds us of the twelve saviors... Obviously, it is evident that the final labor of Heracles has to always be performed in the twelfth planet of the solar family...

We can and must relate the last of his zodiacal achievements with Scorpio, whose constellation is the most appropriate for representing the task of seizing the three-headed dog Cerberus from the zealous subterranean world (the kingdom of shadows, where the truth disguises itself with darkness)...

Naturally, Heracles can only achieve this task with the consent of Hades or Pluto and with the simultaneous help of Hermes and Minerva...(Sex Yoga and wisdom).

I, with infinite veneration, passed through the threshold of the temple. I was longing for the final liberation...

The spermatic waters within the sacred pool were gloriously resplendent inside the fortress-walls of the priests' patio...

The representant initiatic lake of the ancient mysteries, eternal scenario of any temple, could never be missing from there...

Unquestionably, what I then asked within this Lemurian **sancta** was granted unto me... My labor was initiated with the descent into the Tartarus of that twelfth planet of our solar system...

Three delectable females, dangerously beautiful, appealed in vain with their irresistible enchantments...

These provocative female devils tried the impossible in order to make me fall, but I knew how to dominate myself...

The zodiacal sign of Scorpio untied all of its ardent passion in my creative organs. However, I won all the battles against myself...

"The guide dog" (the sexual instinct) always conduces the knight along the narrow path that leads from darkness to light, from death to immortality...

The dog pulls the leash of his lord in order to take him through the steep path until the end. Posteriorly, the dog has to rest; then, the "great renunciation" comes.

The ineludible, supreme detachment from all material things and the radical elimination of the desire for existance is in harmonious rhythmic concordance with this cosmic-sexual event...

The transcendental idea of the breath of darkness moving itself upon the sleeping waters of life, that is to say, the primeval matter with the latent Spirit within it, invites us to reflect...

"The water" (**the ens seminis**) executes the same important play in all cosmogonies. It is the base and origin of the material existence, and the foundation of all authentic "**Realizations of the Innermost Self.**"

Nonetheless, it is urgent, undeferable, and unpostponable to never ignore that within the primeval abyss, within the depth of the waters, many dangerous beasts abide...

If the divine Titans of the old continent "**Mu**," those angels who fell into animal generation, had not have forgotten this tremendous truth, if they had kept themselves alert and vigilant as watchmen in an epoch of war, they would still be in a paradisiacal state...

To completely seize the tricipite dog without any weapon factually signifies absolute control of sexuality...

When I seized that dog, I victoriously ascended from the depth of the horrifying precipice...

Then, the Being of my Being incarnated within me. The Being of my Being is the one who is beyond "**Brahma, Vishnu,** and **Shiva**..." This Being is the divine, solar Absolute Prototype.

I joyfully entered inside a small sanctuary of the sacred Absolute Sun when this mystic event came to pass...

Since that extraordinary instant, I could feed myself with the fruits of the "Tree of Life" beyond good and evil...

I had returned to the original point of departure. Unquestionably, I had came back into my dwelling...

Each one of us has in this radiant sphere of light and happiness his own Divine Prototype...

The sacred individuals who inhabited the central sun prepare themselves in order to enter into the "**Abstract Absolute Space**." This is always happening at the end of the **mahamanvantara** (cosmic day).

Each universe of the infinite space possesses its own central sun, and the addition of such spiritual suns constitutes the "**Protocosmos**."

The emanation of our "omni-merciful and sacred Solar Absolute" is that which H. P. Blavatsky denominates "the Great Breath which is profoundly unknown to itself..."

Obviously, this active and omnipresent principle, even when participating in the creation of the worlds, does not fuse itself within them. This principle remains independent, omni-present, and omni-penetrating...

It becomes easy to comprehend that the emanation of the "Solar Absolute" unfolds itself into the "three primary forces"—**Brahma**, **Vishnu**, **Shiva**—with the evident purpose of creating and creating anew...

When any cosmic manifestation concludes, then the three original forces are integrated in order to mix or fuse themselves with the incessant Breath profoundly unknown to itself...

That which happens in the macrocosm is repeated in the microcosmic man (human being). Such was so in my particular case...

Thus, this is how I could return into the bosom of the sacred Solar Absolute. However, I continued living for million of years with the Lemurian physical body... I converted myself into another stone of "the Guardian Wall."

This wall is formed by the masters of compassion, those masters who renounce all happiness for the love of humanity...

Inverencial peace,
Samael Aun Weor

Glossary

Absolute: Abstract space; that which is without attributes or limitations. The Absolute has three aspects: the Ain, the Ain Soph, and the Ain Soph Aur.

"The Absolute is the Being of all Beings. The Absolute is that which Is, which always has Been, and which always will Be. The Absolute is expressed as Absolute Abstract Movement and Repose. The Absolute is the cause of Spirit and of Matter, but It is neither Spirit nor Matter. The Absolute is beyond the mind; the mind cannot understand It. Therefore, we have to intuitively understand Its nature." - Samael Aun Weor, *Tarot and Kabbalah*

"In the Absolute we go beyond karma and the gods, beyond the law. The mind and the individual consciousness are only good for mortifying our lives. In the Absolute we do not have an individual mind or individual consciousness; there, we are the unconditioned, free and absolutely happy Being. The Absolute is life free in its movement, without conditions, limitless, without the mortifying fear of the law, life beyond spirit and matter, beyond karma and suffering, beyond thought, word and action, beyond silence and sound, beyond forms." - Samael Aun Weor, *The Major Mysteries*

Adam Kadmon: (Hebrew) This term Adam Kadmon has many applications, including the first manifestation of the Abstract Space; The Archetypal Man; Humanity; The Heavenly Man, not fallen into sin.

"The body of Adam Kadmon is formed by the Sephiroth." - Samael Aun Weor, Tarot and Kabbalah

Adhyatmic: (Sanskrit) Spiritual.

Aditi: (Sanskrit) The Vedic name for Mulaprakriti, the abstract aspect of Parabrahman, though both are unmanifested and unknowable. In the Vedas, Aditi is the indivisible conscious-force and ananda of the Supreme; the Mother; the infinite Mother of the gods; supreme Nature or infinite Consciousness.

Adytum: (Greek) The Holy of Holies of any temple. A name for the secret and sacred precincts or the inner chamber, into which no profane could enter; corresponds to the sanctuary of the altars of the Christian churches.

Agathodaemon: (Greek) The beneficient, good Spirit as contrasted with the bad one, Kakodaemon. The Ophites called Agathodaemon the Logos and divine wisdom, which in the Bacchanalian mysteries was represented by a serpent erect on a pole.

Akashic Records: Permanent impressions held in nature of everything that has ever occurred, i.e. "the memory of nature." By means of awakening consciousness, it is possible to access past, present, and future events within these records.

"The Akasha is a subtle agent that penetrates and permeates the whole space. All the events of the Earth and its races, the life of Jesus etc., are depicted as an eternal and living film within the Akasha. [...] We already

know that all movement is relative and that there is only one constant. This one is the velocity of light. Light travels at a certain constant velocity. With their lenses astronomers perceive stars that have already ceased to exist. What they see and even photograph of these stars is the memory, the Akasha. Many of these stars are so distant, that the light coming from them could have begun its journey before the formation of the world. This slowness of light, this constant, may in reality make the invention of certain special instruments with which the past can be seen possible. None of this is impossible. Thus, with a very special telescope, with a very special radio-television apparatus, it is possible to capture sounds and light, events and happenings that have occurred on our Earth since the formation of the world. [...] The devotee will be able to study the Akashic Records of Nature with the Astral Body and know all past, present and future events."
- Samael Aun Weor, *The Perfect Matrimony*

Alchemy: Al (as a connotation of the Arabic word Allah: al-, the + ilah, God) means "The God." Also Al (Hebrew) for "highest" or El "God." Chem or Khem is from kimia which means "to fuse or cast a metal." Also from Khem, the ancient name of Egypt. The synthesis is Al-Kimia: "to fuse with the highest" or "to fuse with God." Alchemy is one of the oldest sciences in the world, and is the method to transmute our inner impurity into purity. It is also known in the East as Tantra.

Ambrosia: In Greek mythology, ambrosia is food and drink with which the Olympian gods preserved their immortality; a symbol of sexual energy. Also known in India as Soma and in the Judeo-Christian scriptures as manna.

Amadis of Gaul: A famous prose romance of chivalry from the 13th or 14th century. It was immensely popular in France and Spain until superseded by Don Quixote, and it was, in fact, considered a sign of elegance to be acquainted with its code of honor and knightly perfection. The story became the subject of a lyric tragedy by Philippe Quinault (1684), with music by Lully, and it inspired the opera Amadigi (1715) by Handel.

Anagarika: (Sanskrit) Literally, "homeless one." The term is commonly applied to Buddhist monks, but Samael is referring to the use of this name among Black Magicians.

Anaxagoras: c. 500 – 428 B.C., a Greek philosopher. He is credited with having moved the seat of philosophy to Athens. He may have been the teacher of Socrates, Euripedes, Archelaus and many other distinguished Athenians. He was a highly educated astronomer and was the first to teach openly what Pythagoras taught secretly, namely the movement of the planets, the eclipses of the sun and moon, etc. His belief that the sun was a glowing mass and that the moon was made of earth that reflected the sun's rays resulted in a charge of atheism and blasphemy, forcing him to flee to Lampsacus, where he died. He taught the theory of the Chaos, on the principle that "nothing comes from nothing," and he rejected Empedocles' four elements (earth, air, fire, and water) as the original of matter. Anaxagoras suggested an infinity of particles, or "seeds" (atoms), each unique in its qualities. He said that all natural objects are composed of particles having all sorts of qualities; a preponderance of similar though not identical particles creates the difference between wood and stone. Anaxagoras' universe, before separation, was an infinite, undifferentiated mass. The formation of the world was due to a rotary motion produced in this mass by an all-pervading mind (nous). This led to the separating out of the "seeds" and the formation of things. Although Anaxagoras was the first to give mind a place in the universe, he was criticized by both Plato and Aristotle for only conceiving of it as a mechanical cause rather than the originator of order. Moreover, he stated that he was thoroughly convinced that the real existence of things, as perceived by our senses, could not be proven.

Archon: (Greek) In profane language, "rulers." In esotericism, "primordial planetary spirits."

Artemis: An Olympian goddess in Greek religion and mythology, daughter of Zeus and Leto and twin sister of Apollo. Artemis' early worship, especially at Ephesus, identified her as an earth goddess, similar to Astarte. In Classical Greek literature she was portrayed as a deliberate and unshakable virgin, a symbol of having perfect chastity; she punished anyone who attempted to violate this state and required all of her attendants to maintain their chastity as well. She defended chastity among men and women. In later legend, however, she was primarily a virgin huntress, goddess of wildlife and patroness of hunters. As the complement to Apollo, she was often considered a moon goddess and as such was identified with Selene and Hecate; the confusion with Hecate arose because Artemis was considered the bringer of death to women, while her twin brother Apollo brought death to men. In ancient Greece, the worship of Artemis was widespread. The Romans identified her with Diana. She is mentioned in the biblical book of The Acts of the Apostles.

Asana: (Sanskrit) Posture or position.

Astral: This term is derived from pertaining to or proceeding from the stars, but in the esoteric knowledge it refers to the emotional aspect of the fifth dimension, which in Hebrew is called Hod. Related terms are below.

Astral Body: The body utilized by the consciousness in the fifth dimension or world of dreams. What is commonly called the Astral Body is not the true Astral Body, it is rather the Lunar Protoplasmatic Body, also known as the Kama Rupa (Sanskrit, "body of desires") or "dream body" (Tibetan rmi-lam-gyi lus). The true Astral Body is Solar (being superior to Lunar Nature) and must be created, as the Master Jesus indicated in the Gospel of John 3:5-6, "Except a man be born of water and of the Spirit, he cannot enter into the kingdom of God. That which is born of the flesh is flesh; and that which is born of the Spirit is spirit." The Solar Astral Body is created as a result of the Third Initiation of Major Mysteries (Serpents of Fire), and is perfected in the Third Serpent of Light. In Tibetan Buddhism, the Solar Astral Body is known as the illusory body (sgyu-lus). This body is related to the emotional center and to the sephirah Hod.

"Really, only those who have worked with the Maithuna (White Tantra) for many years can possess the Astral Body." - Samael Aun Weor, *The Elimination of Satan's Tail*

Asuramaya: Also known as Mayasura; an Atlantean astronomer well-known in Vedic Astrology.

Bacchantes: (Greek) Also called maenads or bacchae (for Bacchus). In Greek and Roman religion and mythology, female devotees of Dionysus. They roamed mountains and forests, adorned with ivy and skins of animals, waving the thyrsus, a staff topped by a pine cone. When they danced, they often worked themselves into an ecstatic frenzy, during which they were capable of tearing wild animals to pieces with their bare hands. Samael explains that there were two groups of these women: those who utilized the positive aspect of the Dionysian energy (chastity) and those who utilized the negative aspect through fornication and lust.

Being: Our inner, divine Source, also called the Innermost or Monad, which is not easily definable in conceptual terms. The use of the term "Being" is important though, in relation to its roots:

From the Online Etymology Dictionary: "O.E. beon, beom, bion "be, exist, come to be, become," from P.Gmc. *beo-, *beu-. This "b-root" is from PIE base *bheu-, *bhu- "grow, come into being, become," and in addition to the words in English it yielded German present first and second person sing. (bin, bist, from O.H.G. bim "I am," bist "thou art"), L. perf. tenses of esse (fui "I was," etc.), O.C.S. byti "be," Gk. phu- "become," O.Ir. bi'u "I am," Lith. bu'ti "to be," Rus. byt' "to be," etc. It also is behind Skt. bhavah "becoming," bhavati "becomes, happens," bhumih "earth, world."

Black Lodge: An organization or intelligence that seeks to pull souls into attachment to desire-sensation and the awakening of the consciousness (negatively) that is trapped within desire (lust, anger, pride, envy, etc.).

"From the dawn of life, a great battle has raged between the powers of Light and the powers of Darkness. The secret root of that battle lies in sex. Gods and Demons live in eternal struggle. The Gods defend the doctrine of chastity. The Demons hate chastity. In sex is found the root of the conflict between Gods and Demons... There are Masters of the Great White Lodge. There are Masters of the Great Black Lodge. There are disciples of the Great White Lodge. There are disciples of the Great Black Lodge. The disciples of the Great White Lodge know how to move consciously and positively in the Astral Body. The disciples of the Great Black Lodge also know how to travel in the Astral Body... The White Magician worships the inner Christ. The Black Magician worships Satan. This is the I, the me, myself, the reincarnating ego. In fact, the I is the specter of the threshold itself. It continually reincarnates to satisfy desires. The I is memory. In the I are all the memories of our ancient personalities. The I is Ahriman, Lucifer, Satan." - Samael Aun Weor, *The Perfect Matrimony*

"Understand that every association of fornicators forms a black lodge, and each lodge or school of this kind has its boss or manager who they venerate as a saint or master." - Samael Aun Weor, *The Major Mysteries*

Black Magic: Magic comes from "mag," priest. Black magic is the science of the impure priesthood, or those who awaken the consciousness within the ego (pride, anger, lust, etc).

"Black Magic appeals to the mass mind. It appeals to the principles of our civilization. It offers something for nothing. As long as there is cupidity in the human heart, it will remain as a menace to the honesty and integrity of our race." - Manly P. Hall, from *Magic: a Treatise on Esoteric Ethics*

"The black magicians have their mysticism, and they always firmly believe that they walk on the good path. No black magician believes that he walks on the evil path. The path of black magic is a broad way filled with vices and pleasures." - Samael Aun Weor, *The Revolution of Beelzebub*

"Multitudes of schools of black magic exist, many of them with very venerable traditions that teach Sexual Magic with the spilling of semen. They have very beautiful theories that attract and captivate, and if the student falls in that seductive and delicious deceit, he becomes a black magician. Those black schools affirm to the four winds that they are white and that is why ignorant ones fall. Moreover, those schools talk of beauty, love, charity, wisdom, etc., etc. Naturally, in those circumstances the ignorant disciple attains the belief with firmness that such institutions are not evil and perverse. Remember good disciple, that the Abyss is full of sincerely mistaken ones and people of very good intentions..." - Samael Aun Weor, *Tarot and Kabbalah*

"Evilness is so fine in the world of the mind... Evilness is so delicate and subtle in the plane of cosmic understanding that in reality a lot of intuition is needed in order not to be cheated by the demons of the Mental World." - Samael Aun Weor, *Treatise of Sexual Alchemy*

"The intellect as the negative function of the mind is demoniacal. Everyone that enters into these studies, the first thing that they want is to dominate the mind of others. This is pure and legitimate black magic. No one has the right to violate the free will of others. No one has the right to exercise coaction upon the mind of others because this is black magic. The ones that are guilty of this grave error are all of those mistaken authors that are everywhere. All of those books of hypnotism, magnetism and suggestion are books of black magic. Whosoever does not know how to respect the free will of others is a black magician; those who perform mental works in order to violently dominate the mind of others convert themselves into perverse demons. These people separate themselves from the Innermost and they crumble into the Abyss." - Samael Aun Weor, *Tarot and Kabbalah*

"Black magic is not a fundamental art; it is the misuse of an art. Therefore it has no symbols of its own." - Manly P. Hall

Brahmavidvarishta: (Sanskrit) Brahmavid means "a knower of Brahman," and Vara, Variyan and Varishra are suggestive of ascending comparative degrees of excellence and fullness. The highest, the Brahmavarishta, is the Thureeya (Turiya), the stage of perpetual Samadhi.

Chakra: (Sanskrit) Literally, "wheel." The chakras are subtle centers of energetic transformation. There are hundreds of chakras in our hidden physiology, but seven primary ones related to the awakening of consciousness.

"The Chakras are centres of Shakti as vital force... The Chakras are not perceptible to the gross senses. Even if they were perceptible in the living body which they help to organise, they disappear with the disintegration of organism at death." - Swami Sivananda, *Kundalini Yoga*

"The chakras are points of connection through which the divine energy circulates from one to another vehicle of the human being." - Samael Aun Weor, *Aztec Christic Magic*

Chastity: Although modern usage has rendered the term chastity virtually meaningless to most people, its original meaning and usage clearly indicate "moral purity" upon the basis of "sexual purity." Contemporary usage implies "repression" or "abstinence," which have nothing to do with real chastity. True chastity is a rejection of impure sexuality. True chastity is pure sexuality, or the activity of sex in harmony with our true nature, as explained in the secret doctrine. Properly used, the word chastity refers to sexual fidelity or honor.

"The generative energy, which, when we are loose, dissipates and makes us unclean, when we are continent invigorates and inspires us. Chastity is the flowering of man; and what are called Genius, Heroism, Holiness, and the like, are but various fruits which succeed it." - Henry David Thoreau, *Walden*

Chela: (Sanskrit) Literally, "child." A disciple, the pupil of a guru or sage.

Christ: Derived from the Greek Christos, "the Anointed One," and Krestos, whose esoteric meaning is "fire." The word Christ is a title, not a personal name.

"Indeed, Christ is a Sephirothic Crown (Kether, Chokmah and Binah) of incommensurable wisdom, whose purest atoms shine within Chokmah, the world of the Ophanim. Christ is not the Monad, Christ is not the Theosophical Septenary; Christ is not the Jivan-Atman. Christ is the Central Sun. Christ is the ray that unites us to the Absolute." - Samael Aun Weor, *Tarot and Kabbalah*

Consciousness: "Wherever there is life, there exists the consciousness. Consciousness is inherent to life as humidity is inherent to water." - Samael Aun Weor, *Fundamental Notions of Endocrinology and Criminology*

From various dictionaries: 1. The state of being conscious; knowledge of one's own existence, condition, sensations, mental operations, acts, etc. 2. Immediate knowledge or perception of the presence of any object, state, or sensation. 3. An alert cognitive state in which you are aware of yourself and your situation. In universal Gnosticism, the range of potential consciousness is allegorized in the Ladder of Jacob, upon which the angels ascend and descend. Thus there are higher and lower levels of consciousness, from the level of demons at the bottom, to highly realized angels in the heights.

"It is vital to understand and develop the conviction that consciousness has the potential to increase to an infinite degree." - The 14th Dalai Lama

"Light and consciousness are two phenomena of the same thing; to a lesser degree of consciousness, corresponds a lesser degree of light; to a greater degree of consciousness, a greater degree of light." - Samael Aun Weor, *The Esoteric Treatise of Hermetic Astrology*

Divine Mother: "Among the Aztecs, she was known as Tonantzin, among the Greeks as chaste Diana. In Egypt she was Isis, the Divine Mother, whose veil no mortal has lifted. There is no doubt at all that esoteric Christianity has never forsaken the worship of the Divine Mother Kundalini. Obviously she is Marah, or better said, RAM-IO, MARY. What orthodox religions did not specify, at least with regard to the exoteric or public circle, is the aspect of Isis in her individual human form. Clearly, it was taught only in secret to the Initiates that this Divine Mother exists individually within each human being. It cannot be emphasized enough that Mother-God, Rhea, Cybele, Adonia, or whatever we wish to call her, is a variant of our own individual Being in the here and now. Stated explicitly, each of us has our own particular, individual Divine Mother." - Samael Aun Weor, *The Great Rebellion*

"Devi Kundalini, the Consecrated Queen of Shiva, our personal Divine Cosmic Individual Mother, assumes five transcendental mystic aspects in every creature, which we must enumerate:

1. The unmanifested Prakriti

2. The chaste Diana, Isis, Tonantzin, Maria or better said Ram-Io

3. The terrible Hecate, Persephone, Coatlicue, queen of the infemos and death; terror of love and law

4. The special individual Mother Nature, creator and architect of our physical organism

5. The Elemental Enchantress to whom we owe every vital impulse, every instinct." - Samael Aun Weor, *The Mystery of the Golden Blossom*

Ego: The multiplicity of contradictory psychological elements that we have inside are in their sum the "ego." Each one is also called "an ego" or an "I." Every ego is a psychological defect which produces suffering. The ego is three (related to our Three Brains or three centers of psychological processing), seven (capital sins), and legion (in their infinite variations).

"The ego is the root of ignorance and pain." - Samael Aun Weor, *The Esoteric Treatise of Hermetic Astrology*

"The Being and the ego are incompatible. The Being and the ego are like water and oil. They can never be mixed... The annihilation of the psychic aggregates (egos) can be made possible only by radically comprehending our errors through meditation and by the evident Self-reflection of the Being." - Samael Aun Weor, *The Gnostic Bible: The Pistis Sophia Unveiled*

Eidolon: (Greek) The Astral Body.

Elohim: [אלהים] An Hebrew term with a wide variety of meanings. In Christian translations of scripture, it is one of many words translated to the generic word "God," but whose actual meaning depends upon the context. For example:

1. In Kabbalah, אלהים is a name of God the relates to many levels of the Tree of Life. In the world of Atziluth, the word is related to divnities of the sephiroth Binah (Jehovah Elohim, mentioned especially in Genesis), Geburah, and Hod. In the world of Briah, it is related beings of Netzach and Hod.

2. El [אל] is "god," Eloah [אלה] is "goddess," therefore the plural Elohim refers to "gods and goddesses," and is commonly used to refer to Cosmo-creators or Dhyan-Choans.

3. אלה Elah or Eloah is "goddess." Yam [ים] is "sea" or "ocean." Therefore אלהים Elohim can be אלה-ים "the sea goddess" [i.e. Aphrodite, Stella Maris, etc.]

There are many more meanings of "Elohim." In general, Elohim refers to high aspects of divinity.

"Each one of us has his own interior Elohim. The interior Elohim is the Being of our Being. The interior Elohim is our Father-Mother. The interior Elohim is the ray that emanates from Aelohim." - Samael Aun Weor, *The Gnostic Bible: The Pistis Sophia Unveiled*

Elysian Fields: In Greek religion and mythology, the happy otherworld for heroes favored by the gods. Identified with the Fortunate Isles or Isles of the Blest, Elysium was situated in the distant west, at the edge of the world. In later tradition and in Vergil, Elysium is a part of the underworld and a pleasant abode for the righteous dead.

Ens Seminis: (Latin) Literally, "the entity of the semen."

Épopée: (French) Epic stories.

Eye of Dangma: Dangma is a Sanskrit term for "a purified soul," thus the Eye of Dangma is a reference to the spiritual sight of the elevated Initiate.

Fornication: Originally, the term fornication was derived from the Indo-European word gwher, whose meanings relate to heat and burning (the full explanation can be found online at http://sacred-sex.org/terminology/fornication). Fornication means to make the heat (solar fire) of the seed (sexual power) leave the body through voluntary orgasm. Any voluntary orgasm is fornication, whether between a married man and woman, or an unmarried man and woman, or through masturbation, or in any other case; this is explained by Moses: "A man from whom there is a discharge of semen, shall immerse all his flesh in water, and he shall remain unclean until evening. And any garment or any leather [object] which has semen on it, shall be immersed in water, and shall remain unclean until evening. A woman with whom a man cohabits, whereby there was [a discharge of] semen, they shall immerse in water, and they shall remain unclean until evening." - Leviticus 15:16-18

To fornicate is to spill the sexual energy through the orgasm. Those who "deny themselves" restrain the sexual energy, and "walk in the midst of the fire" without being burned. Those who restrain the sexual energy, who renounce the orgasm, remember God in themselves, and do not defile themselves with animal passion, "for the temple of God is holy, which temple ye are."

"Whosoever is born of God doth not commit sin; for his seed remaineth in him: and he cannot sin, because he is born of God." - 1 John 3:9

This is why neophytes always took a vow of sexual abstention, so that they could prepare themselves for marriage, in which they would have sexual relations but not release the sexual energy through the orgasm. This is why Paul advised:

"...they that have wives be as though they had none..." - I Corinthians 7:29

"A fornicator is an individual who has intensely accustomed his genital organs to copulate (with orgasm). Yet, if the same individual changes his custom of copulation to the custom of no copulation, then he transforms himself into a chaste person. We have as an example the astonishing case of Mary Magdalene, who was a famous prostitute. Mary Magdalene became the famous Saint Mary Magdalene, the repented prostitute. Mary Magdalene became the chaste disciple of Christ." - Samael Aun Weor, *The Revolution of Beelzebub*

Furies: In Greek and Roman religion and mythology, the three daughters of Mother Earth, conceived from the blood of Uranus, when Kronos castrated him. They were powerful divinities that personified conscience and punished crimes against kindred blood, especially matricide. They were usually represented as winged women with serpent hair. Their names were Megaera [jealous], Tisiphone [blood avenger], and Alecto [unceasing in pursuit]. When called upon to act, they hounded their victims until they died in a "furor" of madness or torment. In the myth of Orestes they appear as Clytemnestra's agents of revenge. After Athena absolved Orestes of guilt in the murder of his mother, she gave the Furies a grotto at Athens where they received sacrifices and libations, and became euphemistically known as the Eumenides [kindly ones]. Samael Aun Weor explains that the Three Furies are the same as the Three Traitors of the Christian Gospel, the Three Traitors of the Masonic Legend of Hiram Abiff, and the Three Egyptian Demons who killed Osiris.

Geryon: In Greek mythology, the three-bodied monster who, with his dog Orthus, watched over a great herd of cattle. Hercules, in performing his tenth labor by stealing the cattle, killed Geryon.

Gnosis: (Greek) Knowledge.

1. The word Gnosis refers to the knowledge we acquire through our own experience, as opposed to knowledge that we are told or believe in. Gnosis - by whatever name in history or culture - is conscious, experiential knowl-

edge, not merely intellectual or conceptual knowledge, belief, or theory. This term is synonymous with the Hebrew "daath" and the Sanskrit "jna."
2. The tradition that embodies the core wisdom or knowledge of humanity.

"Gnosis is the flame from which all religions sprouted, because in its depth Gnosis is religion. The word "religion" comes from the Latin word "religare," which implies "to link the Soul to God"; so Gnosis is the very pure flame from where all religions sprout, because Gnosis is knowledge, Gnosis is wisdom." - Samael Aun Weor from the lecture entitled The Esoteric Path

"The secret science of the Sufis and of the Whirling Dervishes is within Gnosis. The secret doctrine of Buddhism and of Taoism is within Gnosis. The sacred magic of the Nordics is within Gnosis. The wisdom of Hermes, Buddha, Confucius, Mohammed and Quetzalcoatl, etc., etc., is within Gnosis. Gnosis is the doctrine of Christ." - Samael Aun Weor, *The Revolution of Beelzebub*

Gnostic Church: (Greek) From γνῶσις, knowledge, and ἐκκλησία, assembly. Thus, strictly defined, the Gnostic Church is a body or gathering of knowledge. The Gnostic Church is the repository of the greatest knowledge in the universe. The Gnostic Church is comprised of all the perfect beings in existence, who are called gods, angels, buddhas, masters, etc. The Gnostic Church is not a physical entity, but exists in the internal worlds in the superior dimensions. The Gnostic Church utilizes whatever means are appropriate in the physical world in order to aid the elevation of humanity out of suffering. Throughout time, we have known that aid through the various religions, philosophies, teachers, etc. For a complete explanation of the Gnostic Church, study the online course The Sacraments of the Gnostic Church.

"In this course, we are going to explain the sacraments instituted since ancient times in the church of Christ, which has its latest roots in Egypt. Internally, the Holy Gnostic Church is situated in the superior dimensions. Yet, in this day and age, the Holy Gnostic Church has in the physical world a physical exponent in every Lumisial of our visible and invisible Gnostic organisations that form the gigantic Gnostic Movement. The Gnostic Church was instituted by the Master Jesus two thousand years ago in the Middle East, but is a church that has a history much longer than that. It is related with the mysteries of ancient Egypt that has its roots in Atlantis, which come from a Neptunian-Amentian epoch directly related with the World of Yesod, the fourth dimension and beyond. As you know, Gnosis comes from a Greek word for knowledge, and this doctrine of knowledge is related with the famous tree of knowledge of the book of Genesis..." - The Sacraments of the Gnostic Church

Golgotha: (Aramaic) Literally, "skull." The name of the hill where Jesus of Nazareth was crucified.

Goya, Francesco de: Spanish artist who developed a series of etchings called "Los caprichos," in which many fantastic and horrific scenes express the dark and twisted nature of the modern psyche.

El Greco: "The Greek," a famous Greek painter who lived and worked in Spain.

Heracles: Also Herakles or Hercules (Greek Ἡρακλῆς) from Hera, "protectress," (that has an intimate etymological relation with Eros - Love - the Son of the Divine Mother Aphrodite), related to heros "hero," originally "defender, protector." And kleos "glory or aura." Therefore Herakles means "the aura or glory of Hera" or the "aura or glory of Eros." The Greek symbol of the Christ.

Hesiod: 8th cent. B.C., Greek poet. He is thought to have lived later than Homer, but there is no absolute certainty about the dates of his life. Hesiod portrays himself as a Boeotian farmer. Little is known of his life, however, except for the few scant references he makes to his family's origin and to a quarrel over property with his brother. His most famous poem, the didactic Works and Days, is an epic of Greek rural life, filled with caustic advice for his brother and maxims for farmers to pursue. The "days" are days lucky or unlucky for particular tasks. Works and Days discourses on the mythic "five races" (i.e., the five ages) of humans; the Golden Age, ruled by Kronos, a period of serenity, peace, and eternal spring; the Silver Age, ruled by Zeus, less happy, but with luxury prevailing; the Bronze Age, a period of strife; the Heroic Age of the Trojan War; and the Iron Age, the present, when justice and piety had vanished. Hesiod's systemization, especially the idealized Golden Age, became deeply entrenched in the Western imagination and was expanded upon by Ovid. Also ascribed to him are the Theogony, a genealogy of the gods, and the first 56 lines of The Shield of Heracles. He gave his name to the Hesiodic school of poets, rivals of the Homeric school. Homer and Hesiod codified and preserved the myths of many of the Greek gods of the classical pantheon

Hiram Abiff: A biblical personage; a skillful builder and architect whom King Solomon procured from Tyre for the purpose of supervising the construction of the Temple. According to the Masonic story, Hiram Abiff was murdered by three traitors who were subsequently found by a group of Master Masons.

Holy Spirit: The Christian name for the third aspect of the Holy Trinity, or "God." This force has other names in other religions. In Kabbalah, the third sephirah, Binah. In Buddhism, it is related to Nirmanakaya, the "body of formation" through which the inner Buddha works in the world.

"The Holy Spirit is the Fire of Pentecost or the fire of the Holy Spirit called Kundalini by the Hindus, the igneous serpent of our magical powers, Holy Fire symbolized by Gold..." - Samael Aun Weor, *The Perfect Matrimony*

"It has been said in The Divine Comedy with complete clarity that the Holy Spirit is the husband of the Divine Mother. Therefore, the Holy Spirit unfolds himself into his wife, into the Shakti of the Hindus. This must be known and understood. Some, when they see that the Third Logos is unfolded into the Divine Mother Kundalini, or Shakti, She that has many names, have believed that the Holy Spirit is feminine, and they have been mistaken. The Holy Spirit is masculine, but when He unfolds Himself into She, then the first ineffable Divine Couple is formed, the Creator Elohim, the Kabir, or Great Priest, the Ruach Elohim, that in accordance to Moses, cultivated the waters in the beginning of the world." - Samael Aun Weor, *Tarot and Kabbalah*

"The Primitive Gnostic Christians worshipped the lamb, the fish and the white dove as symbols of the Holy Spirit." - Samael Aun Weor, *The Perfect Matrimony* Innermost: "Our real Being is of a universal nature. Our real Being is neither a kind of superior nor inferior "I." Our real Being is impersonal, universal, divine. He transcends every concept of "I," me, myself, ego, etc., etc." - Samael Aun Weor, *The Perfect Matrimony*

Also known as Atman, the Spirit, Chesed, our own individual interior divine Father.

"The Innermost is the ardent flame of Horeb. In accordance with Moses, the Innermost is the Ruach Elohim (the Spirit of God) who sowed the waters in the beginning of the world. He is the Sun King, our Divine Monad, the Alter-Ego of Cicerone." - Samael Aun Weor, *The Revolution of Beelzebub*

Hyperborean Root Race: The second Root Race of this terrestrial humanity. A nation mentioned in Greek mythology. The name means "beyond the North Wind," thus they are supposed to have been somewhere north of Greece, but the name also means "beyond the mountains" and "those who carry (merchandise) across." Apollo was said to spend the winter months among them, and his mother Leto was presumed to have been born in their land. Perseus went there searching for the Gorgon, and Heracles chased the Cerynitian hind to their country. The writer Pindar represented them as a blessed people untouched by human afflictions. H. P. Blavatsky places their country around the North Pole, saying it was "The Land of the Eternal Sun," beyond Boreas, the god of winter. She asserts that this land was of a near tropical climate. In universal Gnosticism, they are known to be the Second Root Race of this Terrestrial humanity.

"The second Root Race was governed by Quetzalcoatl; this was the Hyperborean humanity. The degenerated people of the second Root Race converted themselves into monkeys; these are the ancestors of present monkeys. They reproduced themselves by budding, such as the plants do: from their trunk sprout many branches. They were wiped out by strong hurricanes." - Samael Aun Weor, *The Kabbalah of the Mayan Mysteries*

Hyperion: (Greek, meaning "Exists-Above, Watches-From-Above," or "Going-over") A Titan in Greek religion and mythology. It is sometimes said that he was the original sun god. Hesiod said that Hyperion was the son of Gaia (Earth) and Uranus (sky; water/fire) and that he married his sister Theia; their children were Helios (the Sun), Eos (the Dawn), and Selene (the Moon). Hyperion was the Titan-god of watching and observation, the husband of Theia, the goddess of sight. At the end of the Titan-War he was cast into Tartaros with the rest of his brothers. Zeus later released them from this prison and Kronos became King of Elysium.

"Of Hyperion we are told that he was the first to understand, by diligent attention and observation, the movement of both the sun and the moon and the other stars, and the seasons as well, in that they are caused by these bodies, and to make these facts known to others; and that for this reason he was called the father of these bodies, since he had begotten, so to speak, the speculation about them and their nature." – Diodorus Siculus 5.67.1

Inachus: (Greek) The god of the river Inachus; a son of Oceanus and Tethys. Father of Io and first king of Argos.

Initiation: In white magic, the process whereby the Innermost (the Inner Father) receives recognition, empowerment and greater responsibilities in the internal worlds, and little by little approaches his goal: complete Self-realization, or in other words, the return into the Absolute. White initiation NEVER applies to the "I" or our terrestrial personality.

"There are Nine Initiations of Minor Mysteries and seven great Initiations of Major Mysteries. The Innermost is the one who receives all of these Initiations. The Testament of Wisdom says: "Before the dawning of the false aurora upon the earth, the ones who survived the hurricane and the tempest were praising the Innermost, and the heralds of the aurora appeared unto them." The psychological "I" does not receives Initiations. The human personality does not receive anything. Nonetheless, the "I" of some Initiates becomes filled with pride when saying 'I am a Master, I have such Initiations.' Thus, this is how the "I" believes itself to be an Initiate and keeps reincarnating in order to "perfect itself", but, the "I" never ever perfects itself. The "I" only reincarnates in order to satisfy desires. That is all." - Samael Aun Weor, *The Aquarian Message*

Innermost: "That part of the Reality (God) within man that the Yogi seeks to attune himself to before attaining cosmic consciousness." - M, *The Dayspring of Youth*

"Our real Being is of a universal nature. Our real Being is neither a kind of superior nor inferior "I." Our real Being is impersonal, universal, divine. He transcends every concept of "I," me, myself, ego, etc., etc." - Samael Aun Weor, *The Perfect Matrimony*

Also known as Atman, the Spirit, Chesed, our own individual interior divine Father.

"The Innermost is the ardent flame of Horeb. In accordance with Moses, the Innermost is the Ruach Elohim (the Spirit of God) who sowed the waters in the beginning of the world. He is the Sun King, our Divine Monad, the Alter-Ego of Cicerone." - Samael Aun Weor, *The Revolution of Beelzebub*

Intellectual Animal: When the Intelligent Principle, the Monad, sends its spark of consciousness into Nature, that spark, the anima, enters into manifestation as a simple mineral. Gradually, over millions of years, the anima gathers experience and evolves up the chain of life until it perfects itself in the level of the mineral kingdom. It then graduates into the plant kingdom, and subsequently into the animal kingdom. With each ascension the spark receives new capacities and higher grades of complexity. In the animal kingdom it learns procreation by ejaculation. When that animal intelligence enters into the human kingdom, it receives a new capacity: reasoning, the intellect; it is now an anima with intellect: an Intellectual Animal. That spark must then perfect itself in the human kingdom in order to become a complete and perfect human being, an entity that has conquered and transcended everything that belongs to the lower kingdoms. Unfortunately, very few intellectual animals perfect themselves; most remain enslaved by their animal nature, and thus are reabsorbed by Nature, a process belonging to the devolving side of life and called by all the great religions "Hell" or the Second Death.

"The present manlike being is not yet human; he is merely an intellectual animal. It is a very grave error to call the legion of the "I" the "soul." In fact, what the manlike being has is the psychic material, the material for the soul within his Essence, but indeed, he does not have a Soul yet." - Samael Aun Weor, *The Revolution of the Dialectic*

Io: In Greek mythology, daughter of Inachus, a river God. She was a virgin (chaste) priestess of Hera, who earned Hera's wrath by attracting the attention of Zeus. According to Aeschylus (in his Prometheus Bound), Io was exiled and turned into a cow (by either Zeus or Hera) and was stung continually by gadflies (sent by Hera) in order to stop from her from resting anywhere long enough for Zeus to unite with her. Argus, a giant with a hundred unsleeping eyes, was charged by Hera to guard over her for the same purpose. The giant was killed by Hermes (Mercury). She was pursued by the flies and wandered all over until finally arriving in Egypt where Zeus changed her back into a woman and, with a touch of his hand, impregnated her. This is but one of several versions of her story; Ovid in his Metamorphasis tells another. Io came to be worshipped as the goddess Isis and had a son named Epaphus who was worshipped as the bull-deity Apis.

Ixion: (Greek) The king of the Lapithes and the first man to stain his hands with a kinsman's blood. Ixion arranged a marriage with Dia, the daughter of his kinsman Eioneus. Ixion promised Eioneus a large sum for his daughter, and invited him to come collect it. But when Eioneus arrived, he fell in to Ixion's trap: a pit filled with burning coals. Eioneus perished. When no one on earth would purify Ixion of this unprecendented crime, Zeus took Ixion to Olympus and purified him (perhaps because Zeus loved Dia). While there Ixion attempted to seduce Hera, but Zeus created a cloud which perfectly represented her. With this cloud Ixion committed adultery. Zeus caught him in the act and condemned him to spend an eternity in Tartarus, bound to a fiery, winged, four-spoked wheel which revolved unendingly (some say the wheel was covered in snakes). The cloud, Nephele, had a monstrous son, Centaurus, who mated with wild mares and begat the race of centaurs.

Jnana: (Sanskrit) Knowledge; wisdom.

Kabbalah: (Hebrew קבלה) Alternatively spelled Cabala, Qabalah from the Hebrew קבל KBLH or QBL, "to receive." An ancient esoteric teaching hidden from the uninitiated, whose branches and many forms have reached throughout the world. The true Kabbalah is the science and language of the Superior Worlds and is thus objective, complete and without flaw; it is said that "All enlightened beings agree," and their natural agreement is a function of the awakened consciousness. The Kabbalah is the language of that consciousness, thus disagreement regarding its meaning and interpretation is always due to the subjective elements in the psyche.

"The objective of studying the Kabbalah is to be skilled for work in the Internal Worlds... One that does not comprehend remains confused in the Internal Worlds. Kabbalah is the basis in order to understand the language of these worlds." - Samael Aun Weor, *Tarot and Kabbalah*

"In Kabbalah we have to constantly look at the Hebrew letters." - Samael Aun Weor, *Tarot and Kabbalah*

Kundalini: "Kundalini, the serpent power or mystic fire, is the primordial energy or Sakti that lies dormant or sleeping in the Muladhara Chakra, the centre of the body. It is called the serpentine or annular power on account of serpentine form. It is an electric fiery occult power, the great pristine force which underlies all organic and inorganic matter. Kundalini is the cosmic power in individual bodies. It is not a material force like electricity, magnetism, centripetal or centrifugal force. It is a spiritual potential Sakti or cosmic power. In reality it has no form. [...] O Divine Mother Kundalini, the Divine Cosmic Energy that is hidden in men! Thou art Kali, Durga, Adisakti, Rajarajeswari, Tripurasundari, Maha-Lakshmi, Maha-Sarasvati! Thou hast put on all these names and forms. Thou hast manifested as Prana, electricity, force, magnetism, cohesion, gravitation in this universe. This whole universe rests in Thy bosom. Crores of salutations unto thee. O Mother of this world! Lead me on to open the Sushumna Nadi and take Thee along the Chakras to Sahasrara Chakra and to merge myself in Thee and Thy consort, Lord Siva. Kundalini Yoga is that Yoga which treats of Kundalini Sakti, the six centres of spiritual energy (Shat Chakras), the arousing of the sleeping Kundalini Sakti and its union with Lord Siva in Sahasrara Chakra, at the crown of the head. This is an exact science. This is also known as Laya Yoga. The six centres are pierced (Chakra Bheda) by the passing of Kundalini Sakti to the top of the head. 'Kundala' means 'coiled'. Her form is like a coiled serpent. Hence the name Kundalini." - Swami Sivananda, *Kundalini Yoga*

"Kundalini is a compound word: Kunda reminds us of the abominable "Kundabuffer organ," and lini is an Atlantean term meaning termination. Kundalini means "the termination of the abominable Kundabuffer organ." In this case, it is imperative not to confuse Kundalini with Kundabuffer." - Samael Aun Weor, *The Great Rebellion*

These two forces, one positive and ascending, and one negative and descending, are symbolized in the Bible in the book of Numbers (the story of the Serpent of Brass). The Kundalini is "The power of life."- from the Theosophical Glossary. The Sexual Fire that is at the base of all life. "The ascent of the Kundalini along the spinal cord is achieved very slowly in accordance with the merits of the heart. The fires of the heart control the miraculous development of the Sacred Serpent. Devi Kundalini is not something mechanical as many suppose; the igneous serpent is only awakened with genuine love between husband and wife, and it will never rise up along the medullar canal of adulterers." - Samael Aun Weor, *The Mystery of the Golden Blossom*

"The decisive factor in the progress, development and evolution of the Kundalini is ethics." - Samael Aun Weor, *The Revolution of Beelzebub*

"Until not too long ago, the majority of spiritualists believed that on awakening the Kundalini, the latter instantaneously rose to the head and the initiate was automatically united with his Innermost or Internal God, instantly, and converted into Mahatma. How comfortable! How comfortably all these theosophists, Rosicrucians and spiritualists, etc., imagined High Initiation." - Samael Aun Weor, *The Zodiacal Course*

"There are seven bodies of the Being. Each body has its "cerebrospinal" nervous system, its medulla and Kundalini. Each body is a complete organism. There are, therefore, seven bodies, seven medullae and seven Kundalinis. The ascension of each of the seven Kundalinis is slow and difficult. Each canyon or vertebra represents determined occult powers and this is why the conquest of each canyon undergoes terrible tests." - Samael Aun Weor, *The Zodiacal Course*

Lakshmi: (Hindu) In Hinduism, one of the three primary aspects of the Divine Mother. Lakshmi is the wife / feminine aspect — meaning the shakti, power — of Vishnu, the Preserver or Restorer; He is the Second Logos, the Son; He is the sephirah Chokmah in Kabbalah; thus, Lakshmi is the power of Chokmah.

Logos: (Greek) means Verb or Word. In Greek and Hebrew metaphysics, the unifying principle of the world. The Logos is the manifested deity of every nation and people; the outward expression or the effect of the cause which is ever concealed. (Speech is the "logos" of thought). The Logos has three aspects, known universally as the Trinity or Trimurti. The First Logos is the Father, Brahma. The Second Logos is the Son, Vishnu. The Third Logos is the Holy Spirit, Shiva. One who incarnates the Logos becomes a Logos.

"The Logos is not an individual. The Logos is an army of ineffable beings." - Samael Aun Weor, *Fundamental Notions of Endocrinology and Criminology*

Lucifer: (Latin: lux, lucis, luce, luci, and lucu: "light"; fer, fero: "to bear, carry, support, lift, hold, take up"; these synthesize as "Bearer of Light") Before Milton, Lucifer had never been a name of the devil. One of the early Popes of Rome bore that name, and there was even a Christian sect in the fourth century which was called the Luciferians. Lucifer, the "carrier of the light," is Prometheus, the divinity who brings the life-giving fire to humanity, yet is punished for this act, and is only freed when that fire incarnates as Herakles ("the aura of Hera"), the hero (bodhisattva; i.e. Jesus, Krishna, Moses, etc) who liberates the Christic fire from its bondage in the stone (the mountain / Mercury).

"We need to whitewash the devil with maximum expedited urgency. This is only possible through fighting against our own selves, by dissolving all those conjunctions of psychological aggregates that constitute the "I," the "myself," the "itself." Only by dying in ourselves can we whitewash the brass and contemplate the Sun of the Middle Night (the Father). This signifies that we must defeat all temptations and eliminate all of the inhuman elements that we carry within (anger, greed, lust, envy, pride, laziness, gluttony, etc, etc, etc.). A trainer in the psychological gymnasium of human existence is always required. The divine Daimon†, quoted many times by Socrates, is the very shadow of our own individual Spirit. He is the most extraordinary psychological trainer that each one of us carries within. He delivers us into temptation with the purpose of training us, teaching us. Only in this way is it possible for the precious gems of virtue to sprout from our psyche. Now I question myself and I question you. Where is the evil of Lucifer? The results speak for themselves. If there are no temptations there are no virtues. Virtues are more grandiose when temptations are stronger. What is important is not to fall into temptation. That is why we have to pray to our Father, saying, "Lead us not into temptation." - Samael Aun Weor, *Tarot and Kabbalah*

Mahamanvantara: (Sanskrit) "The Great Day." A period of universal activity, as opposed to a Mahapralaya, a cosmic night or period of rest.

"Truthfully, the quantities of years assigned to a cosmic day are symbolic. The cosmic night arrives when the ingathering of the perfect souls is complete, which means, when the cosmic day is absolutely perfected." - Samael Aun Weor, *The Gnostic Bible: The Pistis Sophia Unveiled*

"I was absorbed within the Absolute at the end of that Lunar Mahamanvantara, which endured 311,040,000,000,000 years, or, in other words, an age of Brahma." - Samael Aun Weor, *The Revolution of Beelzebub*

Maithuna: The Sanskrit word maithuna is used in Hindu Tantras (esoteric scriptures) to refer to the sacrament (sacred ritual) of sexual union between husband and wife. Maithuna or Mithuna has various appearances in scripture:

Mithuna: paired, forming a pair; copulation; the zodiacal sign of Gemini in Vedic Astrology, which is depicted as a man and woman in a sexual embrace

Mithunaya: to unite sexually

Mithuni: to become paired, couple or united sexually

By means of the original Tantric Maithuna, after being prepared psychologically and spiritually and initiated by a genuine teacher (guru), the couple learns how to utilize their love and spiritual aspiration in order to transform their natural sexual forces to purify the mind, eliminate psychological defects, and awaken the latent powers of the consciousness. The man represents Shiva, the masculine aspect of the creative divine, and the woman represents Shakti, the feminine aspect and the source of the power of creation. This method was kept in strictest secrecy for thousands of years in order to preserve it in its pure form, and to prevent crude-minded people from deviating the teaching, other people, or harming themselves.

Nonetheless, some degenerated traditions (popularly called "left-hand" traditions, or black magic) interpret Maithuna or sacramental sexuality according to their state of degeneration, and use these sacred teachings to justify their lust, desire, orgies, and other types of deviations from pure, genuine Tantra.

Krishna: "And I am the strength of the strong, devoid of lust and attachment. O best of the Bharatas, I am sex not contrary to dharma." (Bhagavad Gita 7.11)

"The Tantric student must be endowed with purity, faith, devotion, dedication to Guru, dispassion, humility, courage, cosmic love, truthfulness, non-covetousness, and contentment. Absence of these qualities in the practitioner means a gross abuse of Shaktism. Sexual intercourse by a man with a woman who is not lawful to him is a sin. The Vaidika Dharma is very strict on this point. It forbids not merely actual Maithuna but Ashtanga or eightfold Maithuna namely Smaranam (thinking upon it), Kirtanam (talking of it), Keli (play with women), Prekshanam (making eyes at women), Guhya-bhashanam (talking in private with women), Sankalpa (wish or resolve for sexual union), Adhyavasaya (determination towards it), Kriyanishpatti (actual accomplishment of the sexual act). A Tantric can have copulation with his wife. He calls his wife his Shakti. Wife is a house-goddess Griha-lakshmi or Griha-devata united to her husband by the sacramental Samskara of marriage. She should not be regarded as an object of enjoyment. She is his partner in life (Ardhangini). The union of a man and his wife is a veritable sacred scriptural rite." - Swami Sivananda, *Tantra Yoga*

Mantra: (Sanskrit, literally "mind protection") A sacred word or sound. The use of sacred words and sounds is universal throughout all religions and mystical traditions, because the root of all creation is in the Great Breath or the Word, the Logos. "In the beginning was the Word..."

Maya: (Sanskrit, literally "not That," meaning appearance, illusion, deception) Can indicate 1) the illusory nature of existence, 2) the womb of the Divine Mother, or 3) the Divine Mother Herself.

Meditation: "When the esotericist submerges himself into meditation, what he seeks is information." - Samael Aun Weor

"It is urgent to know how to meditate in order to comprehend any psychic aggregate, or in other words, any psychological defect. It is indispensable to know how to work with all our heart and with all our soul, if we want the elimination to occur." - Samael Aun Weor, *The Gnostic Bible: The Pistis Sophia Unveiled*

"1. The Gnostic must first attain the ability to stop the course of his thoughts, the capacity to not think. Indeed, only the one who achieves that capacity will hear the Voice of the Silence.

"2. When the Gnostic disciple attains the capacity to not think, then he must learn to concentrate his thoughts on only one thing.

"3. The third step is correct meditation. This brings the first flashes of the new consciousness into the mind.

"4. The fourth step is contemplation, ecstasy or Samadhi. This is the state of Turiya (perfect clairvoyance). - Samael Aun Weor, *The Perfect Matrimony*

Mental Body: One of the seven bodies of the human being. Related to Netzach, the seventh sephirah of the Tree of Life; corresponds to the fifth dimension. In Egyptian mysticism, it is called Ba. In Hinduism, is it called vijnanmayakosha or kama manas (some Hindu teachers think the mental body is "manomayakosha," but that is the astral body).

"The mental body is a material organism, yet it is not the physical organism. The mental body has its ultra-biology and its internal pathology, which is completely unknown to the present men of science." - Samael Aun Weor, *The Revolution of Beelzebub*

Monad: From Latin monas, "unity; a unit" and Greek monas "unit," from monos "alone." The Monad is the Being, the Innermost, our own inner Spirit. In Kabbalah, the Monad is represented by the sephiroth Chesed, Geburah, and Tiphereth. In Sanskrit, this corresponds to Atman-Buddhi-Manas.

"We must distinguish between Monads and Souls. A Monad, in other words, a Spirit, is; a Soul is acquired. Distinguish between the Monad of a world and the Soul of a world; between the Monad of a human and the Soul of a human; between the Monad of an ant and the Soul of an ant. The human organism, in final synthesis, is constituted by billions and trillions of infinitesimal Monads. There are several types and orders of primary elements of all existence, of every organism, in the manner of germs of all the phenomena of nature; we can call the latter Monads, employing the term of Leibnitz, in the absence of a more descriptive term to indicate the simplicity of the simplest existence. An atom, as a vehicle of action, corresponds to each of these genii or Monads. The Monads attract each other, combine, transform themselves, giving form to every organism, world, micro-organism, etc. Hierarchies exist among the Monads; the inferior Monads must obey the superior ones that is the Law. Inferior Monads belong to the superior ones. All the trillions of Monads that animate the human organism have to obey the owner, the chief, the Principal Monad. The regulating Monad, the Primordial Monad permits the activity of all of its subordinates inside the human organism, until the time indicated by the Law of Karma." - Samael Aun Weor, *The Esoteric Treatise of Hermetic Astrology*

"(The number) one is the Monad, the Unity, Iod-Heve or Jehovah, the Father who is in secret. It is the Divine Triad that is not incarnated within

a Master who has not killed the ego. He is Osiris, the same God, the Word."
- Samael Aun Weor, *Tarot and Kabbalah*

"When spoken of, the Monad is referred to as Osiris. He is the one that has to Self-realize Himself... Our own particular Monad needs us and we need it. Once, while speaking with my Monad, my Monad told me, 'I am self-realizing Thee; what I am doing, I am doing for Thee.' Otherwise, why are we living? The Monad wants to Self-realize and that is why we are here. This is our objective." - Samael Aun Weor, *Tarot and Kabbalah*

"The Monads or Vital Genii are not exclusive to the physical organism; within the atoms of the internal bodies there are found imprisoned many orders and categories of living Monads. The existence of any physical or suprasensible, angelic or diabolical, solar or lunar body, has billions and trillions of Monads as their foundation." - Samael Aun Weor, *The Esoteric Treatise of Hermetic Astrology*

Mukti: (Sanskrit) Liberation.

Mulaprakriti: (Sanskrit) Literally, the "root of Nature." The abstract deific feminine principle. Undifferentiated substance.

Muses: (Greek) Patron goddesses of the arts, daughters of Zeus and Mnemosyne ("memory"). Originally only three, they were later considered as nine. Calliope was the Muse of epic poetry and eloquence; Euterpe, of music or of lyric poetry; Erato, of the poetry of love; Polyhymnia (or Polymnia), of oratory or sacred poetry; Clio, of history; Melpomene, of tragedy; Thalia, of comedy; Terpsichore, of choral song and dance; Urania, of astronomy. Some say that Apollo was their leader.

Ninth Sphere: In Kabbalah, a reference to the sephirah Yesod of the Tree of Life (Kabbalah). When you place the Tree of Life over your body, you see that Yesod is related to your sexual organs.

"The Ninth Sphere of the Kabbalah is sex." - Samael Aun Weor, *The Perfect Matrimony*

The Ninth Sphere also refers to the sephirah Yesod and to the lowest sphere of the Klipoth.

"The great Master Hilarion IX said that in ancient times, to descend into the Ninth Sphere was the maximum ordeal for the supreme dignity of the Hierophant. Hermes, Buddha, Jesus Christ, Dante, Zoroaster, Mohammed, Rama, Krishna, Pythagoras, Plato and many others, had to descend into the Ninth Sphere in order to work with the fire and the water which is the origin of worlds, beasts, human beings and Gods. Every authentic white initiation begins here." - Samael Aun Weor, *The Aquarian Message*

Nirvana: (Sanskrit निर्वाण, "extinction" or "cessation"; Tibetan: nyangde, literally "the state beyond sorrow") In general use, the word nirvana refers to the permanent cessation of suffering and its causes, and therefore refers to a state of consciousness rather than a place. Yet, the term can also apply to heavenly realms, whose vibration is related to the cessation of suffering.

In other words, if your mind-stream has liberated itself from the causes of suffering, it will naturally vibrate at the level of Nirvana (heaven).

"When the Soul fuses with the Inner Master, then it becomes free from Nature and enters into the supreme happiness of absolute existence. This state of happiness is called Nirvana. Nirvana can be attained through millions of births and deaths, but it can also be attained by means of a shorter path; this is the path of "initiation." The Initiate can reach Nirvana in one single life if he so wants it." - Samael Aun Weor, *The Zodiacal Course*

"Nirvana is a region of Nature where the ineffable happiness of the fire reigns. The Nirvanic plane has seven sub-planes. A resplendent hall exists in each one of these seven sub-planes of Nirvanic matter where the Nirmanakayas study their mysteries. This is why they call their sub-planes "halls" and not merely "sub-planes" as the Theosophists do. The Nirvanis say: "We are in the first hall of Nirvana or in the second hall of Nirvana, or in the third, or in the fourth, or fifth, or sixth, or in the seventh hall of Nirvana." To describe the ineffable joy of Nirvana is impossible. There, the music of the spheres reigns and the soul is enchanted within a state of bliss, which is impossible to describe with words." - Samael Aun Weor, *The Revolution of Beelzebub*

Prajna: (Sanskrit, "discriminative awareness," "consciousness" or "wisdom." In Tibetan, shes rab) Literally "perfect knowledge."

In Hinduism: The third of the four states of the consciousness of Atman. In the Mandukya Upanishad, Prajna is described as a state of blissful, cognizant, dreamless sleep.

In Buddhism: This term is defined by its context; it can mean intuitive wisdom, understanding, intelligence, discrimination, or judgment. In Buddhist philosophy, prajna describes the faculty of discriminative awareness that can see the true nature - the emptiness or void - of all things. Prajna is the highest paramita (conscious attitude or virtue).

Sahaja Maithuna: (Sanskrit) Sahaja, "natural." Maithuna, "sacramental intercourse"

Samadhi: (Sanskrit) Literally means "union" or "combination" and its Tibetan equivilent means "adhering to that which is profound and definitive," or ting nge dzin, meaning "To hold unwaveringly, so there is no movement." Related terms include satori, ecstasy, manteia, etc. Samadhi is a state of consciousness. In the west, the term is used to describe an ecstatic state of consciousness in which the Essence escapes the painful limitations of the mind (the "I") and therefore experiences what is real: the Being, the Great Reality. There are many levels of Samadhi. In the sutras and tantras the term Samadhi has a much broader application whose precise interpretation depends upon which school and teaching is using it.

"Ecstasy is not a nebulous state, but a transcendental state of wonderment, which is associated with perfect mental clarity." - Samael Aun Weor, *The Elimination of Satan's Tail*

Second Birth: The creation of the soul as taught by Jesus to Nicodemus:

"There was a man of the Pharisees, named Nicodemus, a ruler of the Jews: The same came to Jesus by night, and said unto him, Rabbi, we know that thou art a teacher come from God: for no man can do these miracles that thou doest, except God be with him. Jesus answered and said unto him, Verily, verily, I say unto thee, Except a man be born again, he cannot see the kingdom of God. Nicodemus saith unto him, How can a man be born when he is old? can he enter the second time into his mother's womb, and be born? Jesus answered, Verily, verily, I say unto thee, Except a man be born of water and of the Spirit, he cannot enter into the kingdom of God. That which is born of the flesh is flesh; and that which is born of the Spirit is spirit." - John 3:1-6

"In Gnosticism and Esotericism, one understands as Second Birth the fabrication of the Solar Bodies and the Incarnation of the Being." - Samael Aun Weor, *The Esoteric Treatise of Hermetic Astrology*

"To incarnate the divine immortal triad (Atman-Buddhi-Manas) signifies the Second Birth, which means to come out of the Ninth Sphere. The child who is born comes out from the womb. Whosoever is born within the superior worlds comes out of the Ninth Sphere (sex). Whosoever reaches the Second Birth is admitted into the temple of the Twice-born. Whosoever reaches the Second Birth has to renounce sex for all eternity. The sexual act is absolutely forbidden for the Twice-born. Whosoever violates this law will lose his solar bodies and will fall into the valley of bitterness." - Samael Aun Weor, *The Doomed Aryan Race*

In order to incarnate the Monad (the Triad) one must first create the solar bodies, which is only possible through White Tantra.

Second Death: A mechanical process in nature experienced by those souls who within the allotted time fail to reach union with their inner divinity (i.e. known as self-realization, liberation, religare, yoga, moksha, etc). The Second Death is the complete dissolution of the ego (karma, defects, sins) in the infernal regions of nature, which after unimaginable quantities of suffering, proportional to the density of the psyche, in the end purifies the Essence (consciousness) so that it may try again to perfect itself and reach the union with the Being.

"He that overcometh (the sexual passion) shall inherit all things; and I will be his God (I will incarnate myself within him), and he shall be my son (because he is a Christified one), But the fearful (the tenebrous, cowards, unbelievers), and unbelieving, and the abominable, and murderers, and whoremongers, and sorcerers, and idolaters, and all liars, shall have their part in the lake which burneth with fire and brimstone: which is the second death. (Revelation 21) This lake which burns with fire and brimstone is the lake of carnal passion. This lake is related with the lower animal depths of the human being and its atomic region is the abyss. The tenebrous slowly disintegrate themselves within the abyss until they die. This is the second death." - Samael Aun Weor, *The Aquarian Message*

"When the bridge called Antakarana,which communicates the divine triad with its inferior essence is broken, the inferior essence (trapped into the ego) is left separated and is sunk into the abyss of destructive forces, where it (its ego) disintegrates little by little. This is the Second Death of which the Apocalypse speaks; this is the state of consciousness called Avitchi." - Samael Aun Weor, *The Zodiacal Course*

"The Second Death is really painful. The ego feels as if it has been divided in different parts, the fingers fall off, its arms, its legs. It suffers through a tremendous breakdown." - Samael Aun Weor, from the lecture *The Mysteries of Life and Death*

Self-realization: The achievement of perfect knowledge. This phrase is better stated as, "The realization of the Innermost Self," or "The realization of the true nature of self." At the ultimate level, this is the experiential, conscious knowledge of the Absolute, which is synonymous with Emptiness, Shunyata, or Non-being.

Semen: In the esoteric tradition of pure sexuality, the word semen refers to the sexual energy of the organism, whether male or female. This is because male and female both carry the "seed" within: in order to create, the two "seeds" must be combined. In common usage: "The smaller, usually motile male reproductive cell of most organisms that reproduce sexually." English semen originally meant 'seed of male animals' in the 14th century, and it was not applied to human males until the 18th century. It came from Latin semen, "seed of plants," from serere `to sow.' The Latin goes back to the Indo-European root *se-, source of seed, disseminate, season, seminar, and seminal. The word seminary (used for religious schools) is derived from semen and originally meant 'seedbed.' That the semen is the source of all virtue is known from the word "seminal," derived from the Latin "semen," and which is defined as "highly original and influencing the development of future events: a seminal artist; seminal ideas."

"According to Yogic science, semen exists in a subtle form throughout the whole body. It is found in a subtle state in all the cells of the body. It is withdrawn and elaborated into a gross form in the sexual organ under the influence of the sexual will and sexual excitement. An Oordhvareta Yogi (one who has stored up the seminal energy in the brain after sublimating the same into spiritual energy) not only converts the semen into Ojas, but checks through his Yogic power, through purity in thought, word and deed, the very formation of semen by the secretory cells or testes or seeds. This is a great secret." - Sri Swami Sivananda, *Brahmacharya* (Celibacy)

Sexual Magic: The word magic is derived from the ancient word magos "one of the members of the learned and priestly class," from O.Pers. magush, possibly from PIE *magh- "to be able, to have power." [Quoted from Online Etymology Dictionary].

"All of us possess some electrical and magnetic forces within, and, just like a magnet, we exert a force of attraction and repulsion... Between lovers that magnetic force is particularly powerful and its action has a far-reaching effect." - Samael Aun Weor, *The Mystery of the Golden Blossom*

Sexual magic refers to an ancient science that has been known and protected by the purest, most spiritually advanced human beings, whose purpose and goal is the harnessing and perfection of our sexual forces. A more accurate translation of sexual magic would be "sexual priesthood." In ancient times, the priest was always accompanied by a priestess, for they represent the divine forces at the base of all creation: the masculine and feminine, the Yab-Yum, Ying-Yang, Father-Mother: the Elohim. Unfortunately, the term "sexual magic" has been grossly misinterpreted by mistaken persons such as Aleister Crowley, who advocated a host of degenerated practices, all of which belong solely to the lowest and most perverse mentality and lead only to the enslavement of the consciousness, the worship of lust and desire, and the decay of humanity. True, upright, heavenly sexual magic is the natural harnessing of our latent forces, making them active and harmonious with nature and the divine, and which leads to the perfection of the human being.

"People are filled with horror when they hear about sexual magic; however, they are not filled with horror when they give themselves to all kinds of sexual perversion and to all kinds of carnal passion." - Samael Aun Weor, *The Perfect Matrimony*

Solar Bodies: The physical, vital, astral, mental, and causal bodies that are created through the beginning stages of Alchemy/Tantra and that provide a basis for existence in their corresponding levels of nature, just as the physical body does in the physical world. These bodies or vehicles are superior due to being created out of Solar (Christic) Energy, as opposed to the inferior, lunar bodies we receive from nature. Also known as the Wedding Garment (Christianity), the Merkabah (Kabbalah), To Soma Heliakon (Greek), and Sahu (Egyptian).

"All the masters of the white lodge, the angels, archangels, thrones, seraphim, virtues, etc., etc., etc. are garbed with the solar bodies. Only those who have solar bodies have the being incarnated. Only someone who possesses the being is an authentic human being." - Samael Aun Weor, *The Esoteric Treatise of Hermetic Astrology*

Tantra: The word Tantra is Sanskrit and literally means, "a continuum, or unbroken stream [of energy]." The term Tantra refers first (1) to the continuum of vital energy that sustains all existence, and second (2) to the class of knowledge and practices that harnesses that vital energy, thereby transforming the practitioner. Tantra is publicly known in two forms: from India, related to Hinduism; from Tibet, related to Buddhism. Each have their own scriptures, schools, traditions, and practices, which vary widely. And, in spite of the opinions—and financial interests—of many people, the term Tantra is not immediately synonymous with sex, spiritual powers, or materialism. For thousands of years the teachings of Tantra had been protected and isolated in order to preserve their purity and to protect the naive from harming themselves. Now that much of Tantra has been made public, it has been completely disfigured by the passions, desires, and ambitions of misguided people. The vast majority of teachings of Tantra have degenerated completely and are now dangerous. One should study extensively before taking on any teachings or practice of Tantra. This has been emphasized by all truly authentic traditions of Tantra:

"Tantra Yoga had been one of the potent powers for the spiritual regeneration of the Hindus. When practised by the ignorant, unenlightened, and unqualified persons, it has led to certain abuses; and there is no denying that some degraded forms of Saktism have sought nothing but magic, immorality, and occult powers." - Swami Sivananda

Genuine Tantra is an exceptional method of purifying the consciousness of all egotistical elements: lust, pride, envy, gluttony, laziness, etc., but it is not easy or accomplished overnight, and requires great temperance, intelligence, education, and dedication. Real Tantra depends completely on robust and perfect ethics.

"[Buddha] Shakyamuni did not teach that people with loose ethics will succeed in Tantra. That is not the way leading to the city of nirvana. How could these evil churls succeed in Tantra? How could people with loose ethics go to the upper realms? They will not go to a high rebirth; they will not have supreme happiness." - *The Manjushri Root Tantra*

Success in Tantra is determined by the ethical discipline that leads up to it.

There are many varieties of Tantra, but they can be classified in three types: White, Grey and Black. These are differentiated by examination of the results they produce.

White Tantra: those schools that produce beings who are clean of all egotistical desire, anger, lust, envy, etc. Such beings are known as buddhas, masters, angels, devas, etc.

Grey Tantra: those schools who want to be White but do not renounce Black methods. They are caught in the middle.

Black Tantra: those schools that produce beings who sustain and develop the causes of suffering, namely lust, anger, greed, pride, etc. Such beings are called demons, sorcerers, Maruts, Asuras, etc.

Wedding Garment: From a parable of Jesus: "Then saith he to his servants, The wedding is ready, but they which were bidden were not worthy. Go ye therefore into the highways, and as many as ye shall find, bid to the marriage. So those servants went out into the highways, and gathered together all as many as they found, both bad and good: and the wedding was furnished with guests. And when the king came in to see the guests, he saw there a man which had not on a wedding garment: And he saith unto him, Friend, how camest thou in hither not having a wedding garment? And he was speechless. Then said the king to the servants, Bind him hand and foot, and take him away, and cast him into outer darkness; there shall be weeping and gnashing of teeth. For many are called, but few are chosen." - Matthew 22

"Let us now concentrate on the constitution of the human being. In order to be a human being in the most complete sense of the word, first of all it is necessary to have or possess Solar Bodies. We have been talking a lot about the Egyptian Sahu, which is the same Wedding Garment from that parable in which one man came to be seated at the table of the Lord without the Wedding Garment. Then the Master commanded that he be cast into the darkness. So then, without a Wedding Garment or Solar Bodies we also cannot enter into the Kingdom of the Heavens. It is logical that whosoever does not possess the Solar Bodies is dressed with the Lunar Bodies, which are cold, spectral, diabolic, and tenebrous bodies. An Anima (Latin for "soul") dressed with Lunar Bodies is not a Human Being, but is an Intellectual Animal, which is a Superior Animal (Anima). The mistake of humanity is to believe that they are already Human Beings, but they are not. Let us remember the story of Diogenes and his lantern; he was looking for a Man (Human Being) and he did not find one. Only Kout Humi, the Master Morya, Saint Germain, etc. are Human Beings; what we have abundantly in this present time are Intellectual Animals. The first body which must be built in the Forge of the Cyclops is the Astral Body. Thus, we become Immortals in the World of 24 Laws. Afterwards, we need to build the Mental Body, which is ruled by 12 Laws. Whosoever builds the Mental Body is Immortal in the World of 12 Laws. Afterwards, one must build the Body of Conscious Will, and become Immortal in the World of 6 Laws. [...] This famous garment is the Egyptian Sahu or the Greek "To Soma Heliakon," in other words, the Body of Gold of the Solar Man. This is the Wedding Garment required in order to attend the Banquet of the Pascal Lamb. It is necessary and essential to understand that in order to have the Body of Gold of the Solar Man, the Great Alliance is necessary, that is, the work in the Ninth Sphere between man and woman." - Samael Aun Weor, *Tarot and Kabbalah*

White Brotherhood or Lodge: That ancient collection of pure souls who maintain the highest and most sacred of sciences: White Magic or White Tantra. It is called White due to its purity and cleanliness. This "Brotherhood" or "Lodge" includes human beings of the highest order from every race, culture, creed and religion, and of both sexes.

Yoga: (Sanskrit) "union." Similar to the Latin "religare," the root of the word "religion." In Tibetan, it is "rnal-'byor" which means "union with the fundamental nature of reality."

"The word YOGA comes from the root Yuj which means to join, and in its spiritual sense, it is that process by which the human spirit is brought into near and conscious communion with, or is merged in, the Divine Spirit, according as the nature of the human spirit is held to be separate from (Dvaita, Visishtadvaita) or one with (Advaita) the Divine Spirit." - Swami Sivananda, *Kundalini Yoga*

"Patanjali defines Yoga as the suspension of all the functions of the mind. As such, any book on Yoga, which does not deal with these three aspects of the subject, viz., mind, its functions and the method of suspending them, can he safely laid aside as unreliable and incomplete." - Swami Sivananda, *Practical Lessons In Yoga*

"The word yoga means in general to join one's mind with an actual fact..." - The 14th Dalai Lama

"All of the seven schools of Yoga are within Gnosis, yet they are in a synthesized and absolutely practical way. There is Tantric Hatha Yoga in the practices of the Maithuna (Sexual Magic). There is practical Raja Yoga in the work with the chakras. There is Gnana / Jnana Yoga in our practices and mental disciplines which we have cultivated in secrecy for millions of years. We have Bhakti Yoga in our prayers and Rituals. We have Laya Yoga in our meditation and respiratory exercises. Samadhi exists in our practices with the Maithuna and during our deep meditations. We live the path of Karma Yoga in our upright actions, in our upright thoughts, in our upright feelings, etc." - Samael Aun Weor, *The Revolution of Beelzebub*

"The Yoga that we require today is actually ancient Gnostic Christian Yoga, which absolutely rejects the idea of Hatha Yoga. We do not recommend Hatha Yoga simply because, spiritually speaking, the acrobatics of this discipline are fruitless; they should be left to the acrobats of the circus." - Samael Aun Weor, *The Yellow Book*

"Yoga has been taught very badly in the Western World. Multitudes of pseudo-sapient Yogis have spread the false belief that the true Yogi must be an infrasexual (an enemy of sex). Some of these false yogis have never even visited India; they are infrasexual pseudo-yogis. These ignoramuses believe that they are going to achieve in-depth realization only with the yogic exercises, such as asanas, pranayamas, etc.Not only do they have such false beliefs, but what is worse is that they propagate them; thus, they misguide many people away from the difficult, straight, and narrow door that leads unto the light. No authentically Initiated Yogi from India would ever think that he could achieve his inner self-realization with pranayamas or asanas, etc. Any legitimate Yogi from India knows very well that such yogic exercises are only co-assistants that are very useful for their health and for the development of their powers, etc. Only the Westerners and pseudo-yogis have within their minds the belief that they can achieve Self-realization with such exercises. Sexual Magic is practiced very secretly within the Ashrams of India. Any True Yogi Initiate from India works with the Arcanum A.Z.F. This is taught by the Great Yogis from India that have visited the Western world, and if it has not been taught by these great, Initiated Hindustani Yogis, if it has not been published in their books of Yoga, it was in order to avoid scandals. You can be absolutely sure that the Yogis who do not practice Sexual Magic will never achieve birth in the Superior Worlds. Thus, whosoever affirms the contrary is a liar, an impostor." - Samael Aun Weor, *Alchemy and Kabbalah in the Tarot*

Index

Sorcerers, 76, 328, 331
Soul, 4, 21-22, 33, 35-37, 41, 51-52,
    58, 74, 78, 90, 94, 97-98, 100-
    102, 112, 116, 125, 133-134,
    140, 163, 182-185, 199, 202-
    203, 207, 211-215, 220-221,
    224-225, 235, 269, 292, 296,
    314, 316, 320, 324-325, 327,
    332
Souls, 12, 24, 38, 70, 76, 100, 169,
    183-184, 193-194, 235, 310,
    323, 325, 328, 332
Sound, 5, 10, 33, 57, 122, 159, 194,
    231-232, 307, 324
Sounded, 75, 240
Sounds, 10, 14, 69, 232, 308, 324
South, 18, 21, 111, 145, 173, 201,
    221, 284
South America, 18, 284
South American, 21, 111, 145
Space, 5, 8, 19, 33, 100, 102, 113-
    114, 128, 131, 142, 155,
    157-158, 213, 217, 229, 287,
    289, 305, 307
Spain, 252, 267, 308, 317
Spanish, 247, 317
Sparrow Hawks, 150
Spasm, 55
Spear, 82-83, 118, 215, 218-219, 252
Specialist, 107, 117, 124, 135
Species, 235
Specter, 25, 173, 310
Specters, 87, 173
Spectral, 75, 332
Speech, 20, 23, 322
Speechless, 134, 142, 331
Sperm, 78
Spermatic, 12, 162, 233, 251, 273,
    304
Sphere, 82, 91, 122, 124-125, 129,
    157, 190, 201, 219, 223, 234,
    266-267, 294, 305, 326, 328,
    332
Spheres, 136, 157, 201, 327
Sphinx, 25, 137
Spill, 176, 315
Spilling, 56-57, 288, 311

Spills, 57, 288
Spinal, 11, 57, 60, 95, 107-108, 132,
    135, 155, 161, 165, 175, 179,
    187, 191, 322
Spine, 55, 57-58, 60, 94-95, 107-108,
    135, 189, 191
Spinning, 32
Spins, 157-158, 172
Spiral, 141, 249
Spiral Path, 249
Spiralling, 206
Spirals, 158
Spirit, 16, 25, 38, 40, 43, 45, 55, 74,
    76, 89, 100, 120, 122, 127,
    139, 159, 166, 170-171, 176,
    187, 194, 249, 261, 293-294,
    299, 304, 307, 309, 317-319,
    322-323, 325, 328, 332
Spirit-Man, 99, 141, 244
Spiritism, 18, 24
Spiritist, 18-21, 24
Spirits, 8, 10, 17, 24, 76, 88, 112,
    188, 274, 309
Spiritual, 1, 3, 36-37, 58, 76, 93, 100,
    135, 140, 159, 180, 183, 185,
    187, 203, 211, 213-215, 217,
    221, 224, 229-230, 267, 283,
    285, 293, 299, 305, 307, 314,
    321, 323, 329-332
Spiritual Body, 180
Spiritual Soul, 100, 183, 185, 211,
    213-215
Spiritualism, 17, 19, 21, 23
Spiritualist, 19, 24
Spirituality, 211, 271
Spit, 181
Splendor, 211
Splendorous, 182, 291
Splendors, 29, 38, 120, 125, 155,
    172, 193, 203
Sport, 277
Sports, 276-277
Spouse, 38, 74, 91, 187, 201, 211,
    225, 271, 273, 275, 296
Spring, 25-26, 29, 40, 74, 188, 202,
    267, 317
Springing, 74

Glorian Publishing is a non-profit publisher dedicated to spreading the sacred universal doctrine to suffering humanity. All of our works are made possible by the kindness and generosity of sponsors. If you would like to make a tax-deductible donation, you may send it to the address below, or visit our website for other alternatives. If you would like to sponsor the publication of a book, please contact us at help@gnosticteachings.org.

Glorian Publishing
PO Box 110225
Brooklyn, NY 11211 US

VISIT US ONLINE AT:
gnosticteachings.org